THE PEOPLE ARE

GOING TO RISE

LIKE THE

WATERS

UPON YOUR

SHORE

THE PEOPLE ARE GOING TO RISE LIKE THE WATERS UPON YOUR SHORE

A STORY OF AMERICAN RAGE

JARED YATES SEXTON

COUNTERPOINT
BERKELEY, CALIFORNIA

The People Are Going to Rise Like the Waters Upon Your Shore

Copyright © 2017 by Jared Yates Sexton

All rights reserved under International and Pan-American Copyright Conventions. No part of this book may be used or reproduced in any manner whatsoever without written permission from the publisher, except in the case of brief quotations embodied in critical articles and reviews.

Library of Congress Cataloging-in-Publication Data is available.
ISBN 978-1-61902-956-9

Jacket design by Matt Dorfman
Book design by Sabrina Plomitallo-González

COUNTERPOINT
2560 Ninth Street, Suite 318
Berkeley, CA 94710
www.counterpointpress.com

Printed in the United States of America
Distributed by Publishers Group West

3   5   7   9   10   8   6   4   2

CONTENTS

PROLOGUE: Ugly Vibrations in These United States

THE TOWN HAD CHANGED. MAIN STREET WAS STILL THERE, BUT the shops I'd gotten used to years ago had closed since I'd left, their hollowed-out fronts winking like sad, beleaguered eyes. The house I'd rented in graduate school, a two-story that'd once upon a time been a doll shop, its walls and stairs lined with porcelain figurines, looked deserted now. Murphysboro, Illinois, had seemed like a logical stopping point in mapping out my drive from Georgia to Iowa in the summer of 2015, a chance to take a stroll down memory lane, but now it just felt abandoned and devastated, a shell of what I could remember.

Luckily the barbeque joint where I'd taken my meals a minimum of three days a week was still open, the clientele lining the bar mostly unbothered. After a day on the road I wanted friendly conversation but didn't find any takers. The TVs over the bar, usually tuned to a Cardinals game, were glowing with Fox News and the story it had been running for the past week.

In McKinney, Texas, a suburb of Dallas, nearly a hundred teenagers had descended on a pool party and police had been called after some of them hopped a fence. The reporting officers were captured on video racing through the gated community like mad men, one of them rolling unnecessarily across the grass before screaming and tossing black teenagers to the ground. One of the teenagers, a girl in a peach and yellow swimsuit, had earned his ire, resulting in him manhandling her. Having dragged her back into the frame, he threw her down, grabbed the back of her head, and pushed while her friends tried to intervene. The officer drew his gun and chased them away before returning to the girl and shoving her into the dirt, commanding, "On your face!"

The video started and stopped and started again on a continual loop. Sometimes beginning with the roll, sometimes the girl in the swimsuit. The host and guests spoke over it, all of them in agreement that things might've gotten a little out of hand in McKinney, but the officer was just doing his job.

"People's too sensitive," said a man at the bar. Seven years before, we'd bought each other beers on a few occasions, usually whenever I wore my faded Cubs hat and he felt like pining over the glory years of Ryne Sandberg and Harry Caray. The guy's name was Bob or Brad or Billy, something with a B, and when he talked about the 1984 team his face would light up like he was bragging on his kids. "I mean, for fuck's sake."

Sentiment in the restaurant seemed in agreement. Another fella I'd drank with and argued with about the best fishing spots in Southern Illinois was nodding at his pint of Bud Light. "Lookit her. Lookit how she's talkin'."

In silence, I polished off my ribs and listened to the men and the tables around them commenting on the girl and how she'd been egging on the officer. Times had changed, was the sentiment. Kids today talk back in a way they never would've even considered in the good ol' days. Especially the black ones.

A few blocks down, the liquor store where I'd spent a few of my graduate assistant checks was still chugging along. Stepping inside was like strolling through years gone by as everything was as I had left it, including the cooler where a six-pack of Miller Lite still held its same position on the same rack. There's something about old haunts that makes a person go on and on like an idiot, an appeal to be recognized, I guess, and I couldn't help but tell the cashier I'd once lived just down the street for three years.

"Huh," he said, unimpressed. I asked how town had been and he handed me my beer in a sack. "When'd you leave?"

"2008."

"Things weren't great," he said. "Recession and all."

"I bet."

"Bunch of folks addicted to a bunch of shit."

"Sure," I said, unsure what else there was to say. I'd graduated from Southern Illinois in August of '08 and moved back to Indiana right before the bottom fell out of the economy. A terrifying time to enter the workforce, I'd made it just fine after a few shaky years. Murphysboro, I could tell, was still reeling from the punch.

My motel for the night was a place I'd stayed only one other time after an ex-girlfriend and I had had a knockdown-dragout and I needed a place to sleep. First I'd driven to the parking lot of the nearby Wal-Mart and tried to rest there, but a homeless man had knocked on my window just seconds after I'd drifted off and I thought better of it. This motel wasn't much of an improvement, truth be told, and had I known what I was getting into beforehand I might've taken my chances at the Wal-Mart.

Parked outside my room was a trio of beat-up pickup trucks, the frames rusting and nicked from years of hard use. Men sat on the ground, some resting in the planters and others popping a squat right in front of my door. Workers, their skin permanently tanned and giving off the kind of hot glow only years of toiling in the sun could earn. Right then, they were only working on pounding silver tallboys of Coors Light and bullshitting to no one in particular. When I got out of the car with my bags, the guy by my door nonchalantly handed me one, and after throwing my luggage inside I came back and lingered in the doorway.

It felt good to drink that beer with a complete stranger. In all honesty, I'm always looking to toss a few back with people I don't know, especially if they're working folk. I grew up in a family of factory people who cursed like they were on the line and didn't have much time for talk that extended far past the weather or who was pregnant with whose kid. The truth is, there's still a part of me more at home in their company, and that's how I felt right then, drinking shit beer and just nodding as the men would say things out of nowhere that had nothing to do with anything.

The guy who handed me the beer seemed in the mood to chat a little, and so I asked what kind of work they were doing. "A little of this, a little of that," he told me and said they'd been working construction that morning and would be landscaping the next day. "After that? Who knows?"

Done with the beer, I retired to my room to get started on the six-pack I'd bought and flip through the TV. More and more I was finding myself suffering through hours of cable news in an effort to discern just how the presidential field was taking shape. It was June 2015 and there were fifteen months left in the race. Donald Trump was still flirting with throwing his name in the ring and already the circus had begun. Everyone was expecting Hillary Clinton and Jeb Bush, a snooze we all should've known wouldn't come to bear considering it didn't even come anywhere near matching the country's level of crazy.

I'd started covering politics as a hobby, a means to avoid finishing a novel and a way to entertain myself in the face of what looked like a predictable election that would probably end up being a soul-crushing slog. Something had sparked inside of me the previous year during the Ferguson, Missouri, riots, a desire to get into the thick of it in a way I'd never wanted before. Sitting on my couch at home, watching the madness in the streets, I felt an itch that made me want to gnaw my fingers off. I had an inexplicable urge to grab my keys and drive the nearly eight hundred miles just so I could stand in the middle of it.

And so there I was, plopped down on a rock-hard bed in a rundown hotel in Southern Illinois. I'd agreed to write political articles for a literary journal that maybe a couple hundred of my closest writer friends might read, and in twenty-four hours I'd be in another bar, this time listening to a former governor of Maryland, Martin O'Malley, address a group of teachers and union members in Iowa City. I'd been to my fair share of rallies, had worked in a handful of campaigns, but I had no clue what to expect or even how to properly chronicle the experience.

Little did I know how much the coming year and a half would change my life, that this part-time gig would lead me into the heart of disgusting rallies where a nightmarish movement was coalescing and gaining power, an experience that would push me into a spotlight where I'd constantly ring the alarm while spending one sleepless night after another keeping an eye out for people who regularly promised to see me hang.

But back then, in that pit of a hotel, I was busy getting drunk and turning from one reality where McKinney was just another piece of evidence that black lives didn't matter to another where police were simply trying to keep the country from exploding in violence. The contrast in coverage was stark and mystifying. With the click of a button, one could dramatically alter how the world was being delivered to them.

On one channel, injustice.

On another, monsters needing slaying.

In my hand was a cheap universal remote that'd probably been bought from the Wal-Mart down the street for five bucks, and it'd somehow become one of the most powerful devices in human history.

I was marveling over it, the easy movement in perception, when an argument sparked between the workers next door. From what I could overhear, they were playing cards with their wages. Somebody wasn't happy. There was cheating or a bad beat, whatever it was, and their voices got louder until they were screaming bloody murder. Then, as it grew in intensity and volume, there was a thump against our shared wall. Hard enough to make my TV shake. It deescalated quickly and soon they'd returned to playing cards for a half hour before the whole thing got called off.

Listening to the aftermath, I wedged a chair under my door handle, hoping that would be enough to protect myself, and then tried in vain to catch some sleep as the glow of a nation in crisis bathed the room.

PART ONE

SLEEP OF REASON BREEDS MONSTERS

CHAPTER 1

CANARIES IN THE COAL MINE

MY FIRST NIGHT IN IOWA WAS SPENT IN SANCTUARY PUB, A DARK, wood-paneled bar haunted by old basketball coaches arguing man-to-man defense versus the 3–2 zone between reminiscing high-school teams of local legend. Outside, the rain pelted the world, wind driving it diagonally into pedestrians hugging themselves and trudging forward. Former governor of Maryland Martin O'Malley was scheduled to hold an event in the back room where University of Iowa students were double-fisting pint glasses of strong IPA while wrestling for position nearest the door where everyone assumed O'Malley would speak.

The governor should've been a perfect candidate for the caucuses, an antiquated system where Iowans met in their local high schools and discussed their candidates. In this unique system, it looked like O'Malley, seven months out, could have been a surprise contender. He was casual, experienced, and just liberal enough to justify Iowans ever-present desire to send a signal to establishment Democrats. In any other presidential cycle, O'Malley would've been a force to reckon with, but 2016 was anything but ordinary. Voters were starving to send more than a signal to the party. I heard them whispering back there, some of them buzzed off a few sips, that they wanted somebody to tear the party apparatus to the ground and start over. It was a discussion I'd grown used to, mostly behind closed doors.

The dyed-in-the-wool liberals were tired of half-measures like President Obama's Affordable Care Act, and they were tired of party leaders refusing to attack fringe-right Republicans who had stalled so much of the government during the Obama administration.

They wanted a single-payer system. A total nationalizing of the health-care industry. Most of all, they wanted Pelosi and Reid and Obama to quit tiptoeing around the renegade Republican Congress and take their case directly to the American people.

O'Malley offered a taste of that outrage, but he wasn't capable of embodying it in full. When he strolled into the room from the opposite end, his jacket already shed and his sleeves rolled up—Iowans love a politician ready to work—he smiled with an air of calm that didn't come anywhere near the level of intensity the crowd wanted from him. His was the type of stump speech perfected by Bill Clinton in the early '90s and adopted by members of the resulting Democratic Party, a laundry list of liberal points of view that could be fought for in a uto-pian system, an agenda that might be presented to an opposition Con-gress but dismissed summarily.

The only sign of anger O'Malley gifted the crowd came when a young woman asked him what his responsibility amounted to from his tenure as mayor of Baltimore, a city that had been recently torn apart by racial strife critics had quickly laid at O'Malley's door. This was the first time he dropped his "I'm most comfortable in a pub" act and let his emotions steer his ship.

"Tell me how we have 5 percent of the world's population," he said, framing the problem of systemic racism, "and 25 percent of the world's incarcerated population."

And like that, the outrage was tucked back into the pocket of his slacks. His smile returned. A couple more questions and he was shaking hands and heading back out the door he'd entered from. Outside, on the rain-drenched sidewalk, I waited for my cab among the small clus-ters of people smoking their cigarettes and hiding beers under their sweaters. Iowans take their responsibility seriously and routinely make it a priority to attend as many events before the caucuses as possible. They'll travel hours just to hear what a contender, and in some cases a non-contender, has to say. At heart, they are prognosticators and pundits, unafraid to share opinions.

"There's something that's not quite there," said a girl in a long-sleeved Iowa Wrestling shirt. "Something's just not hitting."

Her clique of friends agreed, even the young man with expertly coiffed hair and an O'Malley button stuck to his blazer.

In the cab back to my hotel, the driver had on some less-known right-wing talk-show host I couldn't recognize doing everything but begging the listener to vote for Ben Carson. The former neurosurgeon's campaign had grafted the state's landscape with billboards and signs, a grassroots shock-and-awe campaign that had paid early dividends in the polls. The host was assuring Iowans that under Carson's sedated exterior simmered a white-hot anger.

"You ask me," my driver said, "what I want is somebody to get up there and just tell everyone to go fuck themselves." Hooking a turn and nearly sideswiping a delivery truck, the driver looked apologetically in the rearview mirror. "Sorry about my language, man. You know, that's just how I feel about it."

On my way into the hotel I saw, stuck to the back of a minivan, mixed in among a variety of pro-life and anti-gay-marriage stickers, something I'd only started seeing since leaving Georgia: a black-and-white bumper sticker reading IF ONLY HILLARY HAD MARRIED OJ INSTEAD! I'd come across it no less than a dozen times on the thousand-some miles I'd driven, along with a few others, including one that had dropped all attempts at cleverness or charm by simply declaring HILLARY'S A BITCH.

Since the 1990s, the country had grown more and more polarized, and at the heart of that polarization were the Clintons, including Bill, who had been impeached, and Hillary, who many would argue was disliked even more than her husband. Certainly the bumper stickers and T-shirts that were becoming more commonplace with every passing day testified as such.

The next morning, I came across that same O.J. bumper sticker in the parking lot of the headquarters for the Iowa Startup Accelerator. I was there to cover a Chris Christie town hall and was conspicuous from the moment I'd stepped foot in the chic brick building. The audience was middle-aged and dressed in suits and office wear, a collection of bankers, real-estate agents, retired elementary-school secretaries, and corporate farmers who had come to do the business of politics, the for-profit work that traditional Republicans were most concerned with, and here I was, devoid of a tie and hungover from Budweisers I'd had to ice down in a trashcan after discovering my hotel room didn't offer a fridge. The only person who felt as bad or as out of place was a cameraman with shaggy hair and red, glassy eyes, and the both of us took to begging staffers for complimentary coffee.

There was no complimentary coffee though, and the staffers, all of them in blue blazers, straightaway let us know our shit was not going to be tolerated. They were spitting images of their boss, the governor of New Jersey, a brute of a man who had turned his physical, bullying style into one of the most lucrative brands in politics.

Christie stalked into the room as if he were readying himself for a back-alley brawl. He surveyed the crowd, searched for weaknesses, and when he reached out to me it was with as firm a grip as I'd ever felt.

Chris Christie, I realized, was trying to break my hand.

But the style he brought to that town hall, much like the style that had dominated his political life, was a scaled-back version of his usual bullish self. Standing in front of a banner reading TELL IT LIKE IT IS, he hemmed and hawed as to whether he was going to actually throw his hat into the presidential ring, and when he detailed his message it was with the assurance that he knew how to work with Democrats, citing his time wrangling the predominately liberal New Jersey statehouse.

There were moments, much like with O'Malley, where he let his passion shine through. On the topics of ISIS, teachers' unions, and intelligence gathering, Christie would begin with what was obviously his scripted answer and then, once the momentum started rolling, his voice would gather speed and he'd begin barking into his microphone. By the end of his spiel, he'd advocated full-scale war, virtually wiping unions off the map, and doubling down on controversial spying by the National Security Agency.

It would still be a while before Christie announced his decision to seek the Republican Party's nomination. He'd do so on June 30, a full two weeks after Donald Trump took his fateful ride down Trump Tower's escalators. For years, Christie had written the playbook on how bullies could succeed in national politics, and Trump, just over the state line in New York, had read that book in full. Christie had made the calculation that his bare-knuckled style would cost him the Republican base, or the traditional group of middle- to upper-class voters who cared more about economics and national security than identity politics and anger, ceding the impassioned fringe of the GOP to his billionaire neighbor.

Things could've been so different had the governor, or any of his blue-blazered staff, simply taken the time to walk outside and read a few bumper stickers.

★　★　★

Everybody knew Bernie Sanders wouldn't be president, and no one was afraid to say it.

The indictments were numerous.

He didn't look like a candidate, with his oft-feral wisps of white hair and his gruff physical presence.

He didn't talk like a candidate, with his democratic-socialist platform, comprising economic issues with repeated emphasis on poverty and inequality. And he didn't come from a traditional breeding ground for viable candidates. Instead, he hailed from Vermont, which was responsible for Sanders's previous unelectable counterpart Howard Dean, a state so liberal and independent it had continually reelected a democratic-socialist in the first place.

Also, he was old. Seventy-three going on seventy-four. If elected, which seemed then and now like the longest of shots, he would've been a young seventy-nine by the end of his first term.

Admittedly, the odds were astronomical.

Upon entry, Sanders was branded accurately as a candidate whose purpose and ultimate potential was to serve as a counterbalance on the far left of Hillary's center-left juggernaut, a safety that drew her nearer the platform of the emerging Democratic territory while never seriously challenging or damaging her chances.

Again, Bernie Sanders wouldn't be president, but when was someone going to tell him that?

The word in the state was that Uncle Bernie, as his most strident Iowan supporters had taken to calling him, was outperforming. That he was drawing oversize crowds everywhere he went. That he would finish a distant but respectable second, and that he'd already succeeded in pulling Hillary left, as evidenced by her June 13 Roosevelt Island speech that heralded a platform so populist it would've been considered radical five years before and was now only commonsense due to the hard work and diligence of firebrands like Bernie.

He would lose though.

In Iowa.

In New Hampshire, it seemed.

South Carolina and so on and so on, until his modest war chest finally gave up like a suspect engine in a suspect used car.

So, why were the crowds getting bigger?

Why was the word of mouth growing stronger?

The UAW Hall in Marshalltown, in which he spoke that Saturday afternoon, should've seated sixty. Twenty minutes out and there were more people than seats, the old autoworkers scrambling to find extra chairs as the people kept streaming in.

The official numbers put it at more than 200, but what they didn't make note of is that these were not your traditional political event attendees.

They were poor.

Disabled.

Literally hungry, literally tired, and very, very pissed off.

I recognized them because these people are my family. My people are generations of factory fodder, the type of folks bled dry by manual labor and never even given the dignity of wages equal to their sweat before their very jobs were swept out from under their feet by NAFTA and globalism.

These were Iowans who had worked and been hobbled by a fundamentally rigged system that had rewarded morally reprehensible business and trade practices. People who had never, ever put thought into retirement because they were preoccupied with just living another day. People who were suffering even before the Great Recession and people whose suffering had only worsened as the economy left them behind.

The advertised start time was three o'clock, and that's exactly when it began, which is a rarity in a world where promptness has never been even a passing concern. Sanders was obviously ready as he walked out *during* his introduction, drawing a surprised cheer from the crowd.

Bernie was unlike any politician I'd ever seen in person. He obviously despised stagecraft and held the podium like he was bracing for a car crash. He was devoid of polish and I don't think he was even the slightest bit interested in remedying that problem, which is a mortal sin in national politics.

But most of all, he was angry.

Not the type of strategic anger many politicians follow in their scripts—the writers having underlined and bolded certain stress points, or printed them in red as if spoken from God on high—or the type of anger candidates slip on like a blazer when it suits them. Sanders's anger was like a righteous fury a prophet might wield to frighten his wayward flock.

It began with a whisper:

"We . . . live in the wealthiest nation in the history of the world . . ."

And gradually it grew.

". . . problem is . . . that almost all that wealth . . . rests in the hands of super-wealthy families . . ."

And then, it was THERE.

". . . there is something profoundly wrong . . . when NINETY-NINE percent of all new income generated in this country goes to ONE PER-CENT . . . it is GROTESQUE and it is not WHAT THIS COUNTRY IS SUPPOSED TO BE."

It was jarring. People shifted in their seats, not out of fear or discomfort, but because their growing outrage matched Bernie's as he read the roll call of problems: the wages, the lack of sick time and vacation time for workers, the giant banks, outrageous student debt, terrifying infant-mortality rates, widespread inequality affecting women and people of color.

The old standing speakers the hall had set up struggled as they buzzed in and out. There was a palpable tension as to whether they'd survive each successive line.

That is, until they didn't.

As Sanders railed against the proposed Trans-Pacific Partnership, the sound system lost its battle and what few aides there were scrambled to set up a portable speaker as the senator never skipped so much as a beat.

Wrath only carries a politician so far. If that weren't true we would already be living in a military dictatorship, which our political process has thankfully steered us clear of. No—the candidate, in order to have any success, must cut their anger with something else, something more palatable. Some use style, a certain flair that makes the pissed-off more attractive, while others like Mike Huckabee or Chris Christie rely on humor, down-home folksiness. Sanders, it seemed, employed a particular brand of populism that would help the rage go down smooth.

Bernie, who had advocated on every campaign stop and television appearance for political revolution, has been called a radical time and time again, but recent polls had confirmed what a lot of insiders had already been talking about among themselves: A majority of Americans, when they got past the label "democratic socialist," actually *agreed* with where Sanders stood on the issues.

Politics isn't that hard of a business. It is a rough-and-tumble trade that mixes exceptional degrees of joy and heartbreak and narcissism, but it's relatively simple. With the exception of a half-dozen or so hot-button debates, these issues we're always litigating, these wedge topics we're battling over, everyone is mostly on the same page. After that, it's relatively clear that America has a problem with wealth inequality and employment. The difference between Democrats and Republicans and their solutions usually have to do with how these problems are addressed, or even whether they need to be addressed now or later, the former routinely advocating increased taxes for wealthy Americans and the latter denying every proposed raise for fear of slippery-slope wealth redistribution. But nobody on either side would deny that most Americans are working harder and longer for less than they ever have in the past. It's simply untenable to contest that fact.

Bernie was venting the building frustration of the people in no-nonsense terms and reaping the benefits. He had unwrapped the process in the way Americans had begged their leaders to do for years, and the people were coming in droves to simply hear their own frustrations erupting from the mouth of one of DC's own. They wanted and needed somebody to stand behind the podium and toss away the divisive bull-shit and focus on the day-by-day, everyman problems that have plagued their families for generations.

It's an old act, one that has been employed for as long as there's been an America to scrutinize, but very rarely does the actor win an elec-tion. Instead, they serve as the canary in the coal mine, a reminder that eventually the inequality and the criminal neglect must be answered lest the proletariat grabs its pitchfork. When a Bernie Sanders or a Eugene V. Debs emerges from the cracks of the tried-and-true political process and gains some traction, political operatives and bosses know it's time to slide the scale a little toward the middle, but not enough, still, to change much except for perception.

That's why Hillary Clinton found herself in Roosevelt Park on June 13 speaking about leveling the playing field and pledging to "bring the banks in line."

In the meantime, Bernie was beginning to ride the wave.

During the question-and-answer portion of the event, a nervous twen-tysomething girl rose from her plastic seat and momentarily fumbled with the microphone. "I'm a college student and I don't have any money and I don't have a lot of time or power, but I hear what you have to say and I think you're right. About everything. What can I do to help?"

Still holding onto the podium like it might leave him, Bernie chewed his lip, thought it over. He told her to talk to her friends, her family, tell her what she'd heard and what he was saying. Then, a hitch in his voice, he said, "And don't you let anyone tell you that these things we talked about today aren't possible. Don't let them tell you America can't do these things."

And you know, for a second there, you had to believe him.

★   ★   ★

Fifty miles separated Marshalltown from Des Moines, but to go from the Bernie Sanders event to Hillary Clinton's the next day you'd think you'd crossed into an alternate dimension. When the Iowan sun finally peeked out from behind a bank of clouds for the first time in days, the temperature rocketed from fair to torturous and the long line of people standing and waiting for Hillary began sweating and fidgeting.

"When did you decide to support Hillary?" a local radio reporter asked a nearby woman perspiring through her hot pink blouse.

"Um," the woman said, "when Elizabeth Warren decided not to run."

Up and down the line her answer reverberated and carried, a dozen or so supporters murmured among themselves that they too would've preferred Warren, the tremendously popular progressive senator from Massachusetts. As if on cue, the Hillary volunteers sprang into action with all the zest and practiced techniques of Red Bull salesmen on a college campus.

"Hey, are you guys excited about Hillary?" one of them called, holding up a cardboard Hillary logo, a blue "H" embedded with a red arrow pointing right, a dead ringer for the subliminal wonder that is the FedEx emblem. For an answer he got a few cheers, to which he responded, "Come on! This is Hillary! Let's get excited!"

This time the response was a bit louder and more robust. His colleagues handed out more cardboard Hillary logos, along with a pair of cardboard Hillary cutouts. They posed children and their mothers and then tweeted them out before moving on, the whole operation like clockwork as the volunteers peeled off immediately afterward, found the subjects of the photos, and said, "Look! Hillary retweeted you! You guys are practically best friends!"

Obviously excited, the people were encouraged to retweet the retweet to their friends and followers, to follow Hillary's Twitter, and to maybe take a selfie or two at the rally to then tweet out to their followers and friends.

"Get involved!" the volunteer told a friend of the hot-pink tank-top interviewee.

And so she got involved.

I was too hot to get involved. I was too sweaty to get involved. There were rumors that the 10:30 start time, as listed on the Hillary website, was misleading, that the former secretary of state and first lady, the de facto front-runner of the Democratic Party for the 2016 presidential nomination and assumed Winner of It All, wouldn't show up until at least noon. The people around me felt duped and stirred uncomfortably as they soaked through their shirts.

"You get a sticker yet?" a volunteer sporting a MADAM PRESIDENT button asked, and after I told him I was good he peeled one off and slapped it on my chest, all in one practiced motion. "You looked like you needed one."

A volunteer with the cutout was with a family of six a few feet down. He was holding the likeness, saying, "You know, when the light hits her just right, you can't tell the difference between this thing and the real deal."

Down the row, more people were finding out that Hillary or one of her many advocacy accounts had retweeted them.

"You guys are practically best friends!"

Mercifully, the doors opened and the sweaty supporters clomped inside and found, hanging above the huge stage, an impressive *Patton*-like flag for a backdrop and dozens of tables with red-and-white checked tablecloths, a massive media encampment with maybe forty cameras, opposite it a whole field of catered foods, the options being hamburgers and hot dogs to eat and tea and lemonade to drink.

"It's like a picnic," I heard somebody say.

Months out from the actual caucuses, the event was designed to feel like an afternoon in the park with the family, but it was engineered down to the last detail. Tables of ten were soon inundated with more clipboard-toting volunteers who got our information and encouraged us to "talk about what you like best about Hillary," a dry run for when the caucuses met in February. Attendees were being taught by volunteers to explain their support of Clinton and express their enthusiasm when speaking to total strangers. To their credit, most of my table wasn't in the mood to talk about what they liked most about Hillary. Already it was eleven, and the rumor at the moment was that she wasn't coming until twelve thirty.

"What do you like most about Hillary?" a neighboring table could be heard asking.

"Hmmm," somebody said. "That's a good question."

A volunteer nearby answered for her. "Is it her stance on the issues?"

"Sure," the somebody said. "And I like that she's a woman."

There were maybe thirty handmade signs on the walls in the event center that reminded us of both those facts. One said HILLARY'S RIGHT ON THE ISSUES THAT MATTER! Another read ELECT THE FIRST FEMALE PRESIDENT! Another, playing off a shared "H": HELPER, HERO, HILLARY.

A folk duo tuned up on a secondary stage and between songs they asked the crowd if they were excited about Hillary, which a few volunteers, dancing in the aisles and taping everything on iPads, answered in the affirmative.

I was busy talking to a crazy man trying to convince me he'd worked in the White House. "But you'll never find a record of it," he told me before asking for a sheet of paper. "I'm here writing a book, too. HBO's going to pay me a million dollars for the rights."

Next to him was a mother and daughter duo, the mom visiting from Wisconsin. The daughter, twenty years old, was dead-set focused on the issues and told me, once the lunatic laid off, that her friends didn't care about politics. "They just switch it off," she said.

Why?

"I don't know," she answered. "Maybe they don't think they matter. That it's real."

The tenth or so volunteer to canvass our table interrupted, made sure we'd given our information, had signed a pledge to caucus, that we were talking about what we liked most about Hillary. Before he left, he reminded us to tweet and Facebook photos from the event so our friends and followers could know how much fun we were having.

"What's exciting about Hillary for you?" I asked the mother and the daughter.

"She's going to be the first female president," the mom answered.

Would it have made a difference if Elizabeth Warren would've ran?

"Yes," they both said. "It would."

★ ★ ★

Here in Iowa, eight years before, Hillary Clinton was handed the worst loss of her political life. Originally favored to run the table easily, she finished a distant third, behind that monster John Edwards, with 29.4 percent of the vote. Upstart Barack Obama won with a heady 37 percent. An upset, it would turn out, of historic import.

Many postmortems have been made of the defeat, with analysts focusing on Obama's next-level technological operation and call to history, but any analysis of Hillary's failed bid in '08 would be remiss if it didn't mention the utter clusterfuck that was her campaign: a hulking mess that failed to stay on message and presented one of the more unflattering portraits of a candidate in the history of American politics. Due to its dysfunction, Clinton at times came across to the voting public as cold and calculated. She was easily portrayed to Iowans as out-of-touch and uncomfortable with the Politics of the Personal the state demanded, not to mention far too centrist in her policies.

Now, in a more accelerated position, the '16 campaign had attempted to address every nuanced problem it could see from the previous disaster. Clinton was talking about coloring her hair to bring a little personal touch. Dotting her speeches with traces of token populism on loan from Bernie Sanders and even some of the rumble of opposition to the big banks and Wall Street that Elizabeth Warren would have touted had she decided to throw in her hat.

The issue was that the problems that plagued Hillary Clinton in 2008 had never gone away.

The type of general amnesia surrounding her candidacy was a testament to how well designed that initial phase of the campaign was. Gone were the days where Democrats questioned why she'd voted for the war in Iraq or her past opposition to gay marriage. There was absolutely no talk about how close she was to the big banks or how Wall Street had been absolutely flooding her coffers with donations.

Instead, we now had this Frankenstein's monster–like candidate who had taken her cult of personality and draped it over the process like a blanket while appropriating the most popular and strategist-approved stances of her rivals.

Did you want Elizabeth Warren?

Clinton would give you her best impression.

Thinking about Bernie Sanders?

Clinton could do that too.

In a brilliant piece of strategy, Clinton World was giving the electorate whatever it thought they'd want and thus provided Hillary as a blank slate for which all voters could cast their own hopes and interests, a page taken, Clinton World thought, out of the Obama '08 campaign, an outfit that Hillary and Bill had thought was a smoke-and-mirrors show that stood for nothing and everything simultaneously.

Undoubtedly, Clinton was one of the most talented politicians, in terms of policy and thought, but had never mastered the artifice of surface-level politicking, a weakness strategists were grappling with in real time.

The strategy was successful as the campaign began, and gave Clinton an edge in fund-raising and poll numbers, but it left her flank open on the left as a frustrated electorate, many of them tired of President Obama's consistent centrism, looked for the progressivism that other candidates could legitimately offer. Clinton, after all, was not the candidate of those who wanted to see a shift in policy or direction.

And like any brand run on identity loyalty, even the best and the brightest and largest companies in this country reach a saturation point where their product has been consumed by as many people as it can yet the market still forces them to grow with every quarter. This is how Taco Bell starts serving breakfast and McDonald's looks into chicken wings. In an effort to grow an ungrowable product, corporations try to be all things to all people. And once they reach that point, they suffer.

But the secret of advertising, of brand growth, is to take whatever is popular, whatever is new, and consume and cannibalize it before regurgitating it to the culture at large, only now more easily accessible and less threatening.

What we were seeing in the beginning of the Clinton campaign was the next rollout of an Apple product. The iPhone. The Apple Watch. The MacBook Air. The next operating system. The next Thing You Need. It began in its crib as a data-driven campaign to extend and grow the brand while selling to the consumers the idea that their lives would be forever changed once they have the product in their hands, whether that was even remotely true. What mattered was that the product needed to grow.

In comparison to Sanders, Clinton came off looking like the product she was intending to sell. There is, obviously, a fine line between pandering and successful marketing, and with a crotchety, no-nonsense opponent with a consistent record on the stances they were both touting, the optics did Clinton no favors. The rally in Des Moines was slick to a fault and populated with volunteers more or less running market research in real time with real people who came looking for real answers.

So, when Clinton strode on stage after a playlist of millennial pop songs—"Happy," "Stronger," "Best Day of My Life," and Rachel Platten's "Fight Song," which would plague reporters and rallygoers for the next year—it was like existing in a living, breathing car commercial.

The speech was almost exactly like the one she gave in Roosevelt Park to relaunch her campaign, only the language had evolved here and there. Word had spread through political circles that her stump speech had been edited and focused-grouped within an inch of its life and it showed.

In it, she responded to every small piece of criticism from the past forty-eight hours.

Like Bernie Sanders's call for her to take a stance on the Trans-Pacific Partnership treaty.

"I say let's step back and see if we're getting the best deal for workers," she said, completely sidestepping any actual position.

"I will take on big banks!" she said, addressing Martin O'Malley's assertion that she was just a little too cozy with the institutions that melted down the American economy.

It was the same mistake she'd made eight years before in trying to rebut every single criticism lobbed her way, a relic from Bill's campaigns that had the slogan "Speed Kills" because they wanted to get ahead of every possible attack and own every single news cycle.

But we were living in a twenty-four-hour news cycle, which meant each opposing campaign—and she wasn't just running against Sanders and O'Malley but a veritable gymnasium's worth of Republicans all gunning for her—was going to send out an attack once a day, and if she chose to respond to every last one, her message had no chance of remaining cohesive.

Shuffled into the stump speech, the responses were faulty, clumsy, tossed-in, and conspicuous. It threw off the rhythm, making Clinton seem uncomfortable behind the podium. The ebb and flow of a speech is a finely tuned thing that, when it gets off-course, can really hobble an event and campaign. This one was notably unsure and a bit startling in its rambling effect.

It would have mattered more, but from my vantage point, hardly anybody at the rally was actually listening. Some Iowa folks picked at their Styrofoam plates, some sat stoically with their arms crossed, their mouths set in slits, but the majority of the crowd was busy snapping selfies with their back to Clinton. Giving a thumbs-up. Electric smiles. Some trying different filters on their cameras. Some trying their damnedest to keep the frame steady as they recorded snippets of the speech for their feeds and Facebook friends.

The problem was that these were the consumers already standing in line for the New Hillary Clinton. In the wake of Elizabeth Warren foregoing the race, and with Joe Biden only halfheartedly weighing entry, they had already resolved to buy into the Clinton campaign. These weren't the far-left Democratic voters, the millennials who, like their generation mates, were predisposed to distrust politics and its phony dressings. These were the voters who still indulged the pageantry and the selling of a candidate, and they were ready to post their selfies and videos to Twitter and Reddit and Instagram, to wait for their social circles to comment and like.

But Clinton World had made a miscalculation that would plague it through the general election. Voters in 2016 weren't looking for a friend. And they most certainly weren't in the market for a new product.

They wanted representatives decrying inequality.

They wanted angry candidates warring against culture as a whole.

What they wanted, and what they would get, was rage.

CHAPTER 2
THE AMERICAN DREAM IS DEAD

AS NEIL YOUNG'S "ROCKIN' IN THE FREE WORLD" MACHINE-GUNNED through speakers, billionaire Donald Trump, like a deity deigning mortals worthy of audience, joined his wife, Melania, on an escalator and glided down to the ground floor of Trump Tower to announce his intention to run for the presidency of the United States. Before he could even make it official, he had ushered the country into what will forever be known as the Post-Trump Era.

"When Mexico sends its people, it's not sending its best," he said, not two minutes after taking the podium. "They're sending people who have lots of problems . . . They're bringing drugs, they're bringing crime, they're rapists, and some, I assume, are good people."

And with those fateful words the trajectory of American politics was forever altered with a statement that would have sunk most campaigns before they'd ever found their bearings.

There were pundits who heard the rambling mess of a "speech" and predicted he'd be out of the race within days.

Jon Stewart, outgoing host of *The Daily Show*, laughed off Trump's presentation and said, "Thank you, Donald Trump, for making my last six weeks my best six weeks."

Similarly, the speech was fodder for late-night talk shows as hosts lined up to celebrate the inevitable material Trump as presidential candidate would gift them. Jimmy Kimmel called him "a president and an amusement park rolled into one," while Conan O'Brien likened him to the ceremonial groundhog and announced that his candidacy meant "six more weeks of comedy."

Stephen Colbert, between his role at Comedy Central and his new gig at the helm of CBS's *Late Show*, released a teaser wherein he combed down his hair to mimic the eccentric mogul and lambasted the announcement, saying, "It will be the finest, most luxurious, diamond-encrusted campaign that will give hope to a weary nation until, together, we reach that fine fall day when the new season of *Celebrity Apprentice* premieres."

Looking back with the clarity of what Trump's candidacy became, the clips are mortifying. Though, at heart, Trump was a two-bit huckster reality-TV star buffooning his way through a haphazard presidential campaign, the casualness and amusement with which he was treated is startling and, ultimately, telling. While comedians and pundits dismissed him—*The Huffington Post* went so far as to cover his efforts in its entertainment section rather than politics—the dismissiveness and irony always tended to ignore two key factors that would fuel his ascent: the unvarnished anger of his message and the bald-faced bigotry he peddled.

Heading into 2015, a ready-made base was primed for Trump, and the moment he announced his candidacy that base was his to lose. Since the advent of right-wing talk radio, a phenomenon that cut its teeth on the Monica Lewinsky scandal in the 1990s, the Republican electorate had been fed a consistent stream of altered reality that painted liberals and politics in America in an incredibly frightening manner. In some cases, they were being swindled by sex-crazed, godless opportunists like Bill and Hillary Clinton and then, post–September 11, they were under attack by terrorists and unpatriotic liberals, a combination that seemed, at times, like an intentional alliance.

With the election of Barack Obama, the first African-American president, the right-wing media went into full-blown overdrive, the reason being that they had laid dormant as a veritable press wing for the George W. Bush presidency, not to mention the onset of the internet as a politically powerful landscape where social media and web traffic demanded fresh outrage as the grist for the mill.

By the time President Obama introduced his Affordable Care Act, a slight reform of the insurance system that had virtually been written by the companies themselves, the media was more than ready to portray the legislation as nothing short of a totalitarian coup by a power-mad tyrant. Led by paranoids like Glenn Beck and former vice-presidential candidate Sarah Palin, who regularly cited "death panels" that would decide whether the nation's grandparents lived or died, the conservative base was whipped into a fury that felt, at times, like it might lead to armed revolt.

In 2010, as tensions mounted, I'd gone to a "Tea Party Information Session" in my native Greene County in Indiana. The day before, I'd seen an ad in the paper and, after subjecting myself to *The Glenn Beck Program* every afternoon for a year, I was ready to see what all the rhetoric had amounted to. The meeting was held in a barn-like structure on the county fairgrounds and the heat was so oppressive they had to leave the doors open on either end, the temperature obviously affected by the hundreds of bodies in the audience, a lot of them people I recognized from my small hometown.

The program was sloppy and incoherent at times, but the message was clear: President Obama had been exposed as a dictator on the level of Joseph Stalin or Mao Zedong, both of whom were cited by speakers who referred to the millions of people the two communist leaders had killed. Obama, they explained, was capable of that kind of wanton destruction, and what's more, his background proved that that was his main goal.

Over and over the speakers referred to the idea that Obama had been born in Kenya, that he was really Barry Soetoro, a name that had started popping up on fringe-right websites, and that a discerning person could find links to Al Qaeda if they only took the time to look.

They drew parallels to the rise of Adolph Hitler and kept hammering away at the danger America was facing.

The event was nightmarish and only exacerbated my worry that the Tea Party movement, at heart, was a developing fever. I watched people I'd spent my whole life in proximity to, my normally levelheaded teachers and neighbors, nod along to the remarks before asking if it was time to overthrow the government and chatting among themselves about how Obama needed to be assassinated.

They were parroting the paranoia Fox News and conservative talk radio had pounded into them over the past few years, a narrative the Republican Party had been actively engaging in for generations as it had proved a useful tactic that kept working-class people voting against their own financial interests—tax cuts to the wealthy, cutbacks in social-welfare programs—but now the tactic was stoking anger to the point it could no longer be controlled.

And honestly, if they were being told, day in and day out, that a despot and his gang of cronies were intentionally ruining the country and threatening freedom, then what other recourse could they have?

Thomas Jefferson had said, as these speakers were always happy to remind them, that "the tree of liberty must be refreshed from time to time with the blood of patriots and tyrants."

The disconnect between what they were being told and how the Republicans governed was certainly too much to bear. Every minute of every day they were hearing how a Hitleresque figure was corrupting their country and possibly conspiring with terrorists. He'd assumed an identity and was obviously operating as a foreign agent with the intention of ruining the America they loved so much.

As a result, it wasn't enough for Republicans to refuse to cooperate with Obama. Nothing short of a revolution would have been sufficient.

Trump's message of unbridled wrath was what they had been looking for. Finally, there was a person pissed-off enough to get onstage and simply scream at the system the way any of them would had they been given the opportunity. And though Trump was inelegant and vulgar, it didn't matter, as desperate times rarely afforded pomp or polished oration.

In years prior, Trump had also gained political capital by positioning himself as the voice of the birther movement and spearheading the effort to demand Obama release his birth certificate. That gambit paid off as voters opposed to Obama, many of them continually questioning his citizenship and right to serve as president, appreciated that Trump, a celebrity and businessman, had been willing to put his status on the line in order to call out an "obvious" wrong.

Of course, birtherism had been a thinly veiled appeal to the closeted racists. By painting Obama as "the other," or as a foreigner, conservatives were able to criticize him for his ethnicity without acknowledging that his blackness played any role in their boiling and irrational hatred.

To a large swath of Americans, primarily in the heartland and rural areas, Obama's reelection represented the final act of what had amounted to a takeover of the United States. I can still remember, growing up, my town's resistance to and growing discomfort with minorities entering the entirely white population. With each black or Mexican family that moved into the town limits, there were whisperings about how things were changing and that it was only a matter of time before more followed.

It didn't help, obviously, that demographics were transforming as America's economy weakened. Bill Clinton's signing of the NAFTA trade agreement, a deal that removed trade barriers between the United States, Mexico, and Canada, and paved the way for many US businesses to move in search of cheaper labor, virtually doomed every small town and family that depended on manufacturing, leaving the working class without much in the way of income or dignity. Meanwhile, those same small towns were sprouting up new businesses and restaurants, many of them owned and managed by minorities new to the area.

Making matters worse, Fox News had banked on these insecurities by programming the channel with every racially divisive story that came across the wire. Entire blocks of programming were spent examining black-on-white and black-on-black crime, not to mention any instance where an undocumented immigrant preyed on a white citizen. Its viewers, Donald Trump included, were treated to a nightmarish vision of a country that had not only lost its way financially, but an America where it wasn't safe to be white anymore.

Further, Fox News' success led to the birth of a new consumerist cultural identity that cashed in on rural white anxiety. New programs were launched that took their fearful narratives to even more frightening places, and because these shows were so successful in frightening their viewers and listeners, they were able to sell them gold bonds for when the economy collapsed, rations for when society fell apart, weapons to defend themselves in the coming race war and/ or the inevitable invasion by the United Nations, not to mention a whole slate of less worrisome shows and popular music designed to reassure "Real Americans" they weren't alone in the new and fearsome world. But regardless, the message was there: Real Americans were under attack.

The reality of the situation was that, while NAFTA had bruised American industry, the rise of automation and a focus on cutting costs had doomed workers, and while globalism and multiculturalism might have made people uncomfortable, it's obviously been a benefit to everyone. But the political manipulations painted a different picture and had produced an angry subclass of Americans who were calling for someone, anyone, to stand up and back the growing tide.

And so, near the end of Trump's announcement, when he claimed that "the American Dream was dead," those people—my family members, the people who lived in my hometown, the ones who had bought the lie hook, line, and sinker—heard exactly what he meant.

White America, long endangered, had succumbed to an ever-present threat.

The old guard that had diagnosed and documented the growing tide of treason and decay had fallen asleep on the watch, or else had been too cowardly to fight it back.

Donald Trump was ready to fight.

He was ready to make American great again.

And millions were ready to join him.

CHAPTER 3
NINE DEAD IN CHARLESTON

AMERICANS ARE NOTORIOUSLY BAD AT PUTTING EVENTS INTO context. Whether it's caused by a deliberate muddying of reality by entrenched interests or simply a result of a weakening attention span, we find ourselves as a country continually missing the big, important picture. A nation forever losing the forest for the trees.

With Donald Trump's emergence in national politics, and his eventual conquering of the electoral system, normally sharp pundits were shocked and filled airtime with head-shaking bafflement.

How had it happened?

It was the kind of handwringing every leader and public figure returns to whenever a maniac with a gun lays waste to a group of unsuspecting people.

Is it our movies?

Our video games?

Our culture as a whole?

So, it was of little surprise when a white man named Dylann Roof shot nine African-American members of the Emanuel AME Church in Charleston, South Carolina, that the immediate response was for the national media to respond with inconclusive and oftentimes maddening uncertainty.

The story itself was sensationalized for days, including live shots in front of the historic church and unending segments where rival talking heads argued over whether this was just an isolated incident or a symptom of some larger societal issue before the host, playing timekeeper, announced an end to the debate with an infuriating media-isms like "We'll have to leave this for future discussion" or "This is certainly something we'll be talking about in the days to come."

This particular story, and its resulting debates, were hamstrung even further when, after some investigation into Roof, pictures were found online of the shooter sporting the Confederate flag. Our current media complex cherishes metaphorical and visual arguments over pertinent and useful introspection, so quickly the dialogue was stolen from the heart of the problem—the growing danger of right-wing propaganda, particularly its ability to inflame racial and societal tensions for political benefit—and directed at an issue that could be framed with stylized shots and video feeds of banners waving in the Southern breeze.

All of this is not to say the Confederate flag wasn't a germane issue. The very fact that statehouses and government institutions were still flying a representation of a past treasonous enterprise that had come to represent racism and the subjugation of African Americans was absurd. Those things should've been ripped off the flagpoles decades, if not a century, ago, but the quick movement from Roof's motivations to a symbol that only tangentially represented those motivations obfuscated a conversation that has plagued our political system for years now and made possible the rise of Donald Trump.

In the wake of the murders, I traveled to South Carolina in order to find some reason in the midst of the chaos. What I found was a state both heartbroken and divided. In Charleston, people mourned and searched for signs of providence or hope, while in Eastover, which Roof called his home, I saw a poor community that had incubated a monster. The type of town where despair could fester.

It seems necessary to mention I have known a lot of young men who reminded me of Dylann Roof. Even writing that phrase makes me feel ill, but it's no less true. I have seen one young white male after another who has found himself devoid of opportunity and rendered bitter. And when that bitterness sets in like a cancer, it's so very easy for that young white male to armor himself with hatred.

Roof was especially susceptible to the messages the news and the internet delivered. He was poor and white and predisposed to narratives that told him his position in life wasn't his fault. He saw the reports on TV about the threat of African Americans, and when he went online to research those reports he found a web of racist sources that were more than happy to confirm his prejudices.

They told him over and over his country was in danger.

That somebody had to do something.

★　★　★

The only thing we can agree on is that on June 17, 2015, a twenty-one-year-old walked into the historic Emanuel AME Church in Charleston and killed nine of its members in cold blood. It was an act of terrorism and hate, though opponents argued against both labels.

Despite eyewitness accounts, and a manifesto in the killer's own words, then–Republican front-runner Jeb Bush said he didn't "know"[1] if the killings were racially motivated.

Pundits on Fox News and right-wing radio lined up to say there was no way we would ever know what made the young man snap.

On the left, the answers came in predictable fashion.

Get the guns.

Strengthen mental-illness protocols.

And, while we're at it, take down the Confederate flag flying over the South Carolina statehouse.

Hillary Clinton said it was time to have long-overdue conversations[2] about guns and race in America, a call that has been echoed time and time again as we've seen these tragedies mount in both number and frequency.

The only thing we know is that Dylann Roof walked into Emanuel AME Church on Wednesday and killed nine of the parishioners in an act of unmitigated cruelty.

Well, besides the fact that we know this won't be the last time this happens or the last time we do this dance.

We'll call it unspeakable.

We'll argue about guns and mental health and race.

And then we'll do nothing until the next time.

★   ★   ★

The South Carolina statehouse sits on unbelievably well-kept grounds featuring beautiful trees and landscaping and sight-angles most state capitols could only aspire to. That Saturday, braving temperatures north of a hundred degrees, I strode through the campus and watched other visitors stand in quiet deliberation as the Confederate battle flag flew over the Confederate war memorial in front.

Throughout my drive, from Statesboro to Columbia, every single flag was at half-mast. The Stars and Stripes. The Christian. The South Carolina Palmetto. All but the Confederate, which still waved at full height in every location. Atop the statehouse, the flags were properly lowered, but there, at the Confederate memorial, no such dignity was bestowed.

Social-media sites circulated a petition demanding South Carolina remove the flag, and its signees numbered in the hundreds of thousands. It'd been a long-standing issue in the state, particularly when the presidential primary season returned and candidates, primarily Republicans, were forced to take sides.

Jeb was the only one to immediately call for its removal, and was joined by an unlikely ally in former nominee Mitt Romney,[3] but other hopefuls were a little more hesitant to join the chorus. To do so, as John McCain showed in 2000, is to put your bid on the line and possibly lose South Carolina's primary, which has a long and storied tradition in prognosticating the eventual winner.

Simply put, the Confederate flag, and accompanying Confederate history, are hardwired into South Carolina's DNA and any attempt to separate the two is met with strong and instant resistance. A walk around the grounds revealed an inexplicably linked history, a past that was at all times both the past and undeniably the present. The area was full of memorials to Confederate soldiers and champions of the Southern cause and Confederate ideals, including a statue of former senator Strom Thurmond, arguably the most powerful and revered politician in the state's history.

Those unfamiliar with Thurmond would do themselves a favor by perusing the man's history, if only for a cursory view of the oft-troubled story of race relations in America. This is a man who broke from the Democratic Party over segregation and famously ran for president as a "Dixiecrat" with a platform of denying the "Nigra race" admission into "our theaters, into our swimming pools, into our homes, and into our churches."[4]

The statue of Thurmond stands not far from the back entrance, directly on a line that extends from the Confederate memorial and dissects the statehouse, and finds the memorial of Strom in mid-step, down the sidewalk, apparently marching, with South Carolina in tow, toward another Confederate memorial of an angel coronating a Confederate with a crown of laurels.

One could argue that these are only symbols. Statues I'm reading out of context. That's fine. You can make the argument that there's even a memorial for African Americans on the same lawn, a fine statue of a fairly modest obelisk surrounded by images from the history of blacks in America, including a map of the slave trade that brought them to the continent in the first place.

Sure.

That memorial is a step in the right direction, but any mention of that honor has to be paired with a description of a nearby statue, that of former governor and lieutenant general in the Confederate Army, Wade Hampton III, atop a horse in his uniform, that dwarfs the African-American display and, from the right angle, appears as if he's watching over them.

Almost like that if they decided to stray, he'd be more than ready to pursue.

★   ★   ★

Dylann Roof's former home was crawling with reporters and cameramen, each scrambling up the dirt driveway to catch a quick glimpse or shot of the house before they were run off. All in all, it's a pretty unremarkable home. Shitty gray siding. Shitty white lattice. A lone American flag flew from a flagpole despite reports that, up until that morning, symbols of white power flew alongside.

Across the road sat Mr. Bunky's Market, a down-and-out kind of establishment lined with advertisements for Budweiser and Mountain Dew. Inside, the rafters were filled with heads. Hogs and boars. Deer. The shelves held giant bags of feed for dogs and hogs and chickens and horses, the smell of all of it, mixing with the cut-rate butcher cabinet shoved in the back, permeated the air. Fridges of live bait by the door—crickets and worms—buzzed along with the badly piped-in radio.

In line, I stood behind a sun-bleached local with two fistfuls of Natural Ice tallboys. He was already drunk enough—I could smell the beer wafting off him. The girl behind the counter said she'd checked out Roof a bunch of times, that this was where he came to get his groceries. She'd already decided she's leaving town. Having just come back from vacation, she had no idea why she didn't just stay gone.

Down the road from a National Guard base, replete with a fighter jet positioned like it's in the middle of a suicide-bombing run, Eastover is the type of town most Southerners can recognize. There's nothing for as far as the eye can see except bullshit that doesn't matter anyway.

Crumbling houses that are either abandoned or soon to be.

Areas and infrastructure leveled by winds from some distant storm that have never been rebuilt or attended to.

The only thing nearby is a stretch of franchise restaurants and stores. Shitty jobs with shitty pay.

As I stood in the gravel parking lot, trying my best to survive 108 degrees, I gazed across the road at a house I wouldn't want anyone to live in and thought of Roof shopping in that store every single day. I could only imagine how hellish life must've been living in that type of poverty with little in the way of hope. He must've sat in there and stewed in hatred for everything.

☆　★　☆

When the manifesto[5] hit the internet, I was sitting on a leather couch Roof must've rested on at some point. It's outside the Shoe Dept. store where a manager called the police on Dylann in March after he hung around and "asked a bunch of out of the ordinary questions."[6] In one of the more unnerving moments of my life, I read the purported statement just ten feet from the entrance.

Any debate about Roof's motives are gone now, as if any existed in the first place. Almost immediately after the shooting, pictures circulated of him wearing a jacket with patches from apartheid-era South Africa and Rhodesia, a pair of despicable, white-dominated cultures. After that, anybody who wanted to debate the racial impetus of the violent event was just lying to themselves.

That didn't stop the right, of course, because reality has never mattered to them in the twenty-four-hour news era. Immediately, Fox News tried its best to contort the tragedy into an attack on Christianity[7] and sought out every black pastor in the country willing to agree. A blitz that stunk of self-preservation. They knew the jig was up. That one of theirs was responsible and the political backlash imminent.

When that crashed and burned, Fox pivoted to a new "who can tell what he was thinking?" and "leave it to the liberals to turn this into a political issue" defense.

But I wasn't thinking about that as I sat outside the Shoe Dept.

I was reading one of the most pure and concentrated accounts of personal prejudice and racism I'd ever come across.

Say what you want about Dylann Roof, and all of it is warranted, but he is not illiterate. When I first heard he dropped out of school after the tenth grade, I expected whatever writings or notes we might come across to be the terribly worded and consistently misspelled rantings of an idiot. Instead, from a syntactical standpoint, we have in our hands an obviously researched and labored-over summation of motivations that, despite their ignorance and totally indefensible politics, are the deeply held and structured thoughts of a young man who, upon first blush, isn't totally insane or mentally incapable.

That puts a giant wrench into the traditional thinking of Why This Happens. We prefer our psychopaths easily dismissible. We want them to be simply wrapped up as loony loners, quiet people who tend to froth at the mouth, outcasts from whom we should've "seen this coming."

Roof, it appears, is the type of person who could've very easily excelled in high school and gone to college, where, I assume, maybe wrongly, he might've been purified of his prejudices. He could've gotten a job, could've gotten out of Eastover, could've escaped whatever gravity held him there and bathed him in a learned and consistent hatred of groups of people who never meant to do him harm.

I think of Roof in the same light as the literally dozens of boys I've known, both in the South and the Midwest, who affixed Confederate flags to their trucks and clothes, to their jacked-up pickups and camou-flage hats. Good ol' boys who self-identify as rednecks and paste every sticker and patch they can find with that word, and any other accompa-nying phrases like PROUD WHITE TRASH and CRACKER in an effort to puff out their chests and assume some identity larger than themselves.

For a long time, I've thought of these people and puzzled over their idolatry of the Stars and Bars. In Indiana, my home state, there shouldn't be a reason for somebody to identify themselves with the Confederacy, be it from a geographical or political standpoint.

But there is.

In the South, obviously, people can claim it's a link to heritage, an argument that holds only the tiniest trickle of truth as anybody with half a brain can retort that it's an instantly recognizable symbol of hate. They can trace their heritage back to the War of Northern Aggression, to their forefathers who either fought for the rebellion or who supplied the goods necessary to continue that fight.

The flag stands for all of that, but, much like it does in the Midwest and other parts of the country, the Confederate flag stands in the South as a symbol of opposition, of a middle finger in the direction of not just the Union, which left the South an economic and social disaster, but the Way Things Are, an ever-pervasive feeling that Maybe Things Aren't the Way They Should Be.

* ★ *

Standing in the middle of a polarized America where race and racism are consistently used to further the divide, it seems self-evident that race is one of those levers of economic influence that have consistently kept the machine of America buzzing along its happy line. It's a manip-ulator allowing political forces, such as the prevailing ruling class in Washington, and primarily the GOP since the Nixon administration, to pit huge numbers of Americans of similar economic status against one another in an effort to produce unlikely voting outcomes.

Since the 1960s, Republican candidates at the federal level, including Barry Goldwater and eventually his successor Richard Nixon, saw an opening in Democratic strongholds in the South, mainly due to the conflict of segregation and civil rights, and dove headfirst into the controversy, adopting what came to be known as the Southern Strategy, and ensured themselves generations' worth of a monopoly that continues to this day by signaling, via carefully created dog-whistle phrases and stances, that the right is perpetually on the side of racist whites.

Anybody who doesn't believe this strategy still exists needs only to turn on Fox News any random night. The programs are littered with thinly veiled criticisms of African Americans, including rants about "thugs" and, during the turmoil in Baltimore and Ferguson, long and stylized shots of looters.

On every one of these issues, be it Trayvon Martin, Michael Brown, Freddie Gray, or the McKinney outrage, Fox News and the Republican right have consistently tied themselves to the viewpoint that we're living in a post-racial world, that calls of racism and studies of continuing racial unrest and mistreatment of minorities in this country are liberal fantasies, even going so far as to shame black leaders for "playing the race card."

Make no mistake, the right still plays by Nixon's rules, and its benefitting wildly. Right-wing media are making more money—mostly via advertising for "safety" and "crisis" goods, including gold bonds, weapons, prepper kits, panic rooms, and lined wallets that prevent "electronic pickpocketing"—than ever, and they are reaching an audience that doesn't believe it's racist but sees the world as it *really* is.

Roof is one of those people, and in his manifesto, interestingly enough, he cites the web pages he frequented, including the Council of Conservative Citizens, a confirmed hate group that backs up its ignorance with a slew of bullshit statistics and out-of-context quotes.[8] Using its long list of racist drivel, and mentioning the media's coverage of the Trayvon Martin killing, Roof said he had no choice, that somebody had to fight back as America was taken from white people, that there was no other way than to kill nine innocent people.

This kind of hatred, this back-against-the-wall mentality, is the feeling of raw panic that Fox News and its predecessors and contemporaries have sought to cultivate for the last forty-some-odd years. Every election is one more opportunity to stop the growing fascist momentum of liberalism, a last chance to slow the rising tide of immigrants and moochers and enemies of the state before they finally kill off the Constitution and come for your family.

"I have to do this," Roof said during the massacre. "Y'all are raping our women and taking over the world."[9]

It's the language of a monster, of a psychopath, of a misogynist in a globalist economic present.

Here, it's "our" women, meaning ownership.

The country is also *theirs*, and in Roof's photos he's posed in front of old plantation homes, slave quarters, a Confederate museum. He yearned for a past in which the economic tables were turned and even poor whites had it better than somebody. For a past where blacks were still just tools of the system instead of economic rivals.

I've often felt that politics is a friendlier face put on economics, and the more I've followed it the more I've come to believe it's true that politics is the public visage we put on the forces that continually affect us, whether we recognize them or are oblivious to their influence. While liberal politics represent a general distrust of the system working fairly, right-wing politics, for the most part, are a manifestation of the fear and uncertainty Americans, primarily white males, are feeling in the face of changing times and economic realities.

They are told, constantly, that there's nothing else for them to do.

Their backs are against the wall.

"I have to do it," Dylann Roof said.

★   ★   ★

On June 21, four days after Dylann Roof robbed nine people of their futures, a little after 6 p.m., I parked my car on a side street in Charleston and ran to join the tail end of a parade headed toward Mother Emanuel. Hundreds marched, some toting signs reading BLACK LIVES MATTER and BLIND JUSTICE: WHEN DO WE GET OURS? Most just carried flowers they'd soon leave on the makeshift memorial outside the Emanuel AME Church.

We covered six or seven blocks before we heard the singing. It was so loud it echoed off the ivy-covered homes and through the shared courtyards of the historic houses we passed. Lining the route were old women and disabled men who handed us flowers to take with us to the memorial. Up ahead, the choir had moved on to "How Great Thou Art."

Calhoun, the street that runs in front of the church, was filled with a strange mix of mourners and media, the latter consistently wrangling the former into teary-eyed interviews where they asked, predictably, "How can something like this happen?"

In the cluster stood a black choir that looked like it had been at this for hours. Sweat dripped down their faces and yet they continued to rouse the crowd in hymns and prayers for healing, protection, and action.

Across the street, a young family in their Sunday best bowed their heads in prayer. I listened to the father, wearing a vest and slacks, maroon shirt and tie, pray that his children, in matching green dresses, will know a safer tomorrow.

When they were done, the choir called for the gathered to join hands. I was sandwiched between two men, both large in stature, and as the prayer wore on I heard both of them sob uncontrollably. In a few minutes, the one on my right would address the crowd and tell them his father had been the victim of a shooting in a Wisconsin Sikh temple, a massacre perpetrated by a white supremacist meaning to start a race war.

"This . . . just . . . keeps . . . happening," I heard somebody say, their voice choked with tears.

Another pastor waded into the circle while more and more people brought flowers. "He meant to bring war between the races and he has brought us together."

A cheer before a trombone player played "When the Saints Come Marching In" and the mourning turned, spontaneously, into revelations of laughter, clapping, a choir of amens and hallelujahs. When the last note was through, "Amazing Grace" began and the tears came in short order.

"Let God touch our leaders," the choir director prayed, "and let God touch our country and keep this from ever happening again."

An amen and then an odd moment as the sun set over the Emanuel AME Church's beautiful white walls, where nobody was certain when or where the songs will begin again.

Where nobody was certain if our prayer had been heard or if it would forever fall upon deaf ears.

Where we were waiting for something, for a deliverance and revival that might never come.

CHAPTER 4
THE EGO IS NOT MASTER IN ITS OWN HOUSE

A MONTH LATER, DONALD TRUMP SAID OF SENATOR AND FORMER Republican presidential nominee John McCain, "He's not a war hero. He was a war hero because he was captured. I like people who weren't captured."[10]

This gaffe came on July 18 at the 2015 Family Leadership Summit in Ames, Iowa, and was so outlandish, so disrespectful, so unthinkable that everyone was quick to point out it was more than likely the moment that Republicans' bizarre love affair with Trump would come to a crashing end.

After all, McCain was untouchable. Not only had he served as his party's standard-bearer but there was no doubt as to his heroism.[11] After being shot down in Vietnam, he'd spent over five years as a prisoner of war, a period that could've been significantly reduced if he would've accepted an early release his captors offered after his father was named commander of US forces in Vietnam. However, McCain chose to stay and for that decision he endured horrific torture that would leave him physically scarred for the rest of his life.

The disrespect shown by Trump felt like the final straw. Since his announcement in June, Trump had spent weeks giving rambling, hateful speeches around the country, speeches the networks had shown in their entirety and then rolled their eyes at. With each one, his racist rhetoric was increasing and to veteran politicians and pundits alike it didn't appear this was a sideshow built to last.

Insulting a hero and a legend like McCain was just more proof Trump wasn't ready for the political arena, much less the presidency, and column after column was penned and published predicting his inevitable decline. Even a week later, when an ABC/*Washington Post* poll showed Trump as the Republican front-runner with 24 percent of the vote and leading the rest of the field by double digits, skeptics were quick to point out another number: Only 34 percent of those interviewed believed that the businessman represented the core values of the party.[12]

I certainly wasn't immune. In a column I wrote while sipping sweating cervezas on a beach in Florida, I reveled in Trump's imminent collapse and wondered if he'd be out of the race before the first Republican debate in less than three weeks. Assuming his campaign would be "an interesting historical footnote," I wrote what amounted to one of several political obituaries that couldn't have been more logically sound nor any more wrong.

The mistake I made is one that people have been making as long as there have been mistakes. I assumed, with an eye to history, that events would continue to unfurl along a predictable path. This is why legendary prognosticators like Nate Silver, the data-driven proprietor of *FiveThirtyEight* who so nailed the 2012 election that he'd gained a reputation as a virtuoso, were so off the mark with Trump.

We assumed Trump was running for the nomination of the Republican Party we had come to know. The traits of this party had long been established, and if there was anything you didn't do it was disrespect the military and veterans. The GOP had long wrapped itself in the banner of patriotism, beginning well before September 11 and only growing in power afterward, and any slight to the military, perceived or otherwise, might as well be a resignation.

This mistake was predicated on what we now know to be an unbelievably large and incorrect assumption that the GOP, long besieged by radicals and fringe elements in the Tea Party, would eventually return to its original parameters just as it had in 2008 with John McCain, and again four years later with Mitt Romney. Both men had dalliances with those fringe elements, much as the rest of the party, but ultimately rejected its more outrageous traits, including birtherism, which Trump had all but monopolized for his own benefit.

Any discussion on this topic would be incomplete without an examination of the October 2008 incident where, just weeks before the general election, John McCain interrupted a member of his audience who'd called his opponent Barack Obama an "Arab" and corrected her, saying, "No ma'am, he's a decent family man . . . that I just happen to have disagreements with on fundamental issues . . ."[13]

There is a moment in the footage when you can see McCain trying his damnedest to play along with the questioner as she says she doesn't trust Obama. The senator wears a telltale grin when he's uncomfortable and it slips onto his face just as she begins speaking. He knows where the conversation is leading—just moments before another supporter had told him "we're scared of an Obama presidency," a bit of paranoia that McCain answered, to a chorus of boos, by telling the crowd there was nothing to be scared of—and he's obviously aware his campaign and the trajectory of his party has led into some very deep and very troublesome waters.

"I have read about him," the woman says as her nominee braces himself, "and he's not, he's not, he's, uh, he's, uh, he's an Arab . . ."

A split second passes as McCain does the terrible math. On one hand, the writing is already on the wall and he knows his chances of winning the presidency are growing slim. A series of missteps, including choosing an incompetent, half-crazy Sarah Palin as his running mate, and then suspending his campaign in the face of the recent economic collapse, have hobbled his bid. The only possibility of snatching victory from the jaws of defeat lies in the strategy of stoking fear in the electorate. It's there for the taking, certainly, as right-wing media outlets have demonized his opponent and all but called him an undercover agent for Al Qaeda.

But McCain, despite occasional lapses in political judgment, is above that type of rhetoric. He corrects the woman and takes the microphone before she can do any more damage. He refuses the poison pill of birtherism, saving his decency but sealing the coffin on his candidacy once and for all.

It's a moment that has been widely praised but certainly forgotten in the wake of Trump's success. Even in 2008, before the pinnacle of the Tea Party movement, there was a strain of the Republican electorate more than happy to embrace the brand of bigotry and distrust that would eventually propel Donald Trump to the party's nomination.

You can hear it in the boos that rain down on McCain when he tells the first questioner he shouldn't fear Obama, and you can certainly hear it in those voters who excuse Trump's slandering of the former nominee, including the multitudes I've heard at rallies who've called McCain "a coward" and the man I heard, at the first Republican debate, who referred to him as "a shitty pilot" as we sat in an open-air bar overlooking the circus outside the Quicken Loans Arena in Cleveland, a carnival featuring ticket holders and party dignitaries milling about with the freaks and the geeks. In the bar, though, populated by men wearing suits and golf shirts drinking wine and whiskey, it was more of an establishment feel as the so-called "happy hour" debate played on one of the bar's many flat-screen TVs.

"Don't get me wrong," the sunburned man with an elephant pin on his lapel told his drinking buddy, "I'm not for Trump, but it's not his fault McCain was a shitty pilot."

In a day of surprises, including watching a well-coiffed and -appareled family laugh as they took pictures of a Hispanic woman's sign calling on the party to rebuke Trump's rampant racism, the criticism of McCain was still eye-opening.

My much-needed third pint jiggered something loose in my memory, though, that I had been desperately trying to repress: the swift-boating of John Kerry in 2004, a political hit job unlike any other in which the Bush campaign levied a group of veterans to consistently call into question the Democratic nominee's service.

Watching Kerry, another Vietnam hero, be repeatedly attacked despite his sterling record of bravery had been a torturous exercise in an already trying time in which American ideals and freedoms, in the wake of 9/11, were routinely betrayed. The strategy had been a shameless excoriation that, despite its absurdity, had done its job and stripped away virtually everything that made Kerry an easy choice over Bush, whose Vietnam activities were, to put it charitably, questionable.

I think most of us, even those most disgusted, chalked up the attack to a divide between parties. Sure, Republicans would disrespect a veteran, but only if that veteran was a Democrat. In this new reality, this Post-Trump Era, however, politics had less and less to do with party affiliation

*   ★   *

No one was even remotely interested in tangling with Trump at that initial debate. Much as he did in every contest, the mogul faded into the background the longer the event wore on, but none of his rivals made him pay by honing in or criticizing any of the many offensive and stupid things he'd said in recent months.

This outright refusal has been attributed mostly to a general lack of courage among the GOP field, most citing Trump's intimidation and reputation as a bully. To have watched post-debate coverage or read the next day's print, you would have thought he'd scared them all half to death. The avoidance of confrontation, however, was much more a political strategy than an act of timidity. Trump had already established himself as the front-runner for the nomination, but the field, much like the pundits who lobbed peanuts from the sidelines, had already decided his lead was only temporary.

Like most of the ones that followed, that debate on August 6 followed a typical pattern. Early on, Trump got in a few highlight-ready lines and then receded and let his opponents squabble for scraps. Among his challengers, the real contest was who could best position themselves as the heir apparent to Trump so when he eventually fell apart they'd be there to scoop up his supporters. It was the same game the Republicans had been playing for generations, a tightrope walk of using racists and malcontents to their political advantage while keeping them at arm's length.

Ted Cruz was probably the most wounded by this strategy. Until too late in the process, he stood next to Trump and passed on attacking. The calculation, and this was shared by many in the media, was that Cruz, as leader of the Tea Party in the Senate, was the undoubted heir and eventual benefactor of Trump's collapse. If he could keep steady and manage to avoid the scrum, he'd undoubtedly perform the magic trick the party had been wielding for years by somehow uniting the evangelicals and the hateful.

The problem was that the party gifted the fringe a foothold and, by treating Trump as if he belonged on the national stage alongside their candidates, the Republicans emboldened that base. If his opponents had simply disavowed him or stated that Trump was unelectable, it would have possibly slammed the door on his candidacy. Those supporting Trump were part of a subset of voters who had been scorned over the years by a progressive culture and spanked by social media into tamping down their rhetoric and racist, misogynistic tendencies. By keeping Trump at the forefront, and using him as an outlet for the more offensive elements of the party, the Republicans unwittingly encouraged and heartened a bloc they had always kept at bay.

And they would have known that had they given the polls any respect. According to a *Real Clear Politics* poll average on the day of the first debate, Trump had maintained his stranglehold.[14] Long heralded as the precursor to his defeat, the McCain gaffe in July had done literally nothing to his numbers, though it had more than likely radically redefined what was inbounds for a Republican candidate. Trump had dropped anchor and nearly a quarter of the Republican electorate quickly rallied around him despite how far offshore he'd led them.

However, there were at least two people who weren't afraid to call Trump to task at the debate. One was John Ellis Bush, son of the 41st president and brother to the 43rd, a wonk everyone expected to walk away with the nomination until he revealed himself to be a pitiful campaigner after Trump humiliated him repeatedly. Perhaps out of self-defense, Bush criticized Trump and called a spade a spade. The decision probably didn't cost him the nomination because he was an objectively terrible candidate and this couldn't have been a worse election for someone with his particular pedigree and experience, but he was quickly turned into a pariah within the party because he took a walk and no one followed.

Surely Jeb must've expected Marco Rubio, Ted Cruz, John Kasich, or even Scott Walker to join him in standing up for the values of the party that had rewarded his family for decades. When they didn't, he was stranded out on a limb with the company of an unlikely compatriot: Megyn Kelly of Fox News.

★ ★ ★

Fox News Channel premiered in October of 1996, almost exactly one month before Bill Clinton would be elected to his second term as president of the United States. The brainchild of Australian-American media mogul Rupert Murdock, FNC was designed to be a splashy, state-of-the-art cable channel that skewed the news in favor of conservative ideals. To helm the project, he found the perfect candidate in Roger Ailes, a longtime force in Republican politics who more or less founded conservative visual media after being hired by Richard Nixon to be his executive TV producer.

Starting with Ronald Reagan, Ailes went on to assist every Republican president of the modern era, leaving his stamp on history at each stop. For George H.W. Bush, he produced one of the most effective ads in campaign history with "Revolving Door," a bleak and racist spot in which criminals entered a prison on the right and then immediately exited on the left. That commercial, partnered with the now-infamous "Weekend Passes," or "the Willie Horton ad" as some know it, was instrumental in raising Bush's "tough on crime" numbers from 23 to 61 percent in a matter of three months, according to a CBS News/*New York Times* poll.[15]

Ailes's fingerprints were all over programming as FNC continuously paired its idolization of conservative figures with a vilification of minorities and the liberals who enabled them. Never shying away from incidents involving African Americans, the channel would later, when politics demanded, turn its eye to illegal immigrants and so-called "radical Islamic terrorists."

For anyone who's managed to avoid exposure to Fox News, the country's leading cable news provider, a cursory glance is enough to incite simultaneous shock and rage. The presentation is an assault on the senses as graphics zoom across the screen while ominous music all but heralds the collapse of society. Meanwhile, the channel's inherent racism, sexism, and xenophobia are barely relegated to subtext. But to the regular FNC viewer, and there are well over 2 million of them, the programming certainly produces rage but little in the way of shock. This is, after all, the reality they are inundated with consistently.

That reality has its roots back in the 1960s when Ailes's former boss Richard Nixon implemented the aforementioned Southern Strategy. As a countermeasure to Lyndon B. Johnson's civil-rights legislation, the Southern Strategy intended to appeal to Southern white voters by exploiting racial divisions via carefully worded appeals that would maintain plausible deniability. These dog whistles granted Republicans the ability to speak to disaffected white voters without having to tout explicitly racist views in an age of burgeoning mass media.

The strategy was wildly successful and resulted in continued Republican successes in the former Confederate states. Under the helm of Ailes and his compatriot Lee Atwater, the Southern Strategy, via ads like "Revolving Door," was unleashed on the nation as a whole as a means of exploiting the inherent racist attitudes around the country.

Take a look at that ad.[16] It's black and white, the contrast between the two striking and unavoidable. And speaking of contrast, all of the prisoners are light-skinned except for the one African-American male the entire commercial focuses on. When we zoom in, he's the one walking through the turnstile. He's the one about to take advantage of his freedom to wreak havoc on an unsuspecting white community.

This is all base-level psychology. If Sigmund Freud were to sit down and look at "Revolving Door," he'd undoubtedly point out that this is an appeal to our id, the most basic and irrational part of ourselves, fearmongering at its very worst, and it's repeated every single time Fox News documents a crime involving minorities.

As Atwater, an architect of the mess we find ourselves in now, once infamously said: "You start out in 1954 saying, 'Nigger, nigger, nigger.' By 1968 you can't say 'nigger'—that hurts you, backfires. So you say stuff like, uh, forced busing, states' rights, and all that stuff, and you're getting so abstract. Now, you're talking about cutting taxes, and all these things you're talking about are totally economic things and a byproduct of them is, blacks get hurt worse than whites . . . 'We want to cut this,' is much more abstract than even the busing thing, uh, and a hell of a lot more abstract than 'nigger, nigger.'"[17]

The subconscious has played an undeniable role in American politics since the country was founded, but the advent of mass media has completely redefined its influence. The Republican Party, for example, has always been a bizarre amalgamation of unrelated parts that resembles, in a way, the human mind, beginning with its superego, a cast of intellectual stalwarts that have always guided the party's course. These are men like William F. Buckley and his cohorts at the *National Review*, George Will and any number of public intellectuals of their sort. This brain trust has always had Ivy League educations from Yale and Harvard, a blueblood aristocracy in favor of free markets that help the rich and interventionism that requires working-class soldiers.

Of course, these men represent a minute portion of the United States and, in the interest of political power, have had to marry themselves to the type of citizens they might very well look down their nose at. As a result, the elites have always had to rely on the support of working- and middle-class voters who have very little in common with the nobility at the heart of the Republican Party. This is why you so often see private-school-educated pundits on Fox News talking about "the Real America." The GOP and its supporting structures have to rely on such blatant ridiculousness to convince people to regularly vote against their own interests, a task that has been made infinitely easier in recent years by the dawn of the mass media.

The propaganda arm of the Republican Party has always held a dramatic advantage over that of the Democrats because Republicans, traditionally, have controlled the means of production. A cursory glance at the rise of Barry Goldwater in 1964 reveals that the conservative movement that has defined the twentieth and twenty-first centuries was instigated primarily by the publicity efforts of the conservative press.

That power, though able to sway a party, was not enough to secure Goldwater the White House, primarily because media interests were held in check by the Fairness Doctrine, a policy maintained by the Federal Communications Commission that mandated all media present opposing viewpoints on subjects of national importance. This meant that even the most devoted partisans had to be exposed to differing opinions on a consistent basis.

In 1987, under the direction of Mark Fowler, a former communications attorney for Ronald Reagan, the FCC voted 4–0 to discontinue its enforcement of the Fairness Doctrine. It seems unlikely that Fowler, who likened TV to "a toaster with pictures," understood the ramifications of his decision, but now, nearly thirty years later, we see a dire political landscape that has been polarized by unregulated partisan media.[18]

The "first man to proclaim himself liberated," in the words of Daniel Henninger of *The Wall Street Journal*, was right-wing windbag Rush Limbaugh, a larger-than-life figure who bloviated on his radio show for hours and skewered liberals with more and more outrageous attacks.[19] Limbaugh enjoyed before-then-unseen success in the era of deregulation and was so pivotal in ensuring Republicans victories in the 1994 midterm elections—an uprising that led to the first GOP majority in the House of Representatives since 1952 and was later coined "the Republican Revolution"—that the freshmen class of Republicans invited Limbaugh to speak and named him an honorary member of their caucus. In his speech, Limbaugh told the victorious Republicans to stay "rock-ribbed, devoted, in almost a militant way to your principles" and asked them to "leave some liberals alive" as artifacts so "we can show our children what they were."[20]

Limbaugh, as an unelected voice of the party, only had loyalties to himself and his brand as an agitator and was thus unrestrained by public sentiment. There was no need to compromise or find common ground with his enemies. His continued and ever-expanding influence made certain the Republicans he'd spoken to fell in line behind his often-extreme positions and guided them into one unnecessary spat after another.

Not long after producing Limbaugh's short-lived foray into television, Roger Ailes launched Fox News in 1996 and built on the legacy of Atwater and Limbaugh by helming a news channel undeterred by the Fairness Doctrine or interested in conciliation. Twenty-four hours a day, FNC broadcast unabashedly conservative content while forever denying bias. "Fair and Balanced" and "We Report, You Decide" its slogans read, and that, coupled with omnipresent right-wing radio, was enough to convince viewers looking to believe that the world existed as reported by FNC.

Prior to 1996, American citizens might've carried a political bias, but they weren't able to go so far as to sequester themselves from challenging information. Before the Fairness Doctrine was dismantled, they were forced to listen to dissenting opinions on the radio and on television, and then, before Fox News, they were watching coverage on their local networks and CNN, both of which still operated within the spirit of the doctrine. By nodding to impartiality while presenting a subjective worldview, the channel gave its viewers exactly what they hadn't even realized they wanted so desperately: skewed news with the comfort of tertiary neutrality.

Without question, Fox News was effective as its unrelenting inequity and willingness to dredge muck and fear ensured its place at the top of the ratings and allowed the network to wield unbelievable sway over the country's direction. Fox played an integral role in Bill Clinton's impeachment in 1998, the election of George W. Bush in 2000, the rise of unconstitutional measures like the Patriot Act following September 11, the eventual invasion of Iraq, and the effective hobbling of the Obama administration.

Fox's success, though, sowed the seeds for the GOP's eventual crisis of self-identity. To counteract Obama's Affordable Care Act, a corporate-penned update of our health-care system, Fox pushed its chips into the pile and portrayed the effort as something amounting to a tyrannical coup determined to kill American citizens and plunge the country into a postapocalyptic wasteland. Perhaps Fox's biggest mistake was underestimating its own power as its dedicated viewership took the campaign at its word and prepared for a final showdown that looked more like something out of the Book of Revelations than legislative process.

Since its inception, Fox News has masterfully played these contests in the same vein as the Republican Party. Between elections, Fox portrays the country as being torn apart by racial struggles and withering economically. The end of the American Experiment is near, and Democrats might very well be rooting for its failure. If voters, most of them working- and middle-class, don't put aside their own economic interests and suspicions, they could be complicit in losing everything.

Then, when it comes time to pick a nominee, the Republican Party presents a slate of competitors, most of them unreasonable candidates who personify the panic and fear that's been fed to them. There's Mike Huckabee and Rick Santorum warning against the war on Christianity, Ron Paul cautioning that freedom is being eroded, Michele Bachmann more or less reading conspiracy theories straight off the internet. They quell the nervous voters' need for these trumped-up concerns to be heard, but they are ultimately unelectable, meaning the spotlight eventually turns to a more palatable candidate like McCain or Romney who reflects the values and wants of the elite of the party.

In that first debate in Cleveland, you could already see Fox attempting to cure the electorate's addiction to Trump. For long stretches, he was left alone by the moderators and the more palatable alternatives—in this case Rubio and Walker—were given free rein to recite their prepared lines and stump speeches without challenge. Megyn Kelly, an up-and-comer in Fox's ranks, even went so far as to question Trump on his dubious history with women.

"Mr. Trump," Kelly began, "one of the things people love about you is that you speak your mind and you don't use a politician's filter. However, that is not without its downsides, in particular when it comes to women. You've called women you don't like fat pigs, dogs, slobs, and disgusting animals. Your Twitter account—"

"Only Rosie O'Donnell," Trump interjected, recalling his infamous feud with the comedian and drawing an arena's worth of laughter and applause.

Trying to fight through the noise, Kelly said, "No it wasn't . . . for the record, it was well beyond Rosie O'Donnell."

"Yes, I'm sure it was," an annoyed Trump responded.

What was supposed to be the beginning of the end only furthered the problem. The next day a bristling Trump went on CNN and told Don Lemon, "You could see there was blood coming out of her [Kelly's] eyes. Blood coming out of her . . . wherever."

Predictably, the remarks made waves and were repeatedly played on cable news, including Fox, which didn't shy away from litigating the controversy over the air. It was meant to undermine Trump's emerging legitimacy and paint him as the sexist pig everyone knew him to be. Ultimately, though, it deepened a growing fissure among conservatives that had lain dormant for fifty years. The Republican base, comprising mostly working- and middle-class voters, had been given permission by a candidate to question the media apparatus that had manipulated them for most of their lives. Somehow, Fox's constant assurance that it was "Fair and Balanced" had been driven home for so long that viewers eventually believed it wasn't slanted to the right, that it was just another untrustworthy corporate media operation like CNN or MSNBC.

Now, Trump was the arbiter of who could be trusted and who was fair. Never had a Republican candidate called into question Fox's legitimacy. And Trump had already made it routine practice to tell his supporters the media were dishonest and out to get him. To point the finger at Fox, and to have supporters who knew, deep down, that Fox was never on the up and up—the rift was substantial. The base the Republicans had depended on but ignored for generations was ready to fight back.

CHAPTER 5

THEY'RE TRYIN' TO WIN THIS THING

SIXTY-NINE DAYS HAD PASSED SINCE I WATCHED BERNIE SAND-
ers battle a UAW hall's aged speaker system, his gruff Brooklyn voice
eventually defeating it in front of 250-some-odd people. In the traditional Republican stronghold of Greenville, South Carolina, on August
24, 2015, the crowd numbered in the thousands.

What a long way this campaign had come.

Be it the crowd, the enthusiasm, or even the simple means by which
the organization had ordered its base and tuned its mechanics—whether
that was the overwhelming numbers of volunteers toting clipboards or
the walls lined with signage—this had the feel of a growing movement.

All around the country, Sanders had been filling arenas and events
with impressive crowds. In Arizona, it was 11,000[21]; in Seattle, 15,000[22];
and 27,000 Californians packed the Los Angeles Sports Memorial
Arena[23] earlier that month. Before that, 28,000 came to Portland's
Memorial Coliseum.[24]

And despite constant skepticism, the people kept coming.

All five of the Greenville Convention Center's parking lots were filled,
and from them streamed people carrying signs, families in matching
Bernie gear, Southern businessmen, and tie-dyed septuagenarians chatting while crossing roads and scurrying down embankments on their
way to one of the three congested entrances. A series of BERNIE 2016
sign-wielding volunteers guided the column of still-arriving vehicles
down the boulevard and to the parking for the nearby airport, the
gravel lots already choked full.

There was the predictable stock.

Liberal-arts professors still grasping for the sixties' promise of societal revolution.

Artisanal craftspeople who would've been more comfortable at the Saturday-morning farmers' market or taking shifts at the local co-op.

Poet radicals wearing Che Guevara shirts and poet radicals wearing shirts with Sanders's face over Guevara's.

The freaks and geeks who'd been waiting decades for the socioeconomic institutions of this country to tip the scales so far that everyday Americans would finally, finally hear the case for socialism.

And judging by the people in attendance, the time was now.

Waiting for the candidate, the hall was filled to the brim with late arrivers squeezing in from the sets of double doors. Two topics on everyone's lips: Donald Trump and socialism.

Of the former: When would the ludicrousness end? When would the country wake from its collective fever dream and expel Trump like so much questionable food?

The latter: "When did socialism get to be such a bad word?" I heard a woman ask.

"You know," said her companion, sporting Birkenstocks and a straw hat adorned with FEEL THE BERN buttons, "I couldn't even tell you."

Among the many conversations blending and bleeding together, there was talk that the country had transformed into something the Founding Fathers wouldn't have recognized, an oligarchical system serving the biggest of banks and wealthiest of men. For the attendees, Bernie Sanders's talk of a political revolution wasn't just rhetoric, but a call to arms.

"I've been waiting for this my whole life," a woman nearby said. She was wearing a black shirt with a spotty print of Sanders yelling into a microphone. "I just have a feeling that this is *our* guy."

The entire purpose and drive of the Sanders campaign was to evoke the feeling that Bernie was *our* guy. Here was, finally, a politician who had never strayed from his principles or bothered to play the game, a man who wasn't concerned with the usual niceties and business that modern politics demanded. He had one issue—the frightening and ever-growing inequality between the haves and have-nots—and refused to engage in the tricks of the trade, including super PACs, high-rolling donors, and media glad-handing.

Bernie Sanders was simply an ideologically pure candidate who could not, and would not, be bought or sold.

But that didn't mean he wasn't capable of what some pundits refer to, tongue firmly planted in cheek, as "evolving."

In the era of twenty-four-hour news coverage, one of the hardest parts of running for national office is the incorporation of new sound bites and policy matters in a stump speech that has been honed and pruned within an inch of its life. Some orators are naturally gifted—say President Obama or Bill Clinton—and make the fresh subjects feel as if they're points of discussions or simply off-the-cuff assertions, as if the speaker were realizing, in real time before the audience, a development regarding a matter of national concern. Those who can't come off as insincere or, even worse, opportunistic.

Bernie was somewhere in the middle of that pack. His speeches were strongest when he'd chew the fat of inequality and plead, in plainspoken and passionate language, the plight of the working and middle classes. Back in Iowa, it was as if a terminally frustrated old man had wandered into the hall to say his final peace before retiring to the wilderness in an attempt to escape, at long last, from the inequities of modern life. A wild-haired prophet come to deliver unglad tidings.

In South Carolina, the possibility of actually winning the damn thing had come into full view. Before Sanders ever stepped on the podium, he was preceded by his new national press secretary, Symone Sanders, a twenty-five-year-old social-justice activist and supporter of the Black Lives Matter movement, which had made a recent trend of interrupting

Sanders's rallies and demanding his support. Hoping to kneecap any potential interruption before it got started, she spoke at length of Sanders's civil-rights achievements.

In addition, Sanders had coopted the platform of Black Lives Matters in whole and now dotted his stump speech with references to the movement's stances, sometimes naturally and sometimes awkwardly. One of the biggest applause lines of the afternoon was when Bernie, banging the podium, recited the names of those African Americans recently killed by police, a demand the Black Lives Matters caucus had made during one of their actions.

Perhaps less dramatic was Sanders's latest topics: Supreme Court nominations for justices opposing *Citizens United* and a less-than-specific plan to replace ailing infrastructure. The focus of the speech had changed from all-economics-all-the-time and had developed into the more nuanced and familiar tone of a politician capable of reaching high office.

The evolution of Sanders over the course of those three months reminded me a lot of Rick Santorum's rise in the wake of his surprising showing in the 2012 Iowa caucuses. Though it wasn't then yet obvious that he'd beaten Romney, the presumptive front-runner, something grew in Santorum after his shocking upset. His speeches became clearer, more focused, and with every appearance he began to grow into the role of a Serious Contender. There was a magic to that Santorum campaign that occasionally catches with candidates, particularly fringe upstarts, when they begin to feel the momentum build.

But there's danger as the evolution challenges the candidate to become a better version of him- or herself, to push themselves to fulfill the promise of "the Leap," and for some, let's say Dukakis or George W. Bush in 2000, it entices the contender to explore directions they never would've considered before. Oftentimes, it leads them to personal ruin or damnation.

In Iowa, while addressing a ragtag assortment of Midwest radicals and unionists, Sanders had spoken of winning the presidency as if the contest itself were an afterthought, a less important goal than just saying the important things aloud. Here in Greenville, the presidency was front and center, the job a means to an end of finally leveling the playing field.

"It is immoral to give tax breaks to the wealthiest corporations and citizens when there are children hungry," he declared, his gruff voice fading with every word. "It is immoral to ship jobs and factories to China when there are people struggling here at home."

And then, in a pivot he'd refused to make in the past, he reset the conversation and framed economics as a "family-values issue," the attention firmly on GOP opponents. He filled in his own autobiography, mentioning his wife and children and grandchildren, a piece of personal story he'd avoided since his entry into national politics. Then, when the speech was over, his wife, Jane O'Meara, joined him on stage, and the duo waved at the crowd as "Rockin' in the Free World," the same anthem Donald Trump used to announce his candidacy, blasted over the speakers.

Much like his friend and fellow Vermonter Howard Dean, Sanders had chosen, until then, to campaign without the aid of his partner, a choice that had, at times, cost him in the polls. Male politicians regularly appear alongside their wives to both shore up the female vote and "soften" their image, something Dean needed in the weeks leading to his disastrous Iowa showing as reports painted him as being too angry and unstable. Dean refused, and I'm guessing Sanders did as well, because he saw it as a type of pandering unbefitting a serious candidate. Jane's appearance that Friday, and at subsequent events, was another move Sanders wasn't thrilled about, but I'm sure he was more than happy to jump through hoops as long as polls kept showing him gaining on, and occasionally leading, his rival Hillary Clinton.

They were winning moves—the adoption of Black Lives Matter, the slick rhetorical tactics, and the embracing of the politics of the personal—but if Bernie Sanders had no chance of winning, which was the popular opinion of nearly everyone, what were all these moves going to amount to in the end? And with all that energy, all that enthusiasm, and, yes, all that rage, what would happen if he came up short?

★   ★   ★

Real palpable trouble had been brewing in the Democratic Party since the 1960s, and not since the ascendancy of George McGovern had we seen a power struggle in the Democratic National Committee this explosive and undeniable.

At the heart of the matter was a foregone conclusion that, at times, didn't look as foregone or conclusive as it did a year and a half before, when the party put into place its machinery to ensure that Hillary Clinton's coronation as the first female president of the United States went as smoothly as possible. We were seeing a power struggle that wasn't just about DNC chair Debbie Wasserman Schultz's leadership, but rather a fundamental divide in vision that had plagued the party since the rise of the counterculture and civil-rights movement, a division that certainly played out in the battle between Clinton and insurgent Bernie Sanders, but had been there far longer than any stalwart would like to admit.

The trouble first came to light following the first debate leading up to the Democratic nomination, on October 13. Immediately, there was criticism, primarily from the Martin O'Malley campaign, as to why there weren't more than six scheduled forums, particularly in comparison to the overwhelming number of Republican clashes. O'Malley's concerns had gained little traction until Tulsi Gabbard, the representative from Hawaii and one of five DNC vice chairs, took to cable news to tell everyone who would listen she had been disinvited from the debate due to her shared concern. Eventually, citing her frustrations with the party's apparent favoring of Clinton, Gabbard would resign her leadership post in an incredibly public and bitter repudiation.

Disagreement among party leadership is as old as parties themselves, but the story took a new and more problematic turn as another vice chair, the former mayor of Minneapolis, R. T. Rybak, joined Gabbard in criticizing Wasserman Schultz, going so far as to accuse her of telling out-and-out lies regarding the process. Simultaneously, cracks were showing and anonymous sources talking. A crowd of Democratic insiders were leaking stories to journalists around the country that the DNC had made it clear to its members that the party's weight was, and always had been, behind Clinton's candidacy.

The clash consisted of former Clinton confidants and insiders, collectively referred to as Clinton World among the initiated, like Wasserman Schulz and vice chair Donna Brazile, a longtime Clinton confidant who had worked for nearly every establishment campaign since Bill and Hillary came to DC, and the rising stars of what I like to call the New New Left, a conglomerate of internet-age liberals who had managed to steal a share of the controls via their mastery of developing technologies. The latter group first came to prominence following Howard Dean's failed-but-innovative run in 2004, a campaign that both instilled new life in the long-distrusted tag "liberal" and first harnessed the messaging and fund-raising capabilities of burgeoning social media.

The dispute wasn't new, as this is the type of turf war we see every four years when the primary process hits its stride, but it was fresh in its possibilities as never before had the establishment Democrats needed the New New Left so badly, and never had they needed the establishment less.

★ ★ ★

Back in Greenville, the line to leave the arena snaked around the hallway and down an escalator where volunteers, handing out stickers and signs, were making sure to register every person who crossed their paths.

"I'll be damned," a man a few feet behind me said. "They're tryin' to win this thing."

Outside, pockets of supporters clustered around the building, some cheerfully going over what Sanders had said while others exchanged emails and phone numbers to plan "Feel the Bern" meetups in the coming weeks. From one end of the main parking lot to the other, streams of men and women wore white-and-blue BERNIE 2016 shirts and carried yard signs and tote bags.

Claiming that Bernie Sanders was simply trying to force Hillary Clinton to the left or serve as a counterbalance on the issues was a fool's game at that point. As the man had said, Bernie was trying to win the thing and had built a machine around himself to do just that.

★　★　★

There've been no shortage of books written on the 1972 presidential campaign because, quite frankly, it was one of the weirdest and most unpredictable contests the country had ever seen. Because of a convergence of factors— among them the Vietnam War, public unrest, and rapidly changing demographics—the field was built and ready for absolute pandemonium.

Originally the front-runner to challenge President Richard Nixon was party establishment favorite Ed Muskie, a New England bureaucrat who exemplified all the principles of Democrats in the mid-twentieth century. He was compassionate but tough, hopeful but pragmatic, a descendent of FDR less concerned with utopias and more enamored with JFK's long-heralded sensibilities. At his back was the entire strength of the Democratic Party, including kingmaker Richard Daley, the long-ballyhooed mayor of Chicago who'd directed the party via a series of backroom deals since the late fifties. Undoubtedly, he was the choice for the nod, but Senator George McGovern of South Dakota wrecked that plan.

The purported candidate of acid, amnesty, and abortion, McGovern was an unapologetic liberal who spoke softly and refused to apologize for towing ideological lines. When he opposed the Vietnam War, just as Sanders stood up in the face of the invasion of Iraq, he called into question the very soul of his country. As a candidate, he marshaled the power of a new class of voters, the young college students who flocked to his rallies and volunteered in record numbers, much like Howard Dean's "Perfect Storm" that flooded Iowa in the winter of 2004. And when he eventually overtook Muskie for the nomination, the DNC actively sought to undermine the legitimacy of its primary process and attempted to steal the '72 convention with a series of parliamentary procedures.

McGovern won, but ultimately failed. In the general election, he was destroyed by Nixon to the tune of forty-nine states to one, a bloodbath of historic proportions made possible by a series of mishandlings and a total lack of DNC support.[25] The party turning its back on its insurgent nominee should've been the death of the movement itself, but the betrayal was so potent and unabashed that, forty-some years later, the bruises still linger.

The lessons of McGovern's rout certainly didn't fall upon Bill Clinton's deaf ears. When the governor of Arkansas announced his candidacy in 1992, there weren't many people willing to bet on his success. The party favored stalwarts like Paul Tsongas of Massachusetts and Mario Cuomo of New York, but Clinton's upstart campaign, helmed by renegade James Carville and wunderkind George Stephanopoulos, proved to be more modern and evolved than any of its opponents and claimed control of the party.

Clinton is many things, and among them he is undeniably one of the best person-to-person campaigners in the history of retail politics. Though he has gone on to be a globe-trotting iconoclast for one of the most successful and globally active foundations in the history of the world, he began life as a good ol' boy from Hope, Arkansas, and cultivated a personal charm that has raised tens of billions of dollars, won him the governorship of his home state and two terms as one of the most important presidents of the twentieth century, cemented a legacy of import and persuasion, and solidified an establishment that effectively evolved the party around him.

These things are inarguable, but just as the world was getting smaller via the internet, it was also changing the landscape of what politics was. In the past, it was a handshake, a look in the eyes, an assurance that Politician X *understood* you, that Politician X had your best interests at heart. The truth of modern culture, with readily available stimulation and rampant social media, was that those gestures matter less than ever. What candidates needed was foundation and machinery, a platform that both raised funds and played to the expectations of a class of people more concerned with what their support of a politician said about them than what the politician intended to do.

This revolution had its roots in Joe Trippi, the mastermind of the Dean campaign who pioneered the social-networking approach we all know today and that changed the system much as McGovern and Clinton had done before. It's one of the reasons why Barack Obama was able to win two terms in the White House. The money he raised and the turnout he achieved made both elections afterthoughts as the real battle was never at the ballot but at the keyboard.

The reason Hillary Clinton lost to Obama in '08 had less to do with policy or debate performance and more with how Obama embraced the language of the internet. People sharing statuses, pictures of themselves at rallies, and pinning stickers to their walls or Pinterest boards is about personality politics and self-identification, and Clinton had never been able to establish herself as a presence on that plane. It was a generational divide the Clintons, belonging to the baby-boomer generation, could not fully understand.

The Democratic Party knew this well and first extended an olive branch by bringing Howard Dean in as its chair in early 2005. The decision to embrace Dean led to the fifty-state strategy that would shift funds to traditionally red states and eventually make Obama the first African-American president. It was a strategy that effectively cut the Republicans off at the knees because the GOP, much like the baby-boom establishment, had been slow to understand the possibilities of internet campaigning and had thus been vulnerable.

In Dean's wake, however, the establishment would wrest control of the DNC once again and in doing so would back one of the most qualified and established candidates in Democratic history, a move that made all the sense in the world but essentially alienated an enthusiastic subset that would eventually be faced with a hell of a decision: to fall in line with the Democratic Party, or turn their backs on politics altogether.

CHAPTER 6
LIFE OUTSIDE THE CLOUD

INSIDE THE THEATER, THE ARGUMENT WAS ALREADY HEATED. IT was the fourth such confrontation I'd seen since arriving on the University of South Carolina's campus on September 23 and the third inside the Koger Center for the Arts. Right inside the doors, where volunteers with red lanyards corralled streams of well-tanned and well-coiffed attendees to their seats, two men had disrupted the flow by arguing over whether Donald Trump was a conservative. By the elevators, just past the college Republicans handing out free Trump T-shirts and Trump bumper stickers and Trump buttons, a man in a yellow polo and khakis had leaned forward to invade the space of man wearing a white undershirt and jeans.

An usher pointed me to the open seat between two more arguing men, surprising all three of us. One of them, wearing a sweater with a straw hat, asked if I'd switch seats so he could continue the conversation. I agreed and scooted over to sit next to an insurance salesman whose phone background was a glamour photo of his wife with the words THE HOTTEST surrounding her like magazine print.

"I've just never seen anger like this before," the man with the straw hat said.

The other man shook his head. "Then you've been living in a cloud."

I listened as Straw Hat made the mistake of telling the man he was from a New York publication.

"I don't know what it's like in *New York*," the man said, spitting out the city's name like it tasted bad in his mouth, "but here, we've got a lot to be angry about."

The correspondent assured him: "I'm not telling you there isn't—"

"Well," the man interrupted, "I'm just saying, maybe, in *New York*, there's nothing to be angry about. Maybe that's what it's like when you're living in a cloud."

After recognizing there was no room left for conversation, Straw Hat excused himself and sought asylum elsewhere. The man he'd been talking to leaned over the now empty seat between us.

"Are you from *New York*, too?"

"No," I told him. "I'm a Hoosier."

Relieved, he said, "Good. I don't know if I could've handled another round of that."

★   ★   ★

When Donald Trump first began catching momentum in the summer of 2015, friends and colleagues alike asked me whether I'd ever actually met anyone who supported him. "I don't see Trump signs," one said, shaking his head like it was all some fantasy. "I don't see anything on Facebook. I have a hard time believing they even exist."

Honestly, I had felt the same way. At that point, in my real life and on my social media, I hadn't yet come across any Trump supporters other than members of my family back home in Indiana. This was before Trump signs and flags were populating the landscape, before the MAKE AMERICA GREAT AGAIN hats were being worn all around the country. In the midst of all the articles and quotes my friends posted, never had I noticed anyone taking umbrage with the emerging portrait being painted of Trump, never had I seen a fight erupting over whether or not Trump was a racist. Everyone, it seemed, was in perfect agreement over the repulsiveness of the Republican front-runner.

So Senator Tim Scott's Republican presidential forum series was my first opportunity to really meet the 2016 Republican base up close and personal, and I found the right felt the exact same way about the left. They couldn't believe they were real.

"You're writing a book?" a GOP county official asked after listening in on the conversation I'd had with my neighbor. "What's it about?"

"The election," I told him, trying to be as brief as possible.

"What about it?"

"I don't know," I admitted. "How this whole thing happened. How we got to this point in the country. How we got so divided?"

The GOP official, and most of the surrounding crowd, had a lot of opinions on just how we'd gotten to this point. Most popular among them was that Barack Obama had overstepped his authority as president and was leading the country to ruin.

"Liberals aren't blameless," another man butted in.

"No," the man next to me agreed. "They aren't blameless."

The conversation happened around me, at me, as I struggled to take notes on my phone. There were so many opinions on how Obama and his liberal supporters had not only ruined the country but had salted the earth and ensured continued political division with their lies and socialist designs.

"Truth is," my neighbor said, "there aren't many of them."

"Liberals?" I asked.

"No, sir. There's very, very, very few. Probably 70 percent of this country is conservative. Twenty is independent, but they lean right."

Making sure I understood, I asked him, "You think 10 percent of the country is liberal?"

"If that," he said. "I hardly know any liberals myself."

★　★　★

The fracturing of our political reality is a wound a long time in the making. Some would argue it's been there since the drafting of the

Constitution, and even if that can't be agreed upon it's obvious that the schism of the Civil War and the long-held divisions resulting from Reconstruction have created a rift Americans still suffer from today. But the modern political divide, the schizophrenic-like existence that torments not only our governmental dealings but the daily lives of our citizens, has its roots firmly in the 1990s.

As previously mentioned, the proliferation of right-wing news, both in print and over the airwaves, began after the dissolution of the Fairness Doctrine in 1987 and continued with the deregulation of media ownership provisions. This allowed outlets like Rush Limbaugh and Fox News to present a completely biased opinion to an unsuspecting public more than ready to accept news that confirmed their beliefs. These developments poisoned political discourse and mired the country in partisan squabbles, ailments that critics argued would doom the Republic, but even the most concerned and outspoken voices would have had a hard time understanding the effect the internet and social media would have on our process.

It's necessary for a moment to look back at the nexus of this, the point where these influences intersected: the 1994 midterm elections, when Republicans steamrolled Democrats and seized Congress for the first time in decades. This sweep has much to do with Limbaugh and the rise of right-wing media, but none of it would have been possible without the efforts of Newt Gingrich and his much-ballyhooed Contract With America, a document released during the midterms that laid out a conservative agenda Republicans would undertake if given control of government.

The Contract With America paid off wildly, and one of the reasons it did so is because Gingrich made a bet that, with spreading mass media, local and regional elections could be marketed as being national in scope, a gambit that has been shown to be true time and again. In the era of twenty-four-hour news and in the midst of a gridlocked

Congress, that seems shocking, but there was a time when senators and members of Congress were treated more as representatives of states as opposed to cogs in the national political machine. Gingrich's play to make the '94 midterms a referendum on Bill Clinton and the direction of the country forever shifted the focus from local representation to a battle over whether a party and its shared vision would be enacted in the chambers of power.

Over the years, this shift has only intensified, and that's in no small part because the internet now makes it possible to receive constant and comprehensive reports of how our representatives are voting and whether they tow the party line. Whereas in the past we might have concerned ourselves primarily with our own representatives, we now scan the blogs and reports like someone might have read box scores for a baseball game in the 1960s. And, in its own way, that has made politics like a sporting event in which we, the fans, are either winning or losing, and every move, every decision, every word is dissected and criticized the way someone might armchair-quarterback a *Monday Night Football* game around the Tuesday-morning water cooler.

The result was the passion plays that were the shutdowns of the federal government in 1995 and 1996 and the subsequent impeachment of Bill Clinton two years later. With Gingrich at the helm, the new Republican Party was now fighting a life-or-death struggle with Democrats and more than willing to close the doors of government or take down a president as long as it forwarded its agenda. Constituencies were forgotten as a new countrywide battle took shape.

The casualties, other than the progression of the United States' laws and policies, have been felt primarily on the home front. I cannot put a number on the amount of people who've told me over the years how they've watched their loved ones, their mothers and fathers, sisters and brothers, consumed by the right-wing media machine. It was a long, long process that began with Fox News' founding and resulted in unbelievable changes in behavior and discourse. With every family holiday, there are new anecdotes about uncomfortable confrontations, hurt feelings, tears shed as parents and siblings rage against anyone who dares question the validity of the right-wing lie.

Personally, I first noticed the reality gap in the lead-up to the invasion of Iraq in 2003. Despite the Bush administration's consistent misleading of the public, I was convinced to my core that the war was not only unnecessary but built on false pretenses. I think one of the first clues that tipped me off was hearing those supporting the war, even those who were paid to talk about the situation on the news, routinely confusing Iraq with Al Qaeda, a bizarre mistake as the two could not have been more different. The confusion continued, and soon I heard the conservatives in my life blaming Saddam Hussein and the Iraqi people for the attacks of September 11, a narrative the Bush administration never officially endorsed but certainly used to its advantage.

Many in my family supported that war. Most of them would also later vote for Trump, and much like when I attempted to dissuade them from that choice, when I tried to talk to them about the dangers of invading a sovereign country that hadn't attacked us, the vitriol I received in return was uncharacteristically nasty. I'll never forget, that Fourth of July before the invasion, hearing a family member at a cookout tell me, a red-white-and-blue paper plate in hand, that the president should just "drop a nuclear bomb on the whole Middle East" and "turn it into a glass parking lot."

I asked him about the women and children. About the innocent lives he was more than willing to snuff out without a second thought.

He shrugged. "Kill 'em all."

The fallout from September 11 and the Iraq War was brutal and led to one of the darker periods in American history. Pissed-off and frightened, the Republican faithful, a group that had long touted the virtues of smaller government while worshiping at the altar of Ronald

Reagan, the biggest big-government president, were more than willing to cede to the federal government any authority it wanted, whether it was trampling on civil liberties or fighting an unjust war, and anyone who disagreed was swiftly punished. During those years, I was called a turncoat by loved ones, told that I was un-American, asked by a family member if I knew I was a traitor and that traitors "get what's coming to them."

To look back on that stretch of time now, it's odd to realize, in measure, that at least then we were still talking to one another. Even if it meant fights at the dinner table, confrontations that led to long familial silences and irreparable personal damage, we were still forced to inhabit one space where ideas and opinions commingled. It didn't seem back then that things could get much worse.

Years later, we wouldn't believe how wrong we were.

★　★　★

Donald Trump talked like he was afraid he'd never get the chance to talk again.

Every answer was rapid-fire. Every take hot and loaded. He happily manipulated every single question into a piece of fleshy red meat for his base and marbled it with extra fat. And it all came so fast, and so hot, there was little time to digest any of it or get it all in my notebook.

Reading polls, slagging Rubio.

Three priorities: debt, Obamacare, replace it with something "terrific," military, vets, polls.

POLLS, POLLS, POLLS.

Vets to illegals.

Reviving jobs: I have ten billion dollars.

And those were the first five minutes.

At the forum, Trump was the walking, talking embodiment of the cable news show, a rambling, bombastic blowhard who said nothing at all but said it fucking loud. By my count, Senator Tim Scott asked a total of eight questions, those questions touching on immigration, job creation, ISIS, and pride, and Trump didn't answer a single one straight on.

When Scott pressed him about his plans against ISIS, he leaned down and clasped his hands between his knees like he was about to tell a woman she'd been widowed.

"I know a lot about Syria," he said, "but I'm not going to give specifics."

For the next five minutes, he danced around Syria because he didn't think it was wise to "let enemies know what you're going to do." A few audience members clapped like he'd just won the war. The more traditional Republicans shifted. One heavy man in a navy-blue suit stood up and walked over to the stage while fiddling with a camouflage MAKE AMERICA GREAT AGAIN hat he'd just purchased. The Secret Service quickly intercepted him and, as if to assure them he wasn't a threat, the man held out a Trump button and smiled like he was having the time of his life. An agent gave him a thumbs-up in return as Trump said, "But I'll tell you this: We're gonna let Syria fight ISIS and we're gonna let Russia fight ISIS."

Another question unanswered, another thumbs-up.

★　★　★

While I'm sure the genesis of social media was intended to actually make media more sociable, we're far enough down the road in this experiment to pronounce the returns mixed at best. Certainly, Facebook and Twitter and their like do a fine job of linking us superficially to friends, acquaintances, and family members we might otherwise lose touch with, but the cultural influence of the programs is just now coming into focus.

As the internet has become a ubiquitous presence, a majority of Americans have turned to online platforms for their information, including 62 percent, according to a 2016 Pew poll, who now rely on social media as their main venue for news. This number is astoundingly large and troublesome considering the limitations of social media in conveying information of any sort, much less complicated and nuanced information necessary to the continuing health of the United States government.[26]

First and foremost, attention spans are notoriously short in the online world. Feedback has continually taught users that brevity is key in a platform where space and words are limited, but even if the information is successfully accepted, we can't be trusted to read an entire article, and more often than not we glean what little knowledge we take away from the attached headline. In social media, this effect is only intensified as a multitude of friends bearing links and snippets of information, factual or otherwise, are competing for our already-limited bandwidth, turning the absorption of news into a frenzied free-for-all.

In that maelstrom, it's often the most shocking links that get noticed. As anyone who's navigated social media can tell you, the old axiom of "if it bleeds it leads" has survived mass media's evolution from ink on paper to pixels on a computer screen. Outrage undoubtedly drives the internet, and positive or lukewarm stories often fall by the wayside while controversial pieces go viral and receive fantastic amplification. This emphasis on scandal and discontent has not only affected the way the world seems, but has forever changed the way we interact, or, as is the case, choose not to interact.

The term "intellectual ghetto" was coined by David Bauder in his 2016 Associated Press series "Divided America" and was meant to encapsulate the communities users had segregated themselves into by curating dissenting opinions out of their lives.[27] Because we now have a seemingly infinite number of news outlets to choose from, whether they be historically reputable publications like *The New York Times* or an anti-vaccine blog that only came online the day before yesterday, Americans can now choose the news they consume à la carte and filter out anything that overtly challenges their beliefs, even if those challenges are competent and necessary.

The drive to tune out opposing ideas can be explained by psychology's principles of selective exposure theory and confirmation bias, both being impulses people use to avoid cognitive dissonance, or the stress that occurs when an individual is confronted with evidence that contradicts their beliefs.[28] This is why a conservative turns on Fox News and a liberal prefers MSNBC. What they're tuning in for has less to do with receiving the news of the day than reinforcing their preconceived notions of how the world operates.

But remember, a majority of Americans now say their main source for news is social media. That change has weakened outlets like Fox News and MSNBC and has instead focused the attention on a smattering of websites and blogs that tend to reinforce those preconceived notions in a much more overt and aggressive manner and operate without a need to present empirical or objective fact. The result is a disorganized jumble of outlets growing in power and influence as they realize that power and influence are predicated on how well they serve the public's need for biased information.

As the networks and traditional news providers have lost sway, the task of curating has fallen to the social-media user who now functions as a gatekeeper. Everyone who posts on Facebook, who retweets a story on Twitter, is now essentially one's own news division and their feeds a channel that others can choose to click off the way they might CNN. If the user consuming the feed senses that the gatekeeper doesn't share their opinion or reflect their veracity, confirmation bias leads them to turn away from the gatekeeper and banish their information lest they face cognitive dissonance.

Like Newt Gingrich shifting the focus from local to national, social media has transformed politics from the public to the personal. Whereas, in the past, people associated with their friends and families based on proximity, common history, or blood relation, social media gives the person the power to structure their relationships based on common interests and shared political goals. This grouping, often called an echo chamber, creates a world in which people are rarely confronted by disparate opinions or facts and ensures their persuasion goes unchallenged. And the more they become entrenched in their opinions, and the more they see others touting similar belief structures, the more the user's beliefs deepen.

This past February, I was stunned when I saw a Facebook status come across my feed that gave users directions on how they might discover which people in their circles supported Donald Trump. The person posting the status bragged that she had unfriended no less than a dozen people, including members of her family. Under the status came a flurry of replies from others who took her advice and purged their social media of anyone who dared to consider voting for Trump.

Certainly, the impulse is understandable. At the height of his campaign, Trump represented the most pure and undeniable strand of fascism this country has ever seen from a nominee of a major party. Support for Trump hinted, I think people would argue, at a defect of some sort, some deep and hidden ignorance or bigotry that people might have missed in their friends and relatives, but in exiling those people from their lives, I don't think my Facebook friend or others who have followed her lead understood exactly what they were doing, or that those decisions only made the situation worse.

When we isolate ourselves from those who don't share our opinions, even if they are ignorant or bigoted, we're removing one of the last remaining opportunities for that person to receive feedback that challenges their ignorance or bigotry from a person they could very well trust. In cable news networks and large media conglomerates, there's a built-in wariness that comes simply from the size of the originator. There are thousands upon thousands of people who work for these leviathans, and there's simply no way for the consumer to empathize on a personal level with the whole of the structure, much less know the heart of those providing the news. More than likely, our established relationships are the only remaining avenues by which we can possibly chip away at the intellectual ghettos users have segregated themselves into and challenge, albeit slowly, their preconceived notions.

By isolating them, users only exacerbate the problem of polarization. The moment they hit that unfriend button, the personal face of the opposition is eliminated and suddenly, once the other's life has been cleansed of dissenting views, they see a community populated with only people who agree with them. Suddenly, anybody who doesn't operate within that sphere, anybody who doesn't traffic in the same political persuasion, is seen as being an outlier—unhinged, unrealistic, or, even worse, a person with consciously evil motives.

Suddenly, it's us versus them.

Suddenly, the left's dislike for Donald Trump becomes all the incentive necessary to vote for him.

★ ★ ★

After the forum mercifully came to an end, I made sure to shake the hands of my newfound acquaintances. They'd forgotten my name quickly, but there were no hard feelings. They knew we weren't from the same reality, and maybe it was easier that way.

"Promise me something," the guy who chased off Straw Hat said to me by the door.

"What's that?" I ask.

"In your book . . ."

"Yeah?"

He shook his head and sighed. "Just tell the truth."

I promised him I would and walked toward the exit. It wasn't until I saw another argument on the sidewalk outside that I realized I'd forgotten to ask whose truth I was promising to tell.

CHAPTER 7
THE END OF AN UNEASY TRUCE

"I DISAGREE WITH HILLARY CLINTON ON VIRTUALLY EVERYTHING," Bernie Sanders told *The Boston Globe*'s editorial board for an article that ran November 5, 2015, the day before MSNBC's First in the South Democratic Candidates Forum. "What is important . . . to look at is the . . . track record that Hillary Clinton has had for her long and distinguished career as a public figure."[29]

Nationally, Sanders's distancing himself from the former secretary of state was met with perplexed amusement. Most speculated that Bernie was running to keep Clinton honest on the left, but this public break hinted at something more: the possibility that Sanders really could be running to win.

The media gathering in the pressroom at Winthrop University chatted lazily about whether Sanders's growing crowds were giving him false hope. I was listening to them as I tried to remain inconspicuous. Wearing my first suit that hadn't come off the discount rack at JC Penney, I moved the cursor around my laptop's screen while eavesdropping on the professionals talking shop.

"Maybe he smells it," a cameraman wondered aloud as he deleted images. "I mean, maybe he's thinking of running third-party."

A writer in a corduroy jacket and jeans hiked too high over his gut wasn't so convinced. With a groan, he kicked his feet up on the foldout table and said, "For who? The fucking Green Party?"

The cameraman shrugged. "Maybe."

Not two chairs down slumped another writer charging roughly half a dozen devices on the complimentary power cords. "Only thing Bernie goddamn Sanders cares about is committee assignments."

Despite the group's skepticism, the polls had been tightening by the week, and with the Iowa caucuses just a little over a month away, Clinton had been forced to address her opponent on her numerous television appearances, whereas earlier in the race she'd spent most of her time lambasting the Republicans at large while ignoring Bernie's challenge.

The change came in the initial debate in October, when Clinton jabbed Sanders relentlessly on his gun-control position, a hot-button topic in the wake of a slew of rampage shootings. A representative of rural Vermont, Sanders answered Clinton's concerns by explaining the needs of his constituents differed from urban voters, but the damage was done. Clinton had found the beginnings of an opening and, while she continually cited the civility of the Democrats in contrast to the Republican shitshow, the tone of the campaign had shifted radically.

Evidence of the budding ill will was everywhere on Winthrop's campus. Outside the Byrnes Auditorium, supporters gathered around the cable-news remote sites, waves upon waves of Sanders voters squaring off against Clinton's masses. For hours at a time, they held their signs aloft and chanted "Sanders! Sanders! Sanders!" and "Hillary! Hillary! Hillary!" Though tempers were kept in check, there was no peaceful mingling between the sides.

The contest so far had felt like a respectful disagreement that would probably never move past a terse response or two in the heat of a debate. Now I was hearing Clinton voters calling Sanders's people "unrealistic" and the latter musing over how they'd never trusted the former secretary of state.

"She's one of the worst politicians," a student in a baby-blue FEEL THE BERN shirt told me when I asked why he wasn't supporting Clinton. "She's one of the worst, if not *the* worst."

Worse than Trump?

He considered. "Maybe?"

The conversations I was having with them and the supporters in my life were taking on new shapes and dimensions. Whereas they'd quietly questioned Clinton's trustworthiness and status as an establishment politician just months before, now they were talking about her in tones similar to Republicans, including her email controversy, her past support of the Iraq War and opposition to same-sex marriage, and turning an eye to the primary battle in 2008, when Clinton and Barack Obama had locked horns in one of the most contentious contests the party had ever seen.

The implications of that race have been largely glossed over in a wave of Democratic amnesia, but there are still those who blame Clinton for the ugly tone, including the now infamous speech she gave in Rhode Island in which she mocked Obama's hope-and-change message by saying, "Now I could stand up here and say, 'Let's just get everybody together.[30] Let's get unified. The skies will open, the light will come down, celestial choirs will be singing and everyone will know we should do the right thing and the world will be perfect.'"

Ironically, the playbook Clinton used unsuccessfully against Obama returned in 2016 as she attacked Sanders and his supporters for their pie-in-the-sky attitudes. In many ways, it was becoming clear that Clinton was the legislative heir to the president Obama became, but Sanders was the spiritual successor of the candidate who shocked the political world and inspired a generation.

★ ★ ★

The scars of '08 were already apparent early in the 2016 cycle when in Iowa Sanders came within an eyelash of upsetting Clinton, a moment that members of the Clinton team watched with a particularly toxic feeling of déjà vu, and then predictably routed her in New Hampshire by twenty-two points. For the first time, the political world was coming around to the possibility that Clinton could fall victim to another historic upset.

On February 20, Nevada held its caucuses and many expected Sanders to do well with the state's union voters. In an effort to stem the tide, however, Senator Harry Reid moved behind the scenes to use his influence to focus the labor vote in Clinton's favor. The win felt like a closing of a door on Sanders's upset bid, and when Clinton took the stage to address her supporters, her speech had an air of relief and finality to it.

"The truth is," she began, an eye focused on her opponent, "we aren't a single-issue country. We need more than a plan for the big banks."

Much as the media had underestimated Sanders's viability, the political establishment assumed New Hampshire would be the high-water mark for his revolution. That certainly seemed to be the case after the Nevada loss and then in South Carolina where he fell by nearly fifty points. March 1, the first Super Tuesday of the cycle, Clinton won eight out of the twelve contests, and it seemed, barring a few blips along the way, her march to the nomination was going according to plan.

Then Michigan happened.

In one of the greatest upsets in political history, Sanders managed to stanch the bleeding and capture the state by 17,000 votes. Because polls had shown Clinton enjoying a comfortable lead anywhere from thirteen to twenty-seven points, the question the morning after was how the result could have been so unexpected.[31] Some pointed to '08, the last contested Democratic primary, when Michigan saw its contest disrupted by a dispute with the DNC, thus negating the need for polls that could be used for context. However, the real emphasis should've been on the factors that led to Sanders winning Michigan and that would eventually cost Clinton the presidency.

* ★ *

In November of 1993, I sat in my grandparents' darkened living room and watched Vice President Al Gore debate businessman Ross Perot on *Larry King Live* on the topic of the North American Free Trade Agreement. In two short months, President Bill Clinton would sign NAFTA into law.

Watching that debate was one of the most important moments in my political development. My family consisted of working-class factory people who were always just a step away from financial ruin. The only constant in our lives was the inconsistency of our means. Because we were poor, we supported Democrats. My grandmother, who chain-smoked Pall Malls as Gore and Perot jousted with statistics, had told me for years the Republicans were the party of the rich and to support the GOP was tantamount to being a traitor to our class, but her reaction to what was transpiring on CNN was wholly unexpected.

"My god," she said when Perot held up a picture of Mexican slums and impoverished Mexican workers. "Look at how those people have to live."

Gore held his own, but the feeling coming out of that program was that NAFTA was at best a tenuous step for the country. My grandma admitting as much was a shock. To hear her talk about Franklin D. Roosevelt, you would've thought he was a messiah. She credited him with saving America and pulling her and her family out of the Great Depression, and every Democrat after him was an apostle, a force for good and progress who protected working people. On the walls, commemorative plates honoring F.D.R. and John F. Kennedy hung next to portraits of Jesus Christ. The message was clear: Democrats watched over the poor just as Christ shepherded the meek.

But NAFTA was the moment when it all changed. Even though Bill Clinton had inherited the treaty from his predecessor George H. W. Bush, his signing the law meant my family, and many families around the industrial Midwest, would lay blame with the Democrats when factories that had supported towns around the Rust Belt shuttered their doors. Though the real ramifications of NAFTA were more complex—the agreement bolstered our economy and led to higher standards of living—the immediate reaction was that the Democrats had sold out their constituency.

Because Hillary Clinton was inextricably linked to her husband, whether fair or not, she carried with her the stigma of NAFTA's legacy, and in Michigan she was vulnerable to a liberal in the same mold as F.D.R. The same could be said throughout the Midwest. She lost in Michigan, Wisconsin, Minnesota, and Indiana, states that progressive Obama had previously carried. The Midwest, particularly Michigan and Wisconsin, had traditionally been centers of power for the Democrats, but globalism and changing demographics now rendered them vulnerable.

Clinton's struggles with the working class could've been mended with more careful messaging, but as she watched the center-left defect, she was also staving off a rebellion inside the liberal wing. Sanders's democratic socialism was capturing the hearts and the minds of the same progressives and young voters that Obama's hope-and-change message had reached in 2008 and 2012. Sanders's appeal to dream and imagine widespread revolution hit home for voters who had watched Obama take office and then seemingly drift toward the center. They were ready for the change they'd been promised.

Clinton's painting of Sanders's base as being unrealistic in the same way she'd criticized Obama's only worsened the problem. Certainly, a rawness remained from '08, but it doesn't seem as if the result would've been repeated had Clinton chosen not to go negative. Instead, the campaign repeatedly compared Bernie's populist outrage to the brand of anger that fueled Donald Trump, a comparison that, by extension, meant Sanders's supporters were just as unacceptable.

In May of 2016, the Democratic National Committee took that characterization a step further when Nevada's Democratic convention erupted. Internet rumors circulated that a chair had been thrown and the state's chairwoman reported she'd received harassing phone calls. Debbie Wasserman Schultz furthered the narrative by calling on Sanders to rein in his supporters and made sure to pepper her interviews with thinly veiled comparisons between the Nevada convention and Donald Trump's rallies, which had been descending into chaotic violence since March.[32]

Then came the popularization of the term "Bernie Bro," a label that gained traction online as the Democratic primary grew more competitive. Bandied about social media, and often credited to Robinson Meyer, who wrote "Here Comes the Berniebro" for *The Atlantic*, the pejorative term referred to self-identifying male progressives clashing with Hillary Clinton supporters on Facebook, Twitter, and in comments sections across the internet.[33] The underlying message: Bernie's base was primarily composed of young men who, deep down, were motivated, at least in part, by latent misogyny.

Undoubtedly there were instances of such behavior—political scientists reported[34] in *The Washington Post* that Clinton voters were certainly being harassed by men, though an overwhelming majority favored Donald Trump—but in the heat of the 2016 primary, "Bernie Bro" became a depreciatory shorthand for any Sanders supporter. The Clinton campaign, which had used the term "Obama Boy"[35] in '08 to similar ends, embraced the phrase and used it to further tie Sanders and his voters to Trump.

Emails stolen from the DNC would show that members of the organization, supposedly impartial, had begun using the phrase to discuss Sanders loyalists. Sources inside Clinton World would tell me later that factions of the campaign used the Bernie Bros stigma to help the candidate in the New York primary, an ugly affair that further poisoned discourse between the rivals and their respective voters.

The icing on the cake came June 6, the night before the highly anticipated California primary. For all intents and purposes, Sanders had
lost the fight by then and had been reduced to condemning superdelegates—party officials who enjoy votes that can tip the primary's
scales. Despite imminent defeat, Bernie's supporters were still cau-
tiously optimistic. If Sanders could win California, maybe superdelegates would think twice about supporting Clinton, especially with
her email controversy looming over the process. Some Democrats
were openly hoping she'd be indicted for mishandling state secrets.
The political spectrum had come full circle as the far left shared the
rhetoric of the far right.

Then, at 8:20 p.m. that Monday night, the Associated Press announced that following a survey of Democratic superdelegates, Hillary
Clinton would be the Democratic nominee for president of the United
States of America.[36] The news was reported first on MSNBC, and the
question that quickly emerged was why the AP would risk releasing
news that could affect the California primary.

The truth was that the AP didn't want to be scooped in the pronouncement. Several news agencies were feverishly working the phone
lines and wrestling with delegates to get a commitment one way or
another, and if the AP hadn't released its findings on June 6 another
entity would have in short order. There was a practical explanation
for the announcement, but that wouldn't stop skeptics from wondering
about the ethical implications. The Sanders campaign, sources told me,
was apoplectic about the call. Some argued the decision, at best, was
irresponsible, while others pointed to it as outright proof the Democratic establishment would stop at nothing to rig the primary.

In Brooklyn, the Clinton campaign was just as unhappy. They were
on track to win the California primary the next day and for Hillary to
become the presumptive nominee. The call cast a shadow over the contest and gave Sanders's supporters a reason to question the validity of

the results. The Clinton campaign's hopes to turn the historic night into a celebration of hope and a call for unity had been summarily dashed.

Instead, when Clinton took the stage to celebrate her nomination that night, nearly half of the Democratic base was still fuming over the suspicious pronouncement. Many had become so frustrated with the rhetoric and division they'd unfriended their liberal friends because of consistent bickering. Having seen Sanders's supporters compared to Donald Trump's frothing horde, they didn't bother to celebrate the historic occasion that a woman had just won a major party's nomination.

"Now, I know it never feels good to put your heart into a cause or a candidate you believe in and come up short," Clinton said, appealing to Sanders's faithful. "I know that feeling well. But as we look ahead to the battle that awaits, let's remember all that unites us."

But many weren't listening. They'd already turned their backs on Clinton and eliminated her and her supporters from their clouds. Some would come back to the party when faced with the possibility of a Donald Trump presidency. Others would not. Some would hold their noses in November and vote for Clinton while others would come to support her. Some would return to the Democratic fold while others would make it their life's work to bring the party to its knees. The divisions that'd been present for decades had been brought into the open and, when the smoke finally cleared, would leave the Democrats scrambling to find a new identity.

CHAPTER 8
THE JOKE IS OVER

ON DECEMBER 7, THE CROWD WAITING TO SEE DONALD TRUMP'S speech aboard the USS *Yorktown*, harbored in Mount Pleasant, South Carolina, was abuzz with white people buying the campaign's signature hat, a cheap red number reading MAKE AMERICA GREAT AGAIN that was first adopted when Trump needed something to keep his eccentric head of hair from fluttering out of place in front of the camera. Between purchases, they talked about "ethnic people," "blacks," and other groups they found both unseemly and ungrateful.

As expected, conversation eventually switched to the horrifying attacks that'd been dominating news coverage. A month before, in Paris, extremists had killed 130 people, and just five days earlier a couple with possible ties to ISIS had killed fourteen in San Bernardino, California. Everyone waiting to get in seemed terrified about being killed by Islamic terrorists and certain that America could fall to the barbaric hordes.

The man next to me preached to the line about the merits of dropping the entirety of the United States' arsenal of nuclear weapons on the Middle East and killing every last Muslim before turning to Trump: "I just like that he's not going to bullshit you. If you ask me, it's this political correct bullshit that's got us in all this trouble."

"I like that he's doing this on an aircraft carrier," said a woman who just moments earlier had taken great joy in baiting a desperate vendor into thinking she was going to buy a T-shirt before sending him on his way empty-handed. "It seems right because he's so . . . strong."

In the distance, the sun set behind the USS *Yorktown*. The line, stretched for what someone called "a country mile," sturdied itself against the cold December breeze.

* ★ *

Everyone had it backward and they'd had it backward all along. The pundits had wrung their hands over the poll numbers, wondering what it would take for Trump to finally lose his momentum while *Saturday Night Live* booked him to host and the cable news programs interviewed him every second they weren't showing him live at his rallies.

Between appearances, they'd wonder aloud: How does Trump drag so many people to his extreme point of view?

Trump hadn't dragged anybody anywhere. And he didn't have impressive poll numbers because he'd somehow or another convinced anybody of anything. Trump was, as of that moment, the heartbeat of an America with which many of us were unaccustomed. His was not a proactive candidacy but a pure, unadulterated reaction to what a slice of the American public wanted. This was a group that lived their lives steeped in unbelievable anger. They were either poor or less rich than they thought they should be, they were middle class or upper middle class, and they were, almost to a person, white. They were angry and all they wanted in the fucking world was to blame somebody.

Trump wasn't the cause; he was the disease personified.

He was repeating to this group of people, in a voice they'd been dying for, the very thing they'd always wanted to hear. Someone was to blame. The immigrants. The Muslims. The liberals who wanted nothing more than to marginalize the white working class. And it didn't matter what got in his supporters' way, whether it was the Constitution they claimed to love so much or groups of people they wished to deny basic decency and basic rights.

Trump's true talent was finding the pulse of these ignorant, livid people and playing them like a virtuoso strumming an instrument.

"We put out a statement today," Trump said as he shuffled through his papers that night. "It's impossible to watch this gross incompetence that I watched last night. And we put out a statement a little while ago and these people [the media] went crazy . . . Donald J. Trump is calling for a total and complete shutdown of Muslims entering the United States until our country's representatives can figure out what the hell is going on!"

The crowd surrounding me inside the aircraft carrier exploded. They'd been cheering every custom-made applause line. They'd called President Obama a coward, a criminal, and—this was the dirtiest of words that night—a Muslim. Anything the outside world could see as racist or vile they'd eaten up and shouted back: "Amen!" and "Preach!" as if they were a congregation in a racist church that was just getting going. When protestors interrupted the speech, and at least five of them did, a crowd of men surrounded them, shoved their fingers in their faces, and screamed "Trump! Trump! Trump!" until security carried them away. The look in those men's eyes told me we're only days away from one of these scenes getting out of hand.

"We have no choice," Trump said. "We have no choice. We have no choice."

★   ★   ★

Some would argue that capitalism is a system of competition, while others maintain it's less a matter of innovation and one-upmanship and more about latent opportunism. Trump's success as a businessman and mogul are debatable, but what is not is his uncanny ability to seize an opportunity. The man has a talent at serving his greed and lust for influence by leveraging existing circumstances to his whim.

It's crass, but true, that Trump saw the tragedy in San Bernardino, and Paris before it, as a chance to further his brand. Did he enter the race to tout an anti-Islamic agenda? No, it began as a call to arms against illegal immigration, but the focus of the time has changed and with it the zeitgeist of the White and the Angry. Now, much like Fox News had done for years, it was time to remind the right-wing women of the country that they too could be raped, that the right-wing men could be killed or replaced, much as they already have been, in their own minds, by the forces of political correctness.

To witness it up close and personal was staggering. I've seen some incredible scenes in politics, but none matched the vitriol and hatred I saw that night. Certainly I'd seen the fringe of the right wing bristle with anger, but what was coming into focus that night, what was just rearing its ugly head, was unprecedented. The men and women around me were burning with a rage and ready to fight, to destroy, to dismember—if only Trump gave them permission.

A Black Lives Matter protestor was being led out as Trump said, "Treat her gently," and then joked that the media always criticize him when he takes pity on the protestors. That it makes him look "weak."

He said, "Treat her gently," and you had to wonder what would happen if and when he ever decided to take the gloves off.

Afterward, the protestors were on one side of the street and the Trump supporters on the other. Between them, members of the Mount Pleasant police department, looking like they'd rather be anywhere else in the world. While the college-aged protestors called Trump a racist, the assembled waved their signs and called them "faggots" and "queers" and implored them to kill themselves. As the showdown escalated, one of the supporters stepped toward the group and challenged them to a fight. "I'll whip all your asses," he screamed to the delight of his crowd.

For a response, the protestors chanted "Black lives matter! Black lives matter!" The Trump crowd responded: "All lives matter!" The instigator found the five or so people not chanting and got in their faces. Close enough so that they could smell his breath, he yelled, "Do you hear what they're saying, man? Black lives matter? Are you gonna let them get away with that?"

To get a different angle, I walked away and another thirtysomething man followed me before pointing at a commemorative turret gun near the protest. He nodded at it and then the protestors. He wanted to make his point clear. To be sure, I knew he wanted nothing more than to gun every last one of them down. "I sure wish that thing was working right about now," he said.

There were groups itching to cross the street. Five college kids wanting to "crack some fucking skulls." I heard a few more talk about going back to their cars to get their guns.

When the police finally called the protest off, they marched the kids down the road and away from the property. On either side, numbering in the dozens, hordes of Trump supporters just waiting on somebody to make a move or for the police to give up their escort, whichever came first. Down a ways, somebody rolled down their window and hurled trash at them. Ten minutes later and they were gone, the cars were gone, and the only thing left was the lingering fear that this thing, this vile, retched thing, might somehow get worse.

★ ★ ★

Two months later, Donald Trump would win South Carolina's primary with 32 percent of the vote. The Palmetto State had been called a firewall that would prevent Trump from gaining momentum after his stunning win in New Hampshire, where he beat his closest rival by twenty points. South Carolina has long had a history of picking Republican presidents, and conventional wisdom had it that on February 20 the right's fever would break.

The talk in Republican circles, following the too-close-for-comfort race between Ted Cruz and Trump in Iowa, was that Florida Senator Marco Rubio would emerge as the party's best hope. Cruz had long been hated for his unabashed self-aggrandizing and Rubio had the pedigree of a star in the making. For everyone concerned that Cruz and Trump represented the unbalanced wing of the GOP, Rubio was a fresh face with center-right policies wrapped in a message of leading Republicans into a new era.

Unfortunately, Rubio wasn't up to the task. Clumsy and devoid of political instinct, the great hope of the GOP coasted through debates until the February 6 event in Manchester, New Hampshire, when New Jersey Governor Chris Christie, seeking one last opportunity to energize his withering campaign, singled Rubio out and crushed him on live television. The bully zeroed in on the Florida senator's reliance on talking points and Rubio, flustered by the attack, scurried for cover under a rehearsed line he'd already used twice before.

"This notion that Barack Obama doesn't know what he's doing is just not true," Rubio said, the sound bite awkward and out of place.

Christie couldn't believe Rubio had done it again. "There it is. The twenty-five-second memorized speech."

The governor had him right where he wanted him. The talking point is a time-honored tradition in politics and Christie had been trained to do exactly what he was criticizing Rubio for, but this attack was especially potent, and not just because Rubio floundered under the pressure. It took a toll because Rubio's twenty-five-second memorized speech was the same bit of anti-Obama rhetoric the center-right had been relying on the past seven years to sate its angry base.

Republicans had been portraying Obama as anti-American since he'd announced his intention to seek higher office on the steps of the old State Capitol building, but the check had finally come due. Voters were tired of being told just how dangerous Obama was and then watching their representatives, their voices, treat him like any other president. After John McCain and Mitt Romney talked the talk but later tiptoed away from their more extreme rhetoric, they were ready for someone who backed up their words.

Trump's decision to call for a ban on Muslim immigrants aboard the USS *Yorktown* solidified his status as the candidate the angry base had been waiting for, signaling he was ready to take controversial stances and handle a developing problem with the intensity frightened voters demanded. In that same Manchester debate, Trump had been asked if he supported waterboarding, an intelligence-gathering technique that many have called torture and Obama had outlawed after taking the oath of office, and Trump went even further: "I'd bring back a hell of a lot worse than waterboarding."

Earlier in the debate, Trump had bragged that he had been the first to broach the threat of Islamic terrorism. "Nobody else wanted to mention the problem. I brought it up." It was absurdly untrue as Fox News and other right-wing media had been banging the Islamophobic drum for fifteen years, but the veracity of the claim didn't matter. What Trump was saying was that he was the first person to take the conservative media's portrayal of the threat at face value, the first to react in the way a frightened American public had been trained to expect.

In an era of deep political polarization, that was all that mattered. For years, every issue and debate in the country, whether it was police brutality or same-sex marriage, had fallen into one of two categories, the left and the right, and any dalliance between the two was tantamount to treason. Traditional Republicans had been trying to appeal to their base through rhetoric in public while behaving as traditional politicians in the privacy of Congress, especially in the arenas of immigration and the threat of Islamic terrorism, and Trump was the first to challenge that dichotomy.

Rubio hobbled into the South Carolina primary, but he wasn't alone.

Governor Nikki Haley and Senators Tim Scott and Trey Gowdy had endorsed the Florida senator in a show of unity for the future of the Republican Party. The establishment of the state had fallen in line for the traditional GOP's best hope. The problem was that, in the wake of the Charleston shooting and the resulting controversy over the Confederate flag, the electorate wanted nothing to do with their elected officials.

It was the state party's willingness to turn their back on the flag that cemented the primary in Trump's favor. As the country debated whether South Carolina should remove the Confederate flag from its statehouse grounds, Governor Haley took the lead on the issue. "These grounds are a place that everybody should feel a part of," she said a month after the shooting.[37] "What I realized now more than ever is people were driving by and felt hurt and pain. No one should feel pain."

Those words gained Haley points in the media for her bipartisan leadership while costing her a Republican base who felt she had turned her back on the party and delivered a win in the culture wars for liberal progressives. As a Winthrop University poll showed in September of 2015, 47 percent of South Carolinians viewed the Confederate flag as "a symbol of pride," but what was even more eye-opening was that over 60 percent of whites agreed and nearly 70 percent of Republicans.[38] In the days after the flag was removed, Haley's approval rating was found to have stayed more or less static at 55 percent while her approval with Republicans had plummeted by double digits. The reason was voters like Dianne Lawson, a Trump supporter who told *Think Progress* at a rally in Walterboro, "I'd always been a supporter of Nikki Haley, but I don't believe the package that she's selling anymore."[39]

Public Policy Polling released a poll four days before the primary that showed an even starker reality. Of South Carolinians supporting Trump, 38 percent wished the South had won the Civil War and another

38 percent weren't sure if they would rather have had the Confederacy prevail. Less than a quarter of Trump supporters polled were glad the North had triumphed.[40]

Dylann Roof's crime had come at a time in American history when polarization was so stark and ever-present that the Civil War and white nationalism were issues split between the opposite ends of the political spectrum. With the rise of Black Lives Matter and a continued emphasis on social justice, the Republican base, and working-class whites in particular, felt, much like Roof, as if they were losing the culture wars that had been raging for decades, and thus the Confederate flag became a rallying point in much the same manner as the Trump campaign.

That July, I saw just how bad it was as I visited four separate black churches in four separate Southern states that had been set ablaze following the removal of the Confederate flag from South Carolina's statehouse. After staring into the blackened remains of those houses of worship, what I found was that the communities around them were brimming with the Stars and Bars. Confederate flags waved in the warm summer breeze in seemingly every neighborhood.

Among them was a Confederate flag that hung in Gloverville, South Carolina, a distinctly poor community outside Aiken. The house sporting the flag was directly next door to the Glover Grove Church, which had been gutted by fire. When I found the church, I was shocked to discover the front façade remained while the rest of the building looked like some giant hand had reached down from the heavens and snatched it away. On the other side of the church was a modest house where a family of African Americans sat in the yard, eating lunch and somberly staring in disbelief at the ruins.

In my travels, and throughout my initial reporting on the campaign, I also found a flood of racist graffiti on the walls of bathrooms around the country. These writings were nothing new to me, as in Indiana virtually every truck stop and small-town gas station had this nonsense, whether it was swastikas or racial slurs scribbled in the bad penman-ship of adolescent boys. But this was different. I couldn't get away from them. I suddenly found myself walking out of the public world where whites smiled and chatted with immigrant workers and customers and into private spaces where they'd scrawled unfathomably hateful screeds.

When Trump won in South Carolina, I wasn't surprised. Rubio had been hobbled by his own mistakes and Christie's pummeling, and the call for a Muslim ban had given Trump the ear of a nervous electorate. What did surprise me, however, was that at the victory party in Spar-tanburg I found the assembled supporters to be a group of people who would have never gone to a political event. They milled about the Marriott Hotel, many of them carrying TRUMP 2016 signs and miniature Confederate flags. In the bar, they sipped drinks and talked openly about "retards" at work and the "fags" who protested Trump's rallies.

Other than disparagements, the main topic of conversation was about how Donald Trump was going to make America great again. They were all convinced South Carolina was just the beginning and Trump would gather momentum. They were dead-on, of course, as Trump would go on to receive 14 million votes in the GOP primary and win forty-one contests on his way to secure the Republican nomination.[41]

When Jeb Bush appeared on the hotel's TV screens to announce the end of his pitiful campaign, they cheered wildly, blew raspberries, some of them faking tears to mock Jeb's emotional farewell, some of them flipping him off and calling him a "loser" and a "faggot" to boot. When Jeb receded from public view, they returned to the bar, bought a celebratory round, and toasted to the death of the Grand Old Party.

After Trump finished his speech, most of them left in search of more good times. In their wake, they left piles of trash and empty beer bottles. A man in a sombrero took pictures with revelers who said *queso* and then smiled like it was the funniest joke anyone had ever told. Another group of college Trumpites posed for selfies with their MAKE AMERICA GREAT AGAIN hats turned backward, one suggesting they flash gang signs after another said, "Let's be thugs!" A teenager in a blazer and boat shoes swayed a Trump banner back and forth as a couple nearby, wearing motorcycle leather, waved a tiny Confederate flag.

PART TWO
THE SUMMER OF RAGE

CHAPTER 9
AN AMERICAN HORROR STORY

IN JUNE OF 2016, I DROVE TO GREENSBORO, NORTH CAROLINA, TO discover if the Republican establishment had warmed to the notion of Candidate Trump in the wake of his primary victory. Every step along the way, they'd been cautious, some calling him offensive, others questioning his bona fides, unconvinced the former self-identified liberal wasn't just playing the role of conservative.

The Greensboro Coliseum mirrored the divide at the heart of the party: The traditional Republicans populated the stands while Trump's base crowded into a scrum in front of the stage. The former skewed older in red-white-and-blue blouses and dressed like they were going to a Fourth of July parade or the county fair, decked out in polos adorned with buttons, pins, and broaches featuring the GOP's elephant logo; while the latter strictly wore T-shirts and jeans, a good number of them sporting Trump memorabilia they'd purchased outside. The only crossover came when a grandmother or middle-aged man would come down to the floor to give a thumbs-up and ask to take a picture with someone in a TRUMP THAT BITCH shirt or one reading HILLARY SUCKS BUT NOT LIKE MONICA, which the vendors had yelled over and over again as the line snaked through the doors.

In that line, I'd overheard a Trump official telling security they wouldn't be letting in a young woman and her boyfriend because she "looked too alternative," a phrase, I gathered, that referred to her jet-black hair and leather-studded bracelets. As a working-class white male, I fit in just fine with the majority of the rallygoers, and that was a relief considering they were on the lookout for interlopers. A young black man was consistently watched as whispers spread that he was part of the Black Lives Matter movement, a piece of paranoia that extended (rightly, it turned out) to another young man, this one white, wearing a Steph Curry jersey. Early in the program, another man in a Steph Curry jersey had been thrown out for protesting, and it didn't take long for the kid near me to get fingered as a demonstrator. Soon, members of the crowd were getting in his face and asking what he was doing there as the young man laughed nervously and fidgeted. When Trump spoke later, a man with a shaved head and gray beard turned with every applause line and clapped his hands so hard they must've hurt while screaming at the kid, "Are you going to fucking applaud or what?"

The paranoia in that crowd was a side effect of what was obviously a budding unity developing among the Trump faithful. Aboard the USS *Yorktown*, six months earlier, they'd been a motley crew whose only unifying factor was their support of a candidate no one thought could win. Now they recognized each other as kindred spirits and saw that in their company, contrary to what politically correct culture had pushed, they could say whatever they wanted and act in any manner that suited them without consequence.

Making matters worse, the networks were covering these Trump rallies as if they were like any other political event from years past. The media was penned into an area by railings and the reporters made notes on legal pads or tapped out their reports on laptops while, a few feet away, supporters in the scrum by the stage were busy venting their anger and spewing racist and misogynistic slurs. Before I went into the crowds and reported, there was very little in the way of eyewitness accounts as to just what was brewing among Trump supporters. This meant that for months, the gathered crowds were able to spout one bigoted thing after another without repercussion. Meaning they got comfortable and daring in their hate.

I first saw this when an opening speaker referred to "Crooked Hillary Clinton" and a man yelled "Bitch!" At first, he seemed almost as surprised as anybody that the word had escaped his mouth, but when he took stock of the crowd and heard the others cheering and laughing, a smile broke across his face. Somebody clapped him on the back.

This was a change from the Trump rally in South Carolina aboard the USS *Yorktown*, where the crowd took their cues from the candidate and cheered on his racist rhetoric before retiring to the parking lot and harassing protestors. There, in Greensboro, I could tell Trump voters were beginning to feed off each other and Trump was able to take them up to the line of good taste and let them take over where he could not. As a result, the rallies grew darker, more hateful, the atmosphere simmering with anger and pent-up rage.

One of the people who'd cheered him tested the limits later when Trump referenced the recent Orlando nightclub shooting and made the case that Clinton wouldn't help the LGBTQ community because of her ties to countries that openly discriminated against women and gays, all the while belaboring the shooter's *Muslim immigrant* parents from *Afghanistan.*

"And she's no friend of *L* . . . *G* . . . *B* . . . *T* Americans," Trump said. "She's no friend. Believe me."

"The gays had it coming!" the man shouted and gazed back at the guy who'd called Hillary a bitch. They met eyes, shared a knowing look.

As if it were some kind of joke.

As if forty-nine of his fellow Americans—forty-nine living, breathing human beings—hadn't just been mowed down.

Just as I'd done for all past events, I pulled my phone out of my pocket and began live-tweeting the things I'd been hearing, taking care not to spend too much time staring at the screen lest I attract attention. At times, however, the crowd, searching for possible protestors, took notice and the man who'd confronted Steph Curry gave me a long and questioning glance.

Somebody nearby, in the middle of the program, told me, "You don't look right."

I continued reporting and later, when Trump set his sights on President Obama, I heard several people call him "nigger"; another person nearby went with "sand nigger" and somebody high-fived him. And when Trump bragged about rescinding *The Washington Post*'s media credentials, a smattering of men chanted "Kill them all! Kill them all!"

Afterward, the racial and misogynistic slurs came one after another, as if Trump had given them permission to finally say whatever they wanted, as if his screed against political correctness—saying it had in some way facilitated the growing crisis with Islamic extremism—had broken its spell and assured them it would be fine to walk through the parking lot talking about how you couldn't trust Latinos or telling your child, as she held your hand, that "immigrants aren't people, honey."

A couple of rows down from my car, some college students tailgated in their truck, a Confederate flag waving from the bed. They yelled "Trump train!" between shotgunning beers and slung a bottle at a passing car. On the road outside the coliseum, the lanes were choked with Trump voters blaring their radios and cheering and flipping off people as they passed them on the sidewalk. A man driving by with a Mexican flag draped out his driver's side window was showered with calls of "fucking spic" and "beaner," and threats to have him deported.

I watched all of it in a cold sweat. There was a palpable danger that I'd only sensed after the December 7 rally, only now it was worse and it surrounded me. With every interaction, with every provocation, there was a definite possibility there might be bloodshed at any moment.

White-knuckling my steering wheel, I drove a half a mile through Trump traffic and pulled into a barbecue restaurant to catch my breath. With the window down, I could still hear the music from the highway, could still make out victorious shouting from the cars. To steady myself, I picked up my phone and saw a screen full of texts.

You're trending nationally.

Reading the words, I felt odd, like I was outside of myself. I moved to the next one and the one after that. My friends were telling me about the celebrities who'd retweeted my reports from the rally and asking if I was okay. I opened my Twitter and found my followers had ballooned. The mentions and notifications were zipping by so quickly I couldn't focus.

Still staring at the screen in disbelief, I sleepwalked into the restaurant and had a seat at the bar. I ordered a beer and downed it in one long and anxious gulp.

★   ★   ★

That night, I got home and wrote a dispatch like I had done for every other rally I'd attended. The five-hour drive had done little to ease my nerves so I was crackling with energy. When I finished, I got out of my chair and paced the hallways of the house I'd bought only a few months before and had spent all my time off the campaign trail renovating. I'd lived here less than a month and so the rooms still felt foreign, the shadows strange.

When I got into bed I was still fighting with the toll of what I'd seen and heard. I closed my eyes and could still see the angry faces of the rally. Even in the quiet night, my ears rung with racial slurs and threats. I struggled with sleep and got maybe three hours of fitful rest. After pouring a cup of coffee I sat down at my desk to work and, procrastinating, opened my email instead. Waiting for me were messages from *The New Republic*, *The New York Times*, a slew of literary agents, and friends and colleagues with links to media outlets around the world that had referenced my reporting from the night before.

On one hand, I was still struggling to put the events in Greensboro into context, to wrestle with the reality that my fellow countrymen and neighbors were not only bigoted but potentially dangerous. But the influx of attention, both in the form of interviews and opportunities, meant I didn't have time to sit and dwell on the subject. Soon I was going on radio and television to sound the alarm against the growing threat of Trumpism, a surreal experience as I sat there listening to myself analyze and digest what had happened while, internally, I was still scared as hell of the danger I'd just unearthed.

The attention continued for weeks and I found myself trying to juggle my normal life and this weird existence I'd just stumbled upon. At work and in conversations, suddenly people were asking me if things were really that bad, if Trump really represented the threat I'd communicated, and all I could tell them was that, yes, it was true. And, in all actuality, it was so much worse.

It was nice to be appreciated and receive a bit of notoriety, but the internet is such that things tend to take on lives of their own. I was still trying to find my sea legs and adapt to my newfound existence, and at times it was completely overwhelming, especially whenever I'd open my Twitter and just stare at the activity as the mentions and retweets streamed by like a swiftly flowing river.

While watching the current, I noticed a good number of people questioning my reports, a possibility that'd never entered my mind as I'd been standing there in the Greensboro Coliseum, or even days later as I weighed just what I'd seen. The doubters, of course, were members of another walk of life, Americans who belonged to a much different bubble than my own, though many of them, it seemed, shared a lot in common with my working-class family.

The first were a group I took to calling "the True Believers." These were Trump supporters who had bought into the campaign's narrative that the media couldn't be trusted and weren't able to comprehend that they'd thrown their support behind somebody so hateful. Many were working-class people who posted links about economic disparity or stories about the dangers of globalist trade deals. Convinced I'd fabricated the entire story, they wanted to know *How come you don't have any videos? No photos? Where's your proof?* They demanded to know where I'd stood in the crowd. What I was wearing. Eventually, they wanted to know how much Hillary Clinton and billionaire George Soros had paid me to write my account, a question I considered answering with a snapshot of my monthly bank statement.

Eventually, this group coalesced behind a plot to cost me my professorship at Georgia Southern University. I watched in real time as somebody floated the idea to write the university in order to get me fired, an idea that dozens rallied around. The trolls planned a deluge of calls and emails to my college's dean and Georgia's Board of Regents. Though they were obviously unaware of the protections of academic freedom, and that a few complaints couldn't strip me of my position, they said to "make things up" because "there are no rules with the left."

Next came a group of men I would later learn were connected to the alt-right, an emerging confederation of young conservatives who tended to favor white nationalism. This strand was made up of misogynistic men who called me homophobic slurs and took turns critiquing pictures of me they found online. Threads developed in which men theorized how low my testosterone count was while others signed me up for gay-porn newsletters and mailing services. Eventually I clicked on their profiles and found one site after another that offered anti-feminist screeds and articles on how to properly choke women and use them for their sex.

Then there were the neo-Nazis.

Previously, I'd read articles about how Trump's candidacy and anti-immigration position had attracted extremists, but I'd been ignorant as to exactly how much sway he held over the white-supremacy world. In fact, it wasn't until the summer of 2016 that a lot of people began to take notice of just how popular Trump was with the racist groups of this country, including the resurgent Ku Klux Klan, Aryan groups, and neo-Nazis, many of whom I began to see in the crowds at his rallies. They held Trump up as the Great White Hope and pinned their hopes and aspirations of a white America on him while lashing out at anyone they perceived as a threat.

The first death threat came on Sunday, June 19, five days after my reportage went viral, from a Twitter user named "Warrior Queen," whose handle was @SupaGoy88 and avatar is a meme of a small girl sporting a goat's head. "National Socialist," the bio read. "One more cuck for the tree," this person tweeted, and because I was still learning about these subcultures, I asked @SupaGoy88 what "the tree" meant, and received the answer: *the one you will swing from.*

Over the next hour there were two more, including an assessment from "Marijan," a "European culture & heritage enthusiast" who had added me to his list of "Traitorous whites (purge)." He wrote that I was "a real oven-worthy faggot." Minutes later, @Khazer_Soze (whose Twitter page has since been deleted) told me how fun it would be when "we finally get our boots on your neck."

There were images, too—sloppy Photoshops and crude, Microsoft Paint–like doodles of a smiling Donald Trump throwing a dead Mexican over his infamous wall, a cartoon frog dressed as a member of ISIS beheading a more-than-happy-to-die liberal, a toothy progressive pointing to an African-American man and saying, "Meet my wife's boyfriend."

Then there were the Nazi images. Scenes from the Holocaust. Emaciated Jewish men and women struggling to stand. Mass graves filled with bodies. Lovingly rendered portraits of Donald Trump leading a blitzkrieg. Memes of him in an SS uniform at the controls for a gas chamber. My face and others' awaiting the gas.

When my friends and family found out about the threats, they asked me how I was dealing with it all, and I just shrugged. I think, in part,

I was comforted by the fact that I lived in the twenty-first century. The possibility that somebody would actually attack me never felt real.

That is, of course, until it did.

★ ★ ★

One night I was writing at my desk around four in the morning and just about ready to turn in. Since the Greensboro rally, I'd been working sixteen hours a day and was dog-tired and ready for a break. I was beginning to question whether I could exist in this life and continue following a campaign that made me question the very nature of politics, not to mention my faith in my country's principles. That's when a car pulled in front of my driveway and idled there for a minute. Sometimes cars get lost in my neighborhood, so I watched and figured, when it pulled away, it was just some wayward motorist. Not ten seconds later, though, it returned to my driveway. It must have made six laps, stopping in front of my driveway each time, before it sat there for a full five minutes, occasionally blinking its lights and revving its engine.

When it made another lap, I got up from my desk and grabbed the shotgun I inherited from my dad after his death. I loaded it while I called the police and held it at the ready until they arrived. The officers looked at the threats and broke the bad news: They could look for the car, but there wasn't much they could do in 2016 about online harassment. They told me I could file a report but it probably wouldn't do much of anything. The next morning, I had a security system installed and from the time I got home to the time I went to bed I kept a loaded gun at arm's length.

That person harassing me, the death threats taunting me, that made my decision for me. I was tired and exhausted, but I couldn't abandon my work, especially after I'd found myself with a pulpit and a voice. My little project had transformed seemingly overnight into a crusade larger than myself and way more important than a blog I wrote while downing a beer. But with it had come a new reality in which my life was threatened regularly. I was being recognized by angry men and women at rallies. Word spread that I was "the Trump guy," and when I tried to mingle with the crowds, often I'd be singled out. Daily I was wracked with anxiety and had to check the house room by room when I came home at night. Every time I left I had to set an alarm, an alarm that went off a handful of times, including the night I came back from dinner to find someone had tried to get in through my bedroom window.

I didn't realize how bizarre things had gotten until I had some friends over a couple of months later for a cookout. The people around me, friends, family, and colleagues, had all been supportive, but few asked about the threats, I assume out of an effort not to dwell on the negativity. We tried to talk about anything but what was happening on the news, and when someone would slip up and mention Donald Trump— because, let's face it, there was no avoiding his name in 2016—they'd wince, shoot me an apologetic look, and quickly change the subject.

The night of the cookout, in particular, had been a good one. I'd smoked some ribs outside while people swam in the pool and drank cheap beer. For a few hours, I was able to put aside my newfound responsibilities and the conversation hadn't turned Trump's way. It was the first Sunday in I don't know how long I didn't have to be a political correspondent, that I didn't have to work on a draft of something, an editorial decrying growing fascism, or fend off death threats from my Twitter page.

Somehow, life felt like it was returning to normal.

That changed later when we were all sitting in the living room, enjoying our final beers of the evening. Conversation was light, about movies, I think, and I laughed about something somebody said, before noticing that one of my friends was staring at the shelf under the coffee table.

I followed his eyes: He was staring at the revolver I'd forgotten I was keeping there.

Later, after everyone left, I sat with the realization of just how much life had changed. I logged online, found a handful of angry emails waiting in my inbox, one of them calling me a traitor to my race, another questioning whether I was hiding Jewish ancestry, and then came across somebody on social media who said they wanted to beat my head in.

I put the gun away, but brought it back out a few a nights later after the alarm was tripped while I was out of town.

Real life, it seemed, would have to wait.

CHAPTER 10
THE ROAD TO OHIO

AS MY REPORTING GAINED MOMENTUM, SO TOO DID THE HA-
rassment. Suddenly I was receiving dozens of messages a day, some lau-
datory but most of them hateful. When I felt the most anxiety, I'd sit in
front of my computer and watch the abuse roll in on the screen. It felt
like every Republican in the country had decided to come after me. At
first I tried to respond to every single negative message and attempt to
communicate, but soon there was no possible way of keeping up.

That barrage, and its unrelenting nature, forced me to confront how
I viewed the political state of America. It would have been so much
easier had I just decided conservatives weren't going to respect me and
call it a day. But I wanted to have empathy for them, I wanted to see if
there was some way we could bridge the gap between us.

Late one night, still buzzing from a particularly unpleasant conversation with a Republican on social media, I sent out a call to see if anyone
knew a conservative who'd be willing to take a road trip with me. I
was planning on traveling to Ohio to see Hillary Clinton speak with
Elizabeth Warren, and I thought the hours on the road might present
a chance to get to know a complete stranger with whom I disagreed
completely.

The first time I ever laid eyes on "Dave," he was stepping out of
his car and stretching in the driveway. Instantaneously, I violated
my own rules not to succumb to preconceived notions. From my car,
across the street, he looked exactly like I expected: a young, white
square wearing a pair of khakis with a polo shirt the National Guard
couldn't untuck.

After we introduced ourselves, he sat in my passenger seat, listening while I explained the purpose of this trip. We were about to drive to Cincinnati, Ohio, for a Hillary Clinton rally. Seven hours there, seven hours back. Two strangers who'd never so much as spoken before. A liberal and a man who was seconds away from filling out a survey reporting himself as "very conservative."

"You can do anything in the car," I told him. "Switch the AC on, switch it off. Look through the glove box. Flip through the radio if you want."

"And you want me to fill this out?" he asked.

"This" was a six-question survey I'd hastily thrown together that morning as I was trying my damnedest to get out of the house on time. On it, Dave was asked to rate his level of conservatism, choose words that described conservatives, liberals, President Barack Obama and Secretary Hillary Clinton, and answer how likely he was to vote for the Democratic nominee.

Without hesitation, he circled *Very Unlikely*.

"Do you want to know why we're doing this?" I asked him.

He shrugged. "Sure."

I told him it was an experiment. That in the past two weeks, due to my political writing, I'd received a healthy dose of criticism and harassment, not to mention death threats, and now I wanted to see if complete strangers, on opposite sides of the political spectrum, could transcend these polarized times and find common ground.

"Okay," he said, less than impressed.

I put the car in drive, pressed record on the digital recorder, and tried to get Dave up to speed.

★ ★ ★

The pleasantries were over as we'd met our first disagreement.

We'd been getting along just fine when he had to go and ruin all that good will by saying, "I don't like peanut butter."

I'd gone out of my way to bring a pair of peanut-butter sandwiches for the road. A tactic, I'll admit, I'd planned on using to create a shared experience that would undoubtedly serve as a transition to discovering common ground.

But Dave was picky. Notably so. He didn't like peanut butter or Mexican food or anything spicy. That included chili and certain brands of fried chicken.

I was distraught.

On top of Dave's disappointing gastro preferences, I could now paint a decent portrait. In his twenties, he was the kind of guy who showed up to your college lecture in a full suit and tie, not to mention a brief-case you always wanted to break into. Even at his young age he was already heavily involved in local GOP politics, and when he talked it was with the measure and confidence of a much older politician. In all things, his religion guided him, a fact he underlined when he told me he wasn't worried about Donald Trump because of his faith in God and the divine influence on fate. Dave was what you'd expect if you tried to clone Ronald Reagan but went a little heavy on the America.

The next hiccup, however, wasn't food-based. We were talking about federal-versus-local influence, one of his favorite topics, when Dave told me he didn't feel like the federal government should have enforced desegregation.

★　★　★

I had a brief but interesting conversation one night with Brett Chamber-lain, the founder of *Trump Love Letters*, a project where progressives angered by the Republican nominee were writing respectful, empathetic notes to his supporters in order to broach the communication bubble that divides them. Brett introduced me to a concept I'd always been aware of but never had the vocabulary for.

Attribution bias explains, at least in part, how long-held divisions in politics continue to propagate. It states that rival groups, whether Democrats and Republicans, or Israelis and Palestinians, or so on and so forth, attribute the actions of their adversaries to hate while justifying their own as coming from a place of love. Obviously, this is the basis for the rationalizing at the heart of all partisan conflicts, but it happens so naturally that even those aware of its existence are oftentimes unable to recognize or change the pattern.

I think this explains rather nicely why the hair stood on the back of my neck when Dave told me about his doubt regarding desegregation. Immediately, I was petrified that I'd just doomed myself to hours alone in a car with an unrepentant racist. I'd told myself, before picking Dave up, that I wasn't looking to argue issues. I was hoping to listen and find common ground. But I wasn't going to just sit there and listen to outright intolerance.

"I think ending racism is about winning hearts and minds," he said, and I nearly drove off the road. "I wish the racists had to show who they were instead of being driven underground."

And though I could not have disagreed with him more regarding the federal government's intervention, I came to believe, god help me, that he honestly *believed* what he was saying. In the past, I might have been suspicious that it was a rhetorical trick, a quick pivot to hide hatred and bigotry, but Dave was completely convinced that, while racism is wrong, the federal government had no constitutional authority to legislate on people's minds and hearts.

He could not have been more wrong and he could not have believed this more.

And the only reason I know this is because Dave was nothing if not completely honest. Sitting in the dining room of a Cracker Barrel, he told me he once got into an argument with a girl in his college dorm because she called herself a Buddhist but didn't, in his opinion, live up to the tenets of her faith.

"I bet she didn't like that," I said.

He answered, "Most people don't like being told they're wrong."

Other confessions he made over chicken-fried steak: He's not much into art and thought there should only be artists if there was a market demand; he watched ISIS beheading videos in case one day he needed to speak in an official capacity to families who'd lost loved ones to terrorism; he attended the CPAC conference and loved how Sean Hannity, Fox News bloviater extraordinaire, played matchmaker with audience members during commercial breaks, going so far as to offer to pay for first dates and, if there was a proposal in studio, the wedding of two people who didn't know each other.

Oh. And Dave didn't like reading because "there's so much else" he could be doing.

In his classes, he told me, he was sick of spending so much time on dead philosophers. "Please don't lecture on Kant again," he said and rolled his eyes. "He's *dead*."

When I suggested he probably needed to know Kant as he's considered one of the cornerstones of modern thought, he told me he wished his professors could just hand him a slip of paper containing an easily digestible summary of philosophy. I told him about Bertrand Russell's *A History of Western Philosophy*, a nine-hundred-page weapon I kept handy for light reading, so I could start with Socrates and work my way up to existentialism.

Perplexed, he said, "I like things being in a box."

As the nice Cracker Barrel waitress brought me a fresh Coke, I told Dave that, if liberals had our way, we'd happily smash that box into a million little pieces.

☆ ★ ☆

According to a report published in *Scientific American* in 2012, there are undeniable differences in the makeup of conservatives and liberals, including a study that showed conservatives' eyes lingered on disturbing images—see: ISIS beheadings—15 percent longer than liberals, and that proved conservatives are way more likely to value loyalty.[42]

One study that appeared in *The Journal of Political Psychology* in 2008 caused some waves by positing that these hardwired differences include personalities, interaction strategies, and even the makeup of people's living spaces. According to that research, conservatives were more likely to be "neat" and "organized."[43]

Perhaps one of the most interesting, if not politically relevant, moments in our odyssey to Ohio came when Dave talked at length about the steps he took to simplify his life. Much like his desire for a piece of paper condensing the grand tradition of human thought, Dave had streamlined the decisions he considered wastes of his time, including his wardrobe. Having gone to college and bought four separate differently colored sets of towels—the rationale being that he could use one colored set before throwing them all in the washer and moving on to the next—he transferred the idea to his shirts. Currently, he explained, tugging on his polo, he was onto reds.

"Tomorrow," he said, "it'll be red again."

I couldn't help but break my own rules. Dave's system sounded unnecessarily repressive and inexplicably dull.

Again, he shrugged, and I started thinking about the conversations we'd been having about religion and its place in politics. Just like the Constitution, Dave saw the tenants of Christianity, in his case Southern Baptist, as guideposts for not just personal life but life in the public sphere. If he has dedicated himself to Christ in faith, how could he not dedicate himself to Christ in politics?

I asked him if there are any parallels to his religious dedication and his pledge to support Donald Trump in November, a pledge, I could tell, that troubled him.

"When it comes to campaigning for Trump," he said, "I'll knock on the door and read the card. I don't want my name tied to it."

Dave found Trump offensive and brash, the two traits holding equal concern. He didn't care for Trump's language or how he incessantly bragged about his money, his polls, his support. He wasn't excited about a Trump presidency and actively supported multiple candidates before the field winnowed down.

I told Dave, pledge or not, if I were him, I'd probably have to vote my conscience in the end. That if I ever have children, and they brought home from school a book turned to this page in history, I'd want to tell them I voted against the man.

What would Dave say?

"I'd tell them I took a pledge," he answered, "and that, in the end, I was good on my word."

Outside Lexington, Kentucky, the sun was slipping behind the trees and the faraway mountains. Drifting through the awe-inspiring forests was a soupy, sleepy fog that gave the impression we were driving on air.

"Beautiful," I said.

"Illogical," Dave said.

★ ★ ★

At the hotel, Dave and I were both exhausted and ready to get into our room, but the guy behind the desk wasn't quite finished with his impromptu standup routine. "I used to be a comedian," he said and continued with his off-color act full of jokes both intensely crude and badly constructed.

Dave squirmed in the periphery of my vision. Bad language bothered him on a level I'd never seen before. One of the reasons he'd been so troubled by Trump was the businessman's often-crude demeanor. I'd gone out of my way, as the child of factory workers, to keep myself from swearing, but it all felt for naught as the desk guy kept going and going and going, each joke dirtier than the last.

When we finally got the key, we huffed it upstairs and unpacked for the night. Dave told me he was a deep sleeper—it was confirmed the next morning when I practically had to shake him awake to deal with his obnoxious alarm—and we retired to separate beds to catch a couple of hours of rest before the early-morning call. Dave had a little more life left in him, so he cracked open a novel a friend had given him as a gift. He was a third of the way in and had been for months. Exhausted from the drive and nursing an aching back, I reached to turn off what I thought was the lamp lighting up my side of the room, and the room went pitch black.

Shit!" I yelled, cursing for the first time in Dave's presence.

To my surprise, he laughed.

"I think it's hilarious," he said, "that that's what broke you."

★   ★   ★

Outside Union Terminal, the line into the Clinton rally stretched from the door to Western Avenue. The liberal faithful had shown up in droves, so many that hundreds would be turned away. Local candidates for school boards, benches, and state representative worked the line and pressed the flesh. Vendors were selling MADAM PRESIDENT (GET USED TO IT) shirts and I bought one for Dave, throwing in a big button with Bubba himself and the words FIRST DUDE. Dave joked that he was going to sell them on eBay before posing for a picture to be agreeable.

Less agreeable were the men holding HILLARY FOR PRISON signs by the parking entrance and waving motorists forward, telling them parking was full even though I could see dozens of empty spaces.

"Say what you want," Dave said, "but I've never held a HILLARY FOR PRISON sign."

After passing through security, we found a spot by the stage to discuss the optics of the rally. You couldn't help but get an American flag and the campaign's slogan STRONGER TOGETHER in every shot, a fact especially noticeable when Clinton emerged with Senator Elizabeth Warren in tow and the pair raised their hands, the signs in the background promising a united Democratic Party even though at this point, in June of 2016, that unity still seemed a distant hope.

Warren spoke first and obviously reveled in taking the fight directly to Trump. Hers was the most focused and devastating attack I'd heard yet, and Dave, who recorded the entire event on his phone to watch later and consider, leaned over after she finished and told me his party might be in trouble if Warren ever ran for higher office.

When the Massachusetts senator was done with her attack, Hillary Clinton took the mic and delivered one of her most well-composed and articulate speeches of the campaign. The Clinton I'd seen in Iowa, the candidate wanting to please everyone and thus pleasing no one, had been replaced by a candidate who finally knew who she was and exactly what she was up against. Trump emerging as her opponent had obviously focused her, and Bernie Sanders's challenge had made her a much better candidate. The distinction between her and Trump couldn't have been more evident that morning.

On our way back to the car, Dave admitted he was impressed by Clinton's speech. He appreciated that she didn't attack conservatives directly, that much of what she said was, at least on the surface, what he supported. He even liked the touch she added on her talking points where she'd relate them back to communities and people in Ohio, something he hadn't seen as much of in Republican events.

This was the candidate he'd described in his survey the day before as "immoral," "an opportunist," "underhanded," "likely to lie," and "dangerous."

Was he more likely to vote for her?

Before he answered, we passed a Clinton supporter sharing a heated exchange with a man brandishing a sign reading HELLARY. They had fingers leveled in each other's faces. A fight could've broken out any second.

"No," Dave said. "But I respect her more."

★ ★ ★

A few hours later and we'd reached a compromise on assault rifles, an agreement that the NRA was fundamentally insane, understandings that corporate news was dangerous for democracy, and that social media had enabled echo chambers where we couldn't have been friends before this little excursion. It seemed as if the polarization and political climate holding our government and culture hostage was simply a flimsy myth fabricated by those in power, a lie that could be conquered if only the right and the left talked and compared notes.

But none of that was important right then.

The topic at hand was a young woman Dave knew, a young woman who'd come up in conversations a couple of times already. Dave told me that when it came to his personal life, his brain was "like a Congress" that's always deliberating.

I suggested he should text her, ask how her day's going.

"If she wanted me to know she would've texted me."

I had to explain that sometimes people just want to know they're being thought of, and, after some gentle encouragement, he took out his phone. I was celebrating a small victory, celebrating that my new acquaintance Dave had just put himself out there, that maybe we all really could work together, and was forgetting about politics for the first time in weeks, when a black Elantra rode up on my ass, blinked its lights before passing me on the left shoulder, and rocketed forward to swerve dangerously through traffic.

⋆   ★   ⋆

Matchmaker Sean Hannity was on the radio as I told Dave about the time I called in, way back in 2008, and Hannity hung up on me before claiming I was an Obama campaign plant. The guest as we drove was Gary Byrne, the former Secret Service agent whose book *Crisis of Character* was tantalizing conservatives with hearsay about Hillary Clinton's anger and the Clintons' dysfunctional marriage.

Naturally, I was skeptical. It felt like a cash-in designed to capitalize on the right's obsession with smearing the Clintons, and the interview had such a sleazy, tabloid-esque vibe to it that I felt unclean.

"Do you believe him?" I asked Dave.

He did because, in his observations of Hillary, even this morning, he'd seen what he believed was anger brewing under the surface.

"Well," I said, "let me ask you this: Do you believe what I reported?"

He wasted no time telling me that he did because he had personally been threatened by Trump supporters and so had his colleagues in the GOP offices. He'd known people who've received death threats, who'd had their kids put in danger. The GOP, he told me, had been struggling with an influx of unruly voters who'd been politically inactive before this cycle and were now royally pissed off.

My words. Not his.

Later, sitting at a Fazoli's, he told me how red sauce was too spicy for him before saying, "There's no reason we can't live in the same country. The problem is the people who don't want to try."

Not long after, a Mustang racing well over a hundred miles an hour blasted across three lanes. Close behind was a white Impala that was either chasing the Ford or engaged in a futile street race. Traffic slowed down so as to avoid a pile-up. A minivan ahead of us put on its hazards.

★   ★   ★

We were back in front of Dave's house and had just finished telling each other how much we enjoyed one another's company. I had to admit that I'd expected him to be a wet-behind-the-ears young Republican who lacked the intellectual muster to at least try and back up his opinions. He confessed he'd expected me to be some older, angry liberal professor who was going to yell at him for the entirety of the drive.

"Why would you come then?" I asked.

"I thought it was important to reach out," he answered and then told me how his family and church had been worried he might be in danger on this road trip. That they'd prayed for him in their service the morning we'd left. That no one knew why he'd want to spend so much time with an avowed liberal.

I walked him up to his front door and his mom stepped out to offer me a drink and a cupcake. She produced a digital camera and showed me a segment she'd caught on the Atlanta news about my harassment. She pressed her hand to her heart and said, "I'm so, so sorry."

Before I left, I shook Dave's hand and told him to keep in touch. I meant it too, as I'm fully prepared to argue with Dave for the rest of my life if he's up to it. I disagree with him on many things, but I'm able and willing to at least hear him out now. He assured me he felt the same way, but even then I was still suspicious, a distrust that would lift like so much fog when I found, by the time I reached my car again, that Dave had already sent me a friend request on Facebook.

I hit "accept" and settled into the driver's seat. I still had a three-hour drive back to Statesboro and was intellectually exhausted but happy. I plugged my phone in, shifted my bag in the back seat, and found the second survey I was planning on giving Dave to see if this trip changed his mind. At first, there was a quick flash of panic when I saw the clean paper and all those uncircled responses. I considered rushing back to the front door with pen and paper in hand.

But then it passed as I realized the survey didn't matter. What was important was that even though Dave and I would probably never vote for the same candidate, or see nearly any political happening through the same lens, we were at least living in the same country and more than happy to share that experience. Our counterparts in the Trump movement had little to no interest in sharing a society. On the highway of life, Dave and I were fine staying within the lines and obeying the laws of basic decency, while the Trump supporters would endanger everyone by racing through on the shoulders and swerving dangerously across the highway with little regard.

We could argue about the direction of the country, but still agree there was a country to share.

CHAPTER 11
THERE WILL BE BLOOD

THE RAIN BEGAN IN EARNEST THE SECOND I STEPPED OUT OF THE parking garage and onto the streets of Raleigh, North Carolina. The sky hanging over the city was colorless with rolling tumbles of angry gray clouds. A block away, Trump supporters angled around the courtyard of the Duke Energy Center for the Performing Arts, many of them in cheap plastic parkas, a few holding black umbrellas. Feeling vulnerable, I took my place in line. It was the first Trump rally I'd been to since *The New Republic* and *The New York Times* had published my work. The threats were still fresh in my mind, and whenever a supporter would turn my way I'd have to fight off the fear I'd been recognized and there was going to be trouble. For a disguise, I bought a MAKE AMERICA GREAT AGAIN hat from a vendor working the line. For twenty bucks, I held in my hand the article of clothing that'd come to symbolize the movement terrorizing the country. The tag said it'd been manufactured in Cambodia.

Inching toward the Federal-style columns and the buildings' doors, I listened to the couple behind me talk about how immigrants refusing to learn English was tantamount to treason. The only thing more traitorous, they seemed to think, were the crimes of the presumptive Democratic nominee, Hillary Clinton.

"If you or me did that stuff," the husband said, "we'd be locked up like that."

The "like that" had been punctuated by a snapping of his fingers, the rapidness, I imagine, resembling in his imagination the slam of a prison door. The wife agreed and wondered how it had come to pass earlier in the day that FBI Director James Comey had announced, following an investigation into Clinton's treatment of classified emails as secretary of state, the bureau wouldn't recommend the Department of Justice file charges.

The full history of how Clinton's emails became a driving force in the 2016 election would take a book-length explanation, if not a multivolume tome. It is, even to the security experts I've spoken with, a complicated issue that has been oversimplified consistently by a media and electorate looking for answers. Whether or not Clinton mishandled information is certainly up to debate, and should be taken seriously, despite what some have said while trying to dismiss the severity of the accusations. But what isn't disputable is that those emails greatly affected the trajectory of the campaign and, as a result, the course of American history.

Earlier that July afternoon, Comey had stood in front of the world and bled every second of tension out of the announcement. His tone and step-by-step recital of the investigation led everyone watching to believe he was going to recommend that charges be leveled against Clinton, until, after calling her "extremely careless" in her handling of classified material, Comey surprised the room and an anxious nation by announcing that "no reasonable prosecutor would bring such a case."[44]

The response in the media was to declare the day a "win-lose" for Clinton but to openly speculate if Comey's decision had more or less handed her the election. Some wondered if Trump's supporters, who had been punctuating their rallies with chants of "lock her up," might begin to wind down their calls for Clinton's imprisonment and, in turn, if that might finally deflate Trump's campaign.

Instead, Trump supporters responded to the news by doubling down on their criticisms and incorporating a new element into their developing narratives: Clinton hadn't been charged because the entire federal government was as corrupt as her.

Trump spearheaded this narrative in Raleigh by saying, "Today is the best evidence ever, that we've seen, that our system is absolutely, totally rigged." What happened next was a glimpse into what would be the final evolution of the Trump campaign, a period of time from July to Election Day in which his supporters swallowed every story line the candidate gifted them and in turn raged against the named conspirators.

Within seconds, the concert-theater-sized hall was erupting with calls for Clinton to be locked up, to be executed, one man interrupting the silence by screaming, "Hang that bitch!" Around the auditorium, people cheered and applauded. Others yelled that the FBI director should be locked up too, and when Attorney General Loretta Lynch was mentioned, they wanted her imprisoned.

To make the lie more palatable, Trump painted a scene. The media had made plenty of noise about an impromptu meeting between Bill Clinton and Attorney General Lynch that took place July 2 in Phoenix, and Trump filled in the gaps. "He's waiting around, he's waiting at the airport, 'Oh, look, the AG's coming, let me go say hello.'"

As if that hadn't been enough, Trump took the charge a step further and cited a story run in *The New York Times* that Clinton might consider keeping Lynch on as attorney general.[45]

"That's like a bribe, isn't it? Isn't that sort of a bribe? I think that's a bribe."

After the rally, his supporters clustered around a small crowd of protestors demonstrating against Trump's bigotry. While the two sides screamed at one another, I found a man being interviewed by a TV crew while holding Trump's *The Art of the Deal* the way a Baptist preacher might wield the Good Book. A few feet away, eight or nine young men watched and smoked cigarettes as the man holding Trump's book pontificated that Clinton should be "shot" for "high treason."

Throughout the crowd the story had not only taken hold, but was growing by the second. Everywhere you turned, supporters were taking Trump's narrative and adding new touches and troubling twists.

One woman, confronting a protestor with a NO FASCISM sign, screamed that Clinton's emails had been hacked by ISIS and had resulted in American casualties. Another supporter argued that Clinton had purposefully left her emails vulnerable and had even gone so far as to send information to Islamic terrorists in order to destabilize the United States. In different sectors of the crowd they were split on who all had been part of the plot. Some said it was Clinton while others suspected a deeper conspiracy that included the president, the FBI director, the attorney general, and a nameless, faceless group of billionaire donors.

The mob grew angrier. There were more calls for Clinton and Obama to be lynched, Comey and Lynch to be jailed. Police began shutting down the site and escorting protestors away as Trump supporters leaked into the dark streets of Raleigh, some stopping to get food and eat on the sidewalks. I walked a few blocks to listen, and a group of men joyfully chanting that Hillary Clinton was a "ho" caught up to me. One of them, wearing a HILLARY FOR PRISON shirt, asked if I'd been at the rally and then if I'd heard the guy call for "that bitch to be hung."

"That guy's my hero," one of his buddies said.

We walked a little while longer, the four of them fantasizing about how great America would be after Trump was elected. One of them said he'd be glad when "the pussies aren't in charge anymore," and another was convinced Trump wouldn't put up with "libtards like the fuckers back there."

With my disguise resting in a trashcan, I felt exposed and kept my eyes down. Walking in a pack felt wrong in a myriad of ways. I didn't want anyone to think I was with them, but at the same time I didn't want them to know I was a trespasser. Finally, I gave into my fight-or-flight instinct and veered off without saying anything and headed for the door of a restaurant. The men kept walking into the heart of the city, one of them raising his arms like his favorite team had just won a championship, screaming, "Trump!," the word echoing off the sides of buildings.

*   ★   *

The next morning, I skimmed the news to see how the media handled the outbreak of calls for violence in Trump's crowds and found only cursory reports of his accusations. A scant few far-left blogs and sites focused on the new shift in murderous rhetoric while mainstream sources still struggled to maintain the narrative and concentrated on the conspiracy Trump had crafted.

> *Trump Accuses Hillary Clinton of Offering 'Bribe' to*
> *Attorney General*
> *Trump Suggests Hillary Clinton Bribed Attorney General*
> *Over Email Scandal*
> *Donald Trump Accuses Hillary Clinton of Bribery in*
> *Email Investigation*
> *Trump Accuses Hillary of Offering Bribe to AG Loretta*
> *Lynch*

It was yet another example of how Trump had continued to manipulate and use the media to his own ends. By feeding them a bit of controversy destined to land in the headlines, Trump was building for his supporters a counternarrative to confirm their suspicions while shutting out conflicting information. Now conspiracies that had only existed in the far-reaches of the internet were being introduced into publications of record. If voters wanted to confirm that wild-eyed theories had validity, all they had to do was Google them and find confirmation in the headlines of the biggest newspapers in the world.

In part, this strategy was successful because of the internet's continued emphasis on brevity and social media's allergy to context. On Facebook and Twitter, the importance of an article rarely has anything to do with the actual content. Users share links for a multitude of reasons, but rarely is detailed information among them. As a Columbia University and French National Institute study in 2016 showed, 59 percent of the links shared on social media are never actually clicked, meaning the headlines themselves are the main source of information-transfer.[46]

For those wanting to believe Clinton was a treasonous criminal, all of the components were there. It was easier, with the FBI's findings providing damning cognitive dissonance, to believe a massive conspiracy had taken place to clear her of charges than to accept deeply held convictions that Clinton was a criminal mastermind threatening the country were unfounded. After all, convictions are only strengthened by the amount of time and effort that has been put into them, not to mention the repetition of others confirming those convictions. For years, Republicans had portrayed her as the coldhearted villain who had condemned four Americans to die in Benghazi, and before that Rush Limbaugh and the like had blamed her for the death of deputy White House counsel Vince Foster, not to mention one backroom deal after another. Clinton's public persona had been crafted over decades, and to accept those findings of the FBI her critics might have to accept that all of it had been a political manipulation.

Trump's story, complete with a detailed scene of Bill Clinton meeting with Loretta Lynch, provided a convenient escape route. Not only was Hillary guilty of the crimes she'd been accused of, but it was even worse: To avoid prosecution for mishandling classified secrets, she'd actively undermined the machinery of governmental justice. That possibility opened the door to a whole new realm of possibilities and, as the Trump campaign progressed, his supporters showed an alarming knack for taking the narratives he'd given them and extending them to their logical, or rather illogical, extremes.

Was Hillary Clinton working with ISIS?

Was Hillary Clinton an agent of the New World Order and in league with a cabal of Jewish bankers?

Was Hillary Clinton a Satanist who subsisted on the blood of children? Ridiculous or not, these were some of the questions Trump supporters were asking. Now that Clinton had outmaneuvered the laws, the extent of her evil was only limited by how imaginative a person could be. Suddenly, every story regarding the email controversy could be contorted to fit whatever hole a Trump supporter needed to fill in their forensic trail, and there were plenty of extremist media platforms that were more than happy to provide fodder.

Of course, it didn't help that the mainstream media unintentionally provided hints of authenticity to the claims. A strange relationship had developed between the news and Trump that mutually benefited both parties while muddying the waters for consumers. Since Trump's announcement the previous June, major networks had relied on him to boost their ratings, and over the course of the campaign the cable news channels saw their numbers reach record highs. This resulted in exorbitant advertising fees, including a stretch during the Republican National Convention when CNN charged up to forty times its usual rate.[47] Trump's candidacy was the media gift that kept giving, and the more outrageous he became the better the payday for networks.

As a result, Trump commandeered three major channels that happily pointed a camera at the stage and gave him a national platform free of charge. Some have estimated this exposure had given Trump in excess of three billion dollars of cost-free advertising, a staggering number that no doubt explains in part his success in the Republican primary.[48]

If only it had been limited to that, however, the effect might have been negated come time for the general election. Instead, there was a moment of truth after he captured the nomination, when the media suddenly questioned their influence. They asked in one segment after another if they had created the Trump phenomenon. Articles were published nearly every day in which members of the media gazed at themselves in the mirror and wondered just what they had wrought.

From that point on, a new level of scrutiny was leveled on Trump and his campaign, an atonement of sorts in which every move the candidate made was dissected and put up for public scorn. Trump reacted predictably by criticizing the press and calling them disgusting liars, charges his supporters used to inoculate themselves against dissenting opinions and unfavorable coverage.

Surprisingly, though, Trump's criticism had another effect. Much like how a basketball coach's tirade against an official after a disputable call can lead to a later makeup whistle, the media was so intent on proving Trump and his supporters wrong they began offsetting their coverage of his scandals and gaffes with continued focus on Clinton's emails, a false equivalency Thomas E. Patterson of Harvard Kennedy School's Shorenstein Center on Media, Politics, and Public Policy called a "leveling effect that opens the door to charlatans."[49] This did particular damage as new Trump scandals emerged nearly every day and Clinton's stood alone. Over time, Trump's scandals grew so numerous and overwhelming it was hard to focus on any one thing.

Critics of Clinton had no such problem.

It's especially interesting when considering media coverage to take another look at Trump's remarks that night in Raleigh, particularly in his long and angry litigation of Clinton's crimes that whipped his supporters into a murderous fervor. "The lives of the American people were put at risk by Hillary Clinton," he said, "so she could carry on her corrupt financial dealings, that's probably why she didn't want people to see what the hell she was doing." In addition: "Look at her judgment on emails. Who would do it?"

Ironically enough, there were two separate Trump scandals that perfectly mirrored his accusations against Clinton that never gained traction in the press. One involved a twenty-five-thousand-dollar check from the Donald J. Trump Foundation that had been donated to an organization dedicated to Florida Attorney General Pam Bondi's reelection as she was deciding whether to press charges in a fraud case against Trump University, an endeavor that cost the president-elect $25 million to settle out of court just days after his election.[50, 51] Another attorney general considering fraud charges against Trump, Greg Abbott, who would go on to become the governor of Texas, received $35,000 in donations.[52] Whether Trump had bribed Bondi or Abbott or not, there was certainly more evidence than a chance meeting at an airport in Phoenix.

The second scandal was revealed in a Halloween report from *Newsweek* by Kurt Eichenwald. After an investigation of court documents, Eichenwald wrote that "Trump's companies have systematically destroyed or hidden thousands of emails, digital records, and paper documents demanded in official proceedings, often in defiance of court orders."[53] This pattern of intentional obfuscation had its roots forty-three years prior in a housing-discrimination suit the Justice Department had brought against Trump and his father. The allegations, which Trump settled out of court by paying a hefty fine, were particularly disgusting.

Later, in the first presidential debate, Hillary Clinton herself made mention of the case, saying: "Donald Trump started his career back in 1973 being sued by the Justice Department for racial discrimination because he would not rent apartments in one of his developments to African Americans, and he made sure that the people who worked for him understood the policy."

She was right, and the facts of the case, as well as Trump's consistent record of destroying evidence and widespread corruption (not to mention a whole litany of other disqualifying behaviors), were right there for the whole world to see, if only the world were so inclined.

CHAPTER 12
A NATION FOREVER ON THE BRINK

A LITTLE BEFORE 8 A.M. ON THE MORNING OF JULY 8, ROUGHLY ten hours after shots were first fired in downtown Dallas and less than five since the suspect had been killed, Officer Randall Hancock was dispatched to the Three Oaks apartment complex in Valdosta, Georgia, to investigate a reported vehicle break-in.[54] Nearly twenty minutes later, Officer Hancock stepped out of his cruiser and was struck by three bullets, two of which hit his protective vest and the other of which found his abdomen. Hancock returned fire and disabled his assailant, twenty-two-year-old Stephen Beck, the man who had made the call to 911.

Later, from his hospital bed, Beck would say he'd shot at Hancock so the officer would kill him. Suicide by cop, it's called. In his interview, Beck swore he carried no hatred of law enforcement, but in the early, tempestuous hours of July 8, the ambush was woven into a tapestry of other crimes against police officers that would keep an anxious nation worried it was on the brink of chaos.

When I pulled into Three Oaks, there was virtually no sign of the ambush or resulting shootout. Gone were the strands of crime-scene tape. Missing were the roadblocks. Three Oaks was like any other apartment complex languishing in the dog days of the Georgia summer. Residents walking to and from their homes glistened with sweat. A couple lifting their groceries from the back of their Ford Focus had soaked through their shirts. A man in a white dress button-up, his prism blue tie bouncing too long past his belt, dotted his forehead with a silk handkerchief.

The only sign that anything was amiss was the note taped to the door of the leasing office. The office was closed and it would be closed the next morning as well. On either side of the door stood planters with miniature American flags assumedly left over from the Fourth of July.

*   ★   *

I'd had to tear myself away from the TV the night before. Depending on what channel you watched, who you listened to on Twitter, what your darkest imagination could conjure, the situation in Dallas had either been contained or was spiraling into an ultraviolent anarchy from which our culture might never escape. When I laid my head on my pillow and closed my eyes, I saw the footage.

Crowds of protestors screaming and sprinting for cover.

Police ducking behind their cars.

The raw clip of the shooter scrambling from pillar to pillar and then executing a cop on the screen.

In the morning, I felt like I was fresh off a bender. My head hurt, my eyes were tired, and my stomach seemed incapable of facing the day. The news said the shooter, veteran Micah Xavier Johnson, had been killed by a bomb, either one of his own or one belonging to the Dallas PD, the resolution allowing a new political battle to begin.

The far right laid the blame at the feet of a new black-power organization that no one had ever heard of and nobody could even confirm existed.

The *New York Daily News'* front page screamed CIVIL WAR.[55]

The massacre hadn't even ended by the time *Drudge Report* assigned responsibility to the Black Lives Matter movement, Drudge's headline: BLACK LIVES KILL.[56]

By eleven in the morning conspiracy crackpot Alex Jones had labeled it a race war.[57]

Then, in Bristol, Tennessee, another veteran, Lakeem Keon Scott, mowed down a newspaper carrier and injured three others, including an officer, before confirming he'd been motivated by the recent police killings of black men.[58]

Twenty-five miles outside Ferguson, Missouri, a police officer was conducting a pullover when he was shot three times by suspect Antonio Taylor.[59]

By the time the Valdosta shooting was reported by the Associated Press, it wouldn't take much convincing to think that the United States was sliding into oblivion.

★   ★   ★

Outside Valdosta, a marker stood on the side of GA-122, not far from Meeting House Creek. Across the street was an abandoned trailer in danger of being overtaken by unruly grass. Nearby, a DO NOT TRES-PASS sign kept me from a drive and a cluster of trees I stared at and tried not to wonder if that's where Mary Turner had been hung.

I read the plaque under a vanilla sky strewn with cumulus clouds:

> *Near this site on May 19, 1918, twenty-one-year-old Mary*
> *Turner, eight months pregnant, was burned, mutilated, and*
> *shot to death by a local mob after publicly denouncing*
> *her husband's lynching the previous day. In the days*
> *immediately following the murder of a white planter by*
> *a black employee on May 16, 1918, at least eleven local*
> *African Americans including the Turners died at the hands*
> *of a lynch mob in one of the deadliest waves of vigilantism*
> *in Georgia's history. No charges were ever brought against*
> *known or suspected participants in these crimes. From*
> *1880–1930, as many as 550 people were killed in Georgia*
> *in these illegal acts of mob violence.*

A blood-curdling story, no doubt, but it was sobering to find that even this grotesque account has been sanitized. In all truth, pregnant Mary Turner was hung upside down, soaked with gasoline and oil, set on fire, and then, while still alive, her baby was cut from her and stomped to death. Mary was then shot and buried in an unmarked grave.

All of this took place in 1918. Less than a hundred years ago. When I first happened across Mary Turner's story, I assumed it was from the nineteenth century, the Reconstruction era at the very worst. Instead, the slaughter of Mary Turner and her child coincided with the waning days of World War I. America was still dreaming of Woodrow Wilson's "Fourteen Points" when a mob of monsters did their worst.

As if the indignities visited upon her weren't enough, in 2013 somebody shot the plaque five times, leaving the marker, much like Mary herself, marred and riddled with bullet holes.

☆ ★ ☆

The amazing thing about video is that you can't escape it. In the era of smartphones and high-speed internet, the world is so small it often feels so knowable.

In Baton Rouge, we watch Alton Sterling get held down and shot to death for no reason at all.

In Falcon Heights, Minnesota, Diamond Reynolds streams live footage of her fiancé, Philando Castile, dying as an officer continues to train his gun through the window.

There's something purifying about the transparency. It takes the work out of a situation, leaves us with no choice but to face reality as it is. If you watch these videos—I mean, if you watch them with an open mind—you will see the injustice. It is there and it is unavoidable, and if you have so much as a scrap of a heart it will break that scrap of a heart to the point it can never be repaired.

If you watch, you can't dive into the seedy underbelly of the web and search for prior arrests and traffic violations. You can't blame what the victim was wearing or argue they were carrying themselves in a threatening way. The truth is on display and it is unwavering.

The videos from Dallas are similar, if not as personal. We see officers running toward the gunfire. We see them braced against what the rest of us could only understand as a nightmare.

I watched the videos again that evening. First Alton, then Philando, then the clip where Micah Xavier Johnson, his long gun in tow, carries out his military maneuvers and extinguishes a life well before its time. Then I went back and watched Eric Garner being choked to death on a Staten Island sidewalk. I watched Walter Scott, unarmed, being shot in the back as he ran away.

There is a shared wrong because injustice is injustice is injustice.

★   ★   ★

The radio said a massive protest in Atlanta was teetering on the edge of disarray. People were protesting the recent murders of Sterling and Castile, but they were also calling for an investigation into the death of a black man found hanging in Piedmont Park the day before, a day after reports put the Ku Klux Klan in that park handing out recruitment flyers.[60] Police had told protestors they were free to march as long as they didn't wander onto I-75, a move that would endanger them and disrupt Atlanta's already legendarily unbearable traffic. The crowd disobeyed the order and blocked an entrance. The police were lined up parallel to the protestors, and if you can think of a better metaphor for this moment in American history then damn it, I'm all ears.

From what I heard from a friend marching, the crowd was skittish. Every loud noise lead to a collective jump or, in some cases, a spontaneous sprint for safety. Dallas was still fresh in everyone's mind.

Back in Texas, we were learning more about Micah Xavier Johnson. Investigators had gained access to the house where he'd lived with his mother and had already found bomb-making supplies, weapons, and journals full of detailed military tactics.[61] Neighbors remembered him as an odd man who, clad in camouflage and dressed in his gear, performed "obstacle courses" and "drills" in his mother's backyard.[62]

All day, the media had been painting the portrait of Johnson as a black-power militant, a radicalized Black Lives Matter protestor who took things too far.

By the second, it was growing readily apparent how sick Johnson was. The tour in Afghanistan. The obsession with military maneuvers and playing soldier in his backyard. He didn't take position in that building to further an ideology. He'd been planning something for so long, something awful and murderous, and this march downtown gave him cover and, more important, gave him opportunity. He was, like every other mass murderer in these United States, a deeply disturbed individual.

And then I thought of the men who tortured and brutalized Mary Turner. Who took everything from her as she was made to watch. Men who terrorized entire generations of African Americans, men in white robes and other men in suits and ties, who gave birth to the systemic racism and inequality that still poisons us like an infection gone unchecked. An infection that chokes and shoots our African-American men, that rapes and kills women.

I think fascism is fascism, and I think it's plagued our species since there was a species to plague. It is the sickness of might-makes-right that underpins this unfair economy, this patriarchy, this subjugation of people of color through our judicial system, our social programs, and our very reality. It has been here all along, and it subsists because it so perfectly conceals itself in the cracks of our society.

Fascism can hide behind a badge.

Fascism can hide behind an ideology.

Fascism can hide behind the Confederate flag.

Fascism can hide behind the barrel of a gun.

Fascism can hide in every facet and corner of life.

And when you look at it that way, when you search for the cracks where hatred and its demented sons hide, you can start to see a world where, surprisingly enough, we're all on the same side.

There's Us and there's Them.

There are those of us who just want to live our lives, and there are those who can snuff it all out.

★   ★   ★

The absence of a detectable crime-scene in Three Oaks was so flummoxing I had to circle the complex three separate times before I found the parking lot where Stephen Beck unloaded on Officer Hancock. I cruised past the basketball courts where the backboards lacked rims. Stacks of mattresses sitting in front of dumpsters. A laundry facility where a girl in pajama pants and a tank top was trying her damnedest to balance a hamper on her hip while closing the door and talking on her phone.

Two lots down from the scene of the ambush, I found a black police cruiser with bumblebee yellow stripes and assumed it'd been parked there to calm the tenants' nerves or prevent an aspiring copycat from getting any bright ideas. But there was no driver behind the wheel. It was a tenant. A police officer lived here.

Right there.

And in the time it took for me to gawk at the cruiser, a minivan carrying his neighbors, an African-American family, pulled in three spots down. They stepped out and didn't even acknowledge the cruiser. Just like the rest of us, they were just going about their day.

CHAPTER 13
WHEN THE DEVIL'S AT YOUR DOOR
THE REPUBLICAN NATIONAL CONVENTION

THE NEWS BROKE OVER THE RADIO.

Another ambush.

Another murder in a long line of murders.

Another gaping wound for Baton Rouge, Louisiana, a reeling community that hadn't the chance to heal from Alton Sterling's tragic death twelve days earlier. Three officers killed, another three wounded. The gunman a veteran named Gavin Long who celebrated his twenty-ninth birthday by targeting cops in the streets.[63]

The cable networks breathlessly speculated in the fashion that'd become so commonplace in our era of panic. How many gunmen? Who's responsible? We're just getting video—what is this exactly? What type of weapon are we talking about? What's the feeling out there? All the same whether it's Baton Rouge or Dallas or France.

The only relief came when they would throw to their reporters stationed in Cleveland, preparing for the upcoming Republican National Convention and the possibility that the trend of violence could continue. Are people nervous? they asked. What type of security measures are being taken?

An hour or so later, Stephen Loomis, the president of Cleveland's Patrolmen Association, begged Governor John Kasich to suspend open-carry regulations in the area outside the Quicken Loans Arena, a request Kasich said he couldn't grant. Following his answer—a denial Loomis bemoaned on every available network—the media speculated again, this time what kind of tragedy Cleveland could see if tensions ran too hot.[64]

"I think they're gonna burn down the city," a caller said on talk radio. "I really do."

By Monday morning, the most sought-after picture in Cleveland was someone carrying a weapon in plain view of the entire world. The first I found was Jesse Gonzales, conspicuous because of the large halo of reporters surrounding him. Holding court in the heart of them, Gonzales stood with an AK-47 on his back.

By my count, there were at least four countries and three continents worth of cameras trained on him as he casually answered the most repeated question of why he would ever carry a weapon into a powder keg like this: "Because I can."

Giving a similar answer was a group of Minutemen posting up on a corner outside Public Square. Decked out in body armor and combat boots, tactical communication sets snaking out of their ears, they pontificated on the police union's "illegal request" and, when asked about the weapons, would only say three words: "It's the Constitution."

A few feet away were Ohio police officers in bulletproof vests. I asked one what he thought of the open-carriers and got a roll of the eyes. "No comment," he said, "but it's a pain in my ass."

The scene was interrupted as a truck pulled slowly down the road with a digital screen in the back that sparked to life. Conspiracy mogul Alex Jones's gruff voice avalanched out of the speakers and declared war on globalists and labeled Hillary Clinton a criminal who needed to be locked away.

Soon a black passerby invaded the space, leaving the Minutemen visibly uncomfortable. He carried a sign and ordered random members of the crowd to join him for a picture. "You," he said to a passing girl. "I don't know you from a sandwich, but come on over here."

As the picture of the man and the Minutemen was snapped, the outfit's leader shouted their two-minute warning. Not long after they were marching down the sidewalk, crossing the street, their rifles bouncing as they stepped out of rhythm.

★ ★ ★

Everywhere, outright symbols of hate: Confederate flags. A man dressed in neo-Nazi paramilitary gear. Shirts and buttons and flags and towels with the most misogynistic pictures and slogans you could imagine. The new economy of intolerance and meanness that only Donald Trump could've conjured in twenty-first-century America.

Matching the symbols were moments of confrontation in every corner of the city. In the park, random arguments sparked between ideologically opposed participants, the topics and people ranging from capitalism to eternal damnation, from the ubiquitous country-club uniform of blue blazer, white collar, and khakis to a preacher standing on the steps of Public Square in an ALLAH IS SATAN shirt and carrying an ALL MUSLIMS ARE JIHADISTS sign. The latter was preaching to a crowd of people ignoring him when a Muslim woman climbed up and slipped him a joke pack of gum a protest group had been handing out earlier: ISLAMOPHOBIN, it said, MULTI-SYMPTOM RELIEF FOR CHRONIC ISLAMOPHOBIA. The man took it and told her she was going to hell.

Down on East Fourth Street, the choked thoroughfare where MSNBC and *The Washington Post* rented their headquarters, foot traffic was heavy and people squeezed against each other, bumping and shoving from time to time. At the end, the bottleneck opened onto Prospect Avenue, where impromptu protests were held in the shadow of the Quicken Loans Center.

That's where I found self-proclaimed pickup artist, and founder of the vile misogynistic website *Return of Kings*, Roosh V engaging with a small group of feminists chanting "rapist, rapist, rapist" as he filmed them and asked for more. Roosh, who has published articles about how to train women and stated a preference for girls with "skin tones within two shades" of his own, held his camera aloft to capture the event for his viewers at home and to the delight of his sad pack of an entourage, including one who told a woman, "No one is ever going to rape you, you are so safe . . . unless you go to a refugee camp." When she turned from him: "Aww, you got mad. You've got no emotional control."

Elsewhere, other Trump supporters interrupted speakers and protestors, laughing at them and mock crying when they ruffled. While a revolutionary group rallied against police brutality, a pair of supporters asked them if they knew the meaning of random words and chuckled. A few feet away a group laid black tiles with protest language in the street, gaining the attention of another pair who stood to the side, watching the project and commenting, "These people don't have a moral center" and "Their daddy didn't love them enough."

It took a toll, so I went into Flannery's Pub, grabbed a table by the bar, and while I was ordering a beer the television showed footage of Representative Steve King of Iowa discussing dividing the world into whites and nonwhites: "I'd ask you to go back through history and figure out: Where are these contributions that have been made by these other categories of people you're talking about? Where did any other sub-group of people contribute more to civilization?"[65]

Then footage of Antonio Sabato Jr., idiot soap-opera actor, saying he didn't believe the president was a Christian.

Then that race-baiting, rat bastard Rudy Giuliani.

All leading to Trump entering with a belching fog machine to "We Are the Champions" to introduce his wife Melania.

Enough to make you cry.

I was in a stupor on the train ride back to my room. One day and already so much ugliness. I closed my eyes and listened to the wheels on the track. Then a couple in the seat across from mine, the two of them in their late sixties, Trump buttons on one lapel and a local race on the other, began explaining Black Lives Matter to someone sitting nearby.

"They're paid by George Soros and the Democratic Party," the husband said.

The wife was nodding off beside him.

"They're giving them guns and money and telling them to come to Cleveland and lay waste to the whole damn place."

*   ★   *

In the morning, the main topic of concern was that Melania's speech had been plagiarized from a previous one delivered by Michelle Obama. All down the corridor, correspondents were bloodhounding anyone with a delegate lanyard and pinning them against the walls and fences, asking if it changed their opinion of Trump. The ones who were already iffy about him nodded as they sucked on their bottom lips. "It's a real issue," they said. "This definitely gives me something to think about."

Two hundred yards away were a group of combat veterans calling themselves Vets Vs. Hate, an outfit mostly in T-shirts and shorts, a distinct contrast to the Minutemen from the day before. Ben, an Army vet, told me he'd come because he was tired of how Trump talked about women and Muslims, saying, "These are people we served with proudly."

There was little fanfare for Vets Vs. Hate, though, as all the oxygen was being sucked up by a man dragging the American flag across the ground of Public Square. Quickly he was ringed by media and angry men and women who told him he should be ashamed of himself and occasionally snuck into the circle to snatch the flag off the ground. When they did, the man nonchalantly dipped it back before returning to talk with reporters.

Before long, a biker fought through and grabbed the flag, setting off a tense tug-of-war as photographers rabidly snapped pictures. Police who'd been monitoring the situation wasted no time in breaking up the scuffle and leading both men away from the crowd.

Back on Fourth Street, I found another argument, this one fabricated for the benefit of a reporter. Roosh V and one of his cronies were holding court in an alley, Roosh playing a caricature of a social-justice warrior explaining to his MAKE AMERICA GREAT AGAIN hat-wearing friend just how ignorant he was. A videographer taped the discussion but seemed perplexed: "I don't get it," she said, "why did you two come here together?"

I couldn't stop myself. The heat was stifling and all of the noise and bombast was wearing on me. "This is staged," I interrupted. "This whole thing."

Instantly they dropped the façade, seeming more disappointed than anything. "Why'd you have to do that?" Roosh asked.

Right before Trump's nomination, a protest built up in the park. The revolutionary outfit had returned with larger numbers and soon the police had weaved through the gathering and separated them, the maneuvers nearly causing more problems when they knocked over a pair of African-American men who stood up and shared words. Then, Dr. Cornell West waded into the throng and stopped everything. "There will be no peace until there is justice," he said, a megaphone carrying his voice through the square. "No calmness until justice."

And then Donald Trump became the nominee of a major political party for president of the United States.

★ ★ ★

Earlier in the day, news broke that Milo Yiannopoulos, renowned troll and self-described "most dangerous faggot," had been permanently banned by Twitter for his role in harassing Leslie Jones, actress in the lightning-rod remake of *Ghostbusters*.[66] Divisive by design, Yiannopoulos has made an incredible living and built a fervent following by touring the country and trolling everyone and everything.

As a result, his personal brand was red-hot with the alt-right, a group of young, aggressive conservatives more than willing to spout their

xenophobic, racist, anti-feminist hate speech at the top of their intol-
erant lungs, an ethos that led to them throwing their growing influence
behind Donald Trump. The hottest ticket for the alt-right was Tuesday
night's WAKE UP! Gays for Trump event and the center of their world a
ballroom on Cleveland State University's campus. Hoofing it down the
sidewalk, ears still ringing from Chris Christie's bullish prosecution of
Hillary Clinton, journalist Jerad Alexander and myself were surprised
by a voice we recognized: "These guys."

We turned and found Roosh and his pack of supporters breezing in
around us.

"What are you?" he asked. "Some kind of white knight?"

They kept pace with us for the next two blocks and argued the
reporter they'd tried to dupe earlier had deserved to lose her job. We
were outside the building, Alexander and I telling Roosh and his men
how blatantly disrespectful they were being, when the group peeled off
and skipped nine-tenths of the people waiting in line. It was obvious
right away that this was the alt-right's party, as well as the party of
the *Infowars* T-shirt wearers who stood outside and talked animatedly
about taking down the infrastructure of freedom-hating globalists by
any means necessary.

The walls inside were lined with pictures of rail-thin male models in
various stages of undress. The only consistent article of clothing: the
signature MAKE AMERICA GREAT AGAIN hat of the Trump campaign.
To go with the artwork—including a Gadsden flag hanging over the DJ
booth—were TRUMP/PENCE 2016 signs. Conspicuous as hell was the
name of the governor of Indiana, who in his congressional years had
supported a shift of money from AIDS research to conversion therapy
for homosexuals.[67]

There weren't enough drink tickets to stand around and listen to the
crowd speak in hateful vagaries, or to watch them dance awkwardly
on the small dance floor in front. In line for drinks, I stood near a man

about my age with a fascistic haircut and an obviously high opinion of himself. I'd run across him earlier in the park with a sign reading WANNA TALK TO A RACIST and had asked in passing what he thought he was doing. Now, in line, he asked me the same thing.

I wouldn't know it until later, but I'd had an interaction with Richard Spencer, president of the white-nationalist think tank the National Policy Institute, not to mention the man who'd coined the phrase "alt-right" and would go on to national infamy in just a few months.

Unaware at the time, and a few beers in, I moseyed up as a speaker introduced the first headliner: Dutch politician and founder of the Party for Freedom Geert Wilders. Considered by many to be the Donald Trump of the Netherlands, the far-right and anti-Muslim Wilders came bearing warnings of "Eurabia," a Europe that had been "overrun" by refugees and Muslims. Congratulating the crowd on taking a stand, he told them that if he becomes the prime minister of his country, he'd be opposed to even a solitary new mosque being built in the Netherlands.

The main event, of course, was Yiannopoulos, who sported sunglasses and a tank top with a rainbow Uzi and the words WE SHOOT BACK. He made light of his Twitter banning, the impetus being a fight with a "black Ghostbuster," saying, "What a humiliating end to a wonderful run. It could at least be getting into a fight with somebody serious, but no, no, it was the tertiary star of a fucking terrible feminist flop."

The crowd up front hung on his words, especially as he tied a knot meant to bind the LGBTQ community with the forces of bigotry, the shooting in Orlando serving as the lace, the only problem being that the ballroom was half-full and the people in the back were more concerned with their drinks and socializing than the shitshow on stage. Repeatedly, the crowd of alt-right diehards, the majority of them the same straight kids who'd been following around the likes of Roosh and his cronies, were turning around to tell them to shut up. But it didn't matter. There were better things to do and better places to do them. Soon they were leaving Yiannopoulos and his sycophantic assholes to their hatred, and, I suppose one could argue, their takeover of the Republican Party.

Outside, Cleveland was still awake. Delegates were stumbling from bar to bar with drinks and cigars in hand. Street musicians were still banging drums and strumming guitars on the corners. And, tucked into the corner of campus, were a group of protestors displaying a banner: QUEERS AGAINST RACISM.

"We're here," they chanted, "we're queer, your politics are really weird."

★ ★ ★

Wednesday morning and another disaster.

Pissed off by campaign manager Paul Manafort's calling him a disgrace for not coming to the convention, Governor Kasich went straight to *The New York Times* and said he'd been approached about the VP job before Pence and that, included in the offer, was the possibility of being "the most powerful vice president in history."[68]

Supposedly, Donald Trump Jr. had been in charge of the discussion and assured Kasich he'd be in charge of both domestic and foreign policies.

And what would Trump be in charge of?

"Making America great again."

Two days in and the legitimacy of the candidate and his campaign had been not just questioned but utterly undermined. The only thing more astounding than the revelation was the lack of concern the Trump operation showed or, in concert, how little his supporters cared.

Meanwhile, the cover story for Melania Trump's plagiarism had changed somewhere in the area of four separate times. It'd been a misunderstanding. A common mistake. A nonstory. Melania's fault for writing the speech herself. And finally, mercifully, some speechwriter claimed responsibility, offered her resignation, but was given a reprieve.

The story dominated the news cycle even two days later, taking any and all attention away from the unbelievable tale Kasich had gift-wrapped for the media.

But there were other stories to tell. Like Trump Force One, Donald's 757 campaign craft, coming in for a landing. All the news networks interrupted their coverage for close-ups of the plane entering the air-space. When it touched down, a delegate at the bar where I was having lunch and nursing an early beer applauded. Trump climbed out, said a few words with Pence, and then retreated to his private helicopter, also bearing his name, and choppered off for the city proper.

As the helicopter disappeared into the distance, he clapped again. "There he goes," he yelled, "the next president of the United fucking States."

★   ★   ★

I'd been watching an argument between a man wearing a shirt that said YOU WHORE and his surrounding crowd, not to mention a whole host of other arguments in the vicinity. The altercations had devolved to the lowest common denominator. Ignorance and ad hominem attacks. Sullied and dirtied, I was mulling over whether people had a point when they said the system was beyond saving, that Trump represented a deep and buried psychological defect in the species, when a sound erupted, earning the attention of everyone in the vicinity.

Some ducked.

Some ran for cover.

I hustled across the street, listening to a nearby officer say into his walkie-talkie that he'd heard a gunshot.

A rush of people toward the sound, some with guns and some with cameras.

When we got there, we found a car with a blown tire, the driver outside smoking a cigarette while police changed changed the tire to get the flow of traffic moving again. Inside the car, in the passenger seat, a smiling man displayed his photo ID to journalists asking how to spell his name. The job was done and the driver returned to the wheel and drove off into afternoon traffic. The crowd cheered the police and shook their hands as they got back to work.

Let it be known: The assembled law enforcement in Cleveland, Ohio, were the only ones walking out of that mess with any dignity. Everybody else? Disgusting. The people antagonizing and harassing one another, the media gladly lapping it up, the Republican Party reveling in the slop its organization had become. The police were quick and well-trained, and saved these people from themselves.

The only hiccup I saw came that afternoon when the revolutionary group from earlier returned for an impromptu flag burning and officers crashed into the crowd to arrest the perpetrator despite it being a constitutionally protected right. Some argued it constituted a fire hazard, while for others it was free speech, but in the aftermath things got hairy.

Just a few feet down the road, another spokesman for the group held court on the sidewalk, telling reporters and rubberneckers what they'd hoped to achieve—nothing less than a total overthrow of the system— before attempting to set fire to another flag. The police intervened again and this time clashed with the reporters covering the event, pushing them against barricades and parked cars.

A fleeting moment, perhaps, an excusable trespass in the face of so much chaos and madness. I left feeling sore about it anyway, or maybe it was the drink I'd left behind when the sprinting swarm had raced past the bar and I'd had to chase after them.

★ ★ ★

Aside from a Mike Pence speech only notable for being unnotable—other than a woman who lingered next to me on the street, craning her neck and saying, "He's a good, good man, I can tell . . . maybe he should be president"—the real action Wednesday night was Ted Cruz's address to a divided Republican house.

Word had been spreading all week that a contingent of Cruz supporters, most of them wearing pins or medals bearing his campaign logo, had been making life hell for the pro-Trump crowd at every turn, including a tense moment when the Colorado delegation walked out of the convention following a contentious roll call that shut down the long-ballyhooed Never Trump movement in one fell swoop. Otherwise, Cruz supporters were throwing as many wrenches into the gears as they could find and generally making their disapproval known.

The hope, in Trump circles anyway, was that Cruz would step up to the microphone Wednesday night and put to rest any rumor of division or rancor, a hope Cruz toyed with for the duration of his address. At times, he seemed right on the precipice of endorsing Trump, and the speech was finely tuned to stoke expectations, and then, as it wound its way to conclusion, and when it became apparent he wouldn't endorse Trump that night, the audience booed the living hell out of him.

Pence's speech became an afterthought, even more so than it would've been anyway. In the bars and in the streets, all people could talk about was Cruz's betrayal. "Fuck Cruz," a man sitting at a nearby pub spit out, slapping the bar. A smiling female Cruz delegate passed by looking pleased, and the man repeated himself, saying, "Fuck Cruz," and flipping her the bird.

★ ★ ★

Thursday morning began with more news: Trump had declared he wasn't sure he'd honor all of America's NATO commitments.[69] Reaction in the armed forces community was swift as commanders and strategists alike condemned any insinuation that we wouldn't continue to support the very organization that had been on the front lines of the Cold War against the Soviet Union.

Debate in the streets was less nuanced. Everywhere you turned, the residents of the polarized political spectrum were getting in their final licks. They argued about guns. Supply-side economics. Religion. Everything you could imagine.

I was watching two men disagree about Israel and Palestine when I caught wind of a pair of Trump supporters in HILLARY SUCKS BUT NOT LIKE MONICA and DONALD FUCKING TRUMP shirts orbiting a man sitting on one of the square's steps. The rhetoric was heated and personal.

"You're a fucking scumbag," one of them said, trying to intimidate the man.

"Come on," the resting man said. "You're not going to do shit to me."

As the altercation got uglier, the men seemed to enjoy it more. They laughed to each other about the other man's appearance, his perceived sexual orientation, called him a pedophile and shouted, "Everybody watch your kids, there's a convicted pedophile over here!"

Afterward I talked to both parties.

The pair, Chris and Levi, were from Michigan and had driven down to antagonize protestors and for the Kid Rock concert that night. "This woman over here," Levi said, gesturing to the man sitting feet away, "I'm trying to wake that idiot up. Soros is paying him and everybody else and they want *my fucking money*. They're playing games and I want people to wake up. I don't care if you puff peters or whatever, just get your hands off my paycheck."

Jimi Giannatti, a photojournalist out of Tucson, said the incident began when he interrupted another confrontation across the square and the men followed him back to that spot. He said a friend of his had been assaulted at a Trump rally.

"I was at Kent State yesterday," he said, "and getting yelled at by xenophobic, racist misogynists is nothing."

Asked why he was here, he paused.

"I've always believed that when the devil's at your door you have to tell him to get the fuck out."

☆   ★   ☆

By design, Thursday was intended to be Donald Trump's victory lap, a chance for the insurgent to stick it in the eye of the establishment one last time and revel in his victory. Similarly, the crew at *Infowars*, a new-media empire based in Austin, Texas, and built on the potent brew of paranoia and mainline capitalism, enjoyed a comparable celebration in Cleveland. Alex Jones, the pope of American conspiracy theories, had built an unlikely bridge between his fringe organization and the nominee of a major political party, cementing the strangest partnership in recent memory.

The foundation was built by Roger Stone, a longtime Trump confidant and infamous Nixon ratfucker who did the old man's dirty work with a smile on his face. Trump had gone so far as to appear on Jones's show earlier in his campaign, and Jones had told those close to him that Trump had sought his counsel and was often pleasantly surprised to hear his words coming out of the candidate's mouth.

Jones and Roger Stone were inseparable at the convention and held numerous rallies and events where members of the alt-right and preppers alike mingled and cheered on the destruction of the so-called globalist forces. They were inescapable. Walking down the sidewalk, you'd suddenly get beaten by Jones's voice machine-gunning out of a nearby speaker, or see any of the numerous *Infowars* shirts, including the now notorious HILLARY FOR PRISON one that everyone, conspiracy loon or otherwise, sported in the street.

And then there were the operatives. You could hardly walk for running into wild-eyed young men carrying expensive camera rigs. They were at every protest event, filming the proceedings before interrupting by screaming random questions about Clinton's emails, her ties to Saudi Arabia, her obvious lack of respect for the laws of the country.

The latest was a rally run by the female antiwar group Code Pink, where a man identifying himself as a veteran trained his camera on the group and yelled "Bill Clinton likes to bite women!" Quickly he gained the attention of men nearby who told him to shut up and then the eye of his camera was turned their way.

He was spotted again that afternoon at Roger Stone's book signing on Media Alley, a bustling event where Stone, wearing a shirt calling Bill Clinton a rapist, partnered with Alex Jones in signing and addressing the adoring crowd. With a perimeter of ex-military bodyguards, Jones grinned ear-to-ear and delivered warnings to the global elite he and his supporters wanted to topple.

Next to me, a Republican delegate on her way back to the convention chatted with the bodyguards about the New World Order, an illuminati plot destined to take over the world and enslave the majority of its people. Jones has dedicated his entire life to fighting this perceived threat and pontificates how globalists lace the drinking water with fluoride to hamper resistance and other plots that, to most, sound paranoid at best, but not that delegate who bragged that she had helped Trump land the Republican nomination. She handed Jones a book and when it came back with his and Stone's signature, she hugged it to her chest and said, "I love you guys."

★　★　★

I'm not sure what I expected from Donald Trump's acceptance speech. Walking from one protest to another, I'd read the transcript that'd been released to the press and found it to be the ugliest, darkest, most pessimistic view of America a candidate had probably ever offered from his party's stage. It was pure Nixon, right down to Trump calling himself the candidate of "law and order," only without Nixon's limited charm.

But watching it live in the middle of a crowd of supporters, it felt like an unwavering nightmare of racism, anger, and unrelenting fascism. The biggest cheers came from the trumpeting of "America First," a slogan that closely mirrored the popular "Britain First" slogan that preceded both Brexit and the murder of politician Jo Cox in England, a slaying before which the perpetrator screamed that very phrase.[70] And when Trump was introduced, I watched a pair of supporters in the crowd raise their arms multiple times in an unabashed Nazi salute.

I was stunned. It was the type of gesture most Trump detractors could only assume his base would love to use, but here they were, in full view of the public, sieg-heiling the Republican nominee for president.

Maybe I was naïve. Just the night before, conservative talking head Laura Ingraham had made headlines by offering what looked like, from an angle, the very same salute. I'd seen her in a bar a few hours later. She'd walked in and headed toward the back, a table full of Republican county officials yelling, "There's Laura Ingraham! You kicked its fucking ass tonight! Mic drop! Laura Ingraham in the house!"

Now there was no mistaking what I was watching. Even if there was a chance I had mistaken it the first time, they repeated the gesture when Trump assured the crowd: "I am your voice."

The rest of the speech is a blur now. Just thinking about Trump lording over the street on the electronic board, his orange face contorted in rage as his supporters cheered rabidly and greeted him as a führer, is enough to bring back a sense of nausea. Afterward, they were cheering in the pubs and on the sidewalks.

In the distance, they set off fireworks that couldn't be seen for the buildings lining the street. They boomed loudly, the sound echoing off the sides and rumbling like an angry god.

A man walking ahead of me shoved his friend. "I've been waiting for this fucking thing my entire fucking life."

I thought of the caller from the radio show who'd feared the Republicans were going to burn Cleveland to the ground.

The caller had had it wrong.

They weren't going to set any fires.

The fire had been burning for years.

CHAPTER 14
THE PEOPLE ARE GOING TO RISE
LIKE THE WATERS UPON YOUR SHORE
THE DEMOCRATIC NATIONAL CONVENTION

THE MOOD IN FRANKLIN DELANO ROOSEVELT PARK, SITUATED
just outside the Wells Fargo Center in Philadelphia, was decidedly laid-
back. Just behind the baseball diamond, a roadie checked equipment
on a makeshift stage while people lounged lazily in the hot Philadelphia
sun. Nearby, they lounged at picnic tables, sipping water provided by
the city and discussing fair-trade. A Nora Jones album played over the
speakers. I settled down in the grass to consider how I'd come from the
mad world of the RNC's Cleveland just four days before to this hippie
hangout as I looked over at a man napping in the shade of a tree.

In the distance were encampments where longhaired, shirtless
neo-hippies sprawled out on blankets and in camp chairs. Their phones
and computers played jam-band music, the messages on their signs and
tents all decidedly positive and pro-Bernie. NOT ME, WE. NOT FOR
SALE: BERNIE SANDERS. There were dozens, maybe a hundred or so,
all of them trying to beat the heat and, by all appearances, remain positive despite the fact that the Bernie Sanders campaign that had defied
all expectations and dragged eventual nominee Hillary Clinton to the
left, along with the entire Democratic Party, had been more or less dead
since mid-June. Nearly two weeks to the day, he'd endorsed Clinton and
urged his supporters to follow his lead. The people I saw were maybe in
denial, but at least it was a peaceful denial.

An hour or so later I spied my first BERNIE OR BUST sign, a blue
piece of cardboard with white lettering tethered to the backpack of a

woman with a Sanders tattoo on her right arm, a design with Bernie's trademark unkempt hair and glasses amalgamated with David Bowie's *Aladdin Sane* face paint, and I followed her and her ink around a path and into a gathering under a thicket of shade trees where a band was covering the Beatles' "All You Need Is Love" for a circle of dancing supporters. At the edges of the crowd, people were barefoot in the grass, smoking joints and hand-rolled cigarettes, Sanders signs and memorabilia at their feet. Here it is, I thought, a final farewell to the Sanders campaign. A festival of inspired supporters who came to Philadelphia to revel one last time in a movement that shook politics and inspired a new generation of progressives to buy into the system.

Then I looked over and saw her. A woman lying in the grass next to the baseball diamond, her arm shielding her face from the sun. She was trying to keep her body within the ever-changing shade with little success. Propped up next to her against the fence, a homemade sign: DNC DO YOU HEAR THE PEOPLE SING?

☆ ★ ☆

On July 22, WikiLeaks released over 20 thousand hacked emails that had been stolen from the servers of the Democratic National Committee, emails that exposed the unseemly business of national politics, including bits that brought to light the unpleasant communiqués staffers regularly share, spitballs that read a whole lot worse when the world gets a chance to peek inside.[71]

The timing of the release couldn't have been more damaging. Clinton was announcing Tim Kaine as her running mate, and just as she revealed the new Democratic ticket here came a nagging news story that could, if covered the right way, derail what was universally seen as a paint-by-numbers clinic on how to roll out a VP. Most of the information, however, was banal, the stuff of DC cocktail rumors and Capitol Hill dirt sheets. There didn't seem to be much fire to go along with the smoke, until an email titled *RE: No Shit* from Brad Marshall, the CFO of the DNC, was uncovered:[72]

> *"It might may [sic] no difference, but for KY and WVA can we get someone to ask his belief. Does he believe in a God. He had skated on saying he has a Jewish heritage. I think I read he is an atheist. This could make several points difference with my peeps. My Southern Baptist peeps would draw a big difference between a Jew and an atheist."*

Though Sanders wasn't specifically mentioned by name, the inference was clear. For over a year, Bernie's faithful had been claiming that the DNC was playing favorites in the primary, and now they had their smoking gun. The man in charge of the party's finances had been caught red-handed not just rooting for Clinton but strategizing on her behalf.

The story survived Friday's news dump and the weekend's hangover from the RNC, a virtual miracle in the age of the twenty-four-hour news cycle, and incubated with every passing minute. By Sunday, the writing on the wall was clear: Someone had to go.

Debbie Wasserman Schultz, who had said repeatedly that the DNC manipulating the primary was a "conspiracy theory," was a natural candidate.[73] Her bumbling as chair of the DNC, and her barely hidden allegiance to Clinton, had threatened to tear the party apart, and now the check had come. Someone had to pay. Long a critic of Wasserman Schultz, Sanders seized on the opportunity and publicly stated he thought she should resign. By Sunday afternoon, she relented.[74]

The original plan was for Wasserman Schultz to gavel in the convention and oversee it before leaving her post afterward, but Monday morning, as she addressed her Florida constituents, she was booed mercilessly by crowd members holding up pieces of paper reading EMAILS.

She didn't make it to the gaveling.

★ ★ ★

The protestors outside the DNC gathered in the park with signs calling Clinton a criminal. A woman next to me wore a tie-dye shirt with the words NEVER HILLARY STOP THE DNC'S COUP printed on the back.

The mood soured quickly. Signs were popping up along the street. Rhetoric was intensifying, and soon everyone was talking about Benghazi, using the words "crooked" and "liar," their voices rising as they complained about the conspiracy to steal the nomination from Sanders.

By the free water tent, a guy hadn't lost his faith. "I think he still has a chance. People are saying there's a plan."

The plan, as I gathered, was for Sanders to demand a roll-call vote for the nomination and then, via parliamentary subterfuge that had no precedent, switch delegates' votes and necessitate a second vote in which no one would be bound by primary and caucus outcomes.

"It was voter fraud," another Sanders supporter told me when I asked if it was democratic to go against the will of voters, a majority of whom had voted for Clinton. "There were millions of votes that got erased. Millions of people were disenfranchised."

Then came the delegates.

A block away they exited AT&T Station and walked behind the safety of tall fences that divided them from the protestors. The Sanders supporters flocked to those fences and pressed their signs against the chain links. They chanted "Bernie! Bernie! Bernie!" and then "Bernie Beats Trump! Bernie Beats Trump!" as the delegates streamed by. Some wearing Sanders shirts and gear gave them thumbs-up and paused for pictures with the crowd.

Somebody played "This Land Is Your Land" on the bagpipes.
I heard voices in the distance.

When I turned, I saw them marching. Hundreds more. Some flying the red flags of socialism, others holding signs calling Hillary a criminal, others with Jill Stein, the Green Party candidate for president who'd offered to serve as vice president if Bernie wanted to join her ticket. They were chanting, "Hell no, DNC / We won't vote for Hillary."

The crowd swelled and changed unpredictably. The mood transformed from calm and disgruntled to active and angry, and at moments it felt more like I was in the middle of another Trump rally as people lined the fences, eight to nine deep, and beat them as others waved Sanders signs and chanted right along.

I puzzled over them. Who were these supporters of Sanders, a liberal-as-they-come Vermont senator who delighted the world when a tiny bird landed on his podium and he regarded it with unbound happiness? How had his iconography, his very name, been coopted by a mob of people who sounded a lot like Donald Trump's supporters?

★　★　★

That night, at the start of the Democratic National Convention, Sanders took the stage and did Clinton what could only be described as a solid. Telling his supporters to throw their weight behind her, he attempted to build a bridge between the progressive wing of the Democratic Party and the establishment that has held the reins since Clinton's husband took office in 1992.

In his appeal, Sanders was unequivocal. A Donald Trump presidency was too dangerous a concept for third-party politics or protest votes. Earlier in the day, he'd sent a message through the media that he didn't want his supporters interrupting the convention—which they did anyway, booing whenever Clinton's name was mentioned—or walking out of it altogether.

Back at the park, the signs made his supporters' feelings clear. They were ready to execute what they called "the Dem Exit," a mass exodus from the Democratic National Convention. They were ready to take their ball and go home, whether that meant sitting this one out or giving their vote to Jill Stein. Many had taken their SANDERS 2016 signs and written JILL STEIN underneath, a makeshift ticket they hoped to will into fruition.

To go along with this fantasy, supporters believed Bernie had sent another signal. In his address at the convention, he'd mentioned a preference for a roll-call vote for the nomination, a state-by-state tallying of delegates that would showcase just how much support his campaign had earned in the fight. Delusional stalwarts were certain this was where Sanders would spring his trap and snatch the nomination.

The protest started in the subway, where every platform and car was stuffed full of protestors arguing loudly with commuters how the process had been rigged and manipulated. They started impromptu chants that reverberated through the train and could be heard on the sidewalks outside the stations.

At the fence, there were hundreds, if not thousands of protesters. They chanted, stomped, played drums, and carried more signs. Things were getting uglier. Clinton signs and shirts were being torn apart or defaced. A banner strung across the fence, facing the convention, read PICK $ OR US.

So, when the time came for the roll call, protestors hushed one another and gathered around people streaming the numbers on their phone before making their way into the park with the stage, where Nora Jones had been replaced by a live stream from inside the hall. They lounged in the grass and booed votes for Clinton and cheered like mad for their candidate. One man held an appeal over his head: SAVE US, WIKILEAKS.

Things got ugly when it became apparent the votes weren't going to change, that Sanders didn't have a grand strategy in place, and the couple next to me called Clinton a bitch under their breath and wondered how far into her term she'd be arrested.

South Dakota sent Clinton over the top in delegates, but word didn't immediately disseminate among the crowd, who were still cheering and booing every vote, several wondering when the secret plan would take hold.

Then Vermont passed when it was their turn to allocate their delegates.

"What's that mean?" a girl nearby asked, and I told her there was a rumor that Vermont wanted to go last so they could voice their support of Sanders as a parting gift.

"So they're not being stripped of their votes?"

By the time it came back to Vermont, the deal was long since done. Hillary Clinton was the first female nominee of a major American political party. And then Sanders took the mic and the crowd cheered like mad.

This was the moment, they thought. The time and place for the revolution. Bernie was going to challenge the lawlessness of the primary and seize control. When he moved that the convention suspend their procedure, a man in front of me raised his hand in victory. All of their work, all of Sanders's work, was coming to fruition.

And then he moved that the convention nominate Clinton by acclimation, or a simple majority.

There were tears.

People consoling each other.

Somebody threw down their BERNIE OR BUST sign and stomped on it.

A few tried to start a "Bust! Bust! Bust!" chant, but their hearts weren't in it.

Then: "To the wall!"

It echoed between groups as they marched out of the park and to the fence keeping them from the Wells Fargo Center. They amassed there and in a full-on rage they beat the fences in rhythm with their chants. Charging the DNC with selling out their country. Calling Clinton and Wasserman Schultz every name imaginable while others bent down in the streets and grass and drew and painted Jill Stein.

That night, they'd clash with police, burn flags, and chant that democracy was dead.

★   ★   ★

On February 18, 2004, the night that Howard Dean withdrew his name from the Democratic primaries, I was sitting in a room with all the lights turned out, tears dripping down my face. If I spend enough time and concentrate on it, I can go back to that very evening and feel the sickness in my gut as I realized Dean would not become president.

Twenty-two years old, I was immersed in the counterculture of the left. My undergraduate days were spent reading Kerouac and Ginsberg and Abbie Hoffman. I was drinking too much, smoking too much pot, and generally pissed off at the world. When I went to class, I spent my time slumped down in my seat writing antiwar poetry. When I skipped class, which was often, I'd find some rally against the Iraq War or George W. Bush, usually in the campus square or in front of the Vigo County Courthouse. The movement was real and it was everywhere. It was all I wanted. It was all I had.

Howard Dean was the embodiment of that spirit. It's easy to forget now, but in 2003 and 2004, the Iraq War was impossibly popular. Just questioning the conflict was enough to get yourself labeled a traitor. Dean was among the first public figures to take a stance against the invasion and, for my money, he was a hero of the highest order.

What made it worse was that Dean gained traction. Before he lost the

Iowa caucuses and melted down spectacularly in his post-loss speech, it seemed to the world that Dean had every chance to unseat Bush and return some semblance of sanity to the White House. His was a movement and I bought in big. I made my first political contribution—twenty dollars I couldn't spare—and traveled to Iowa to help the campaign. I gave my time, my blood, my sweat, and my tears to that movement.

When he dropped out, I shut off the TV before he could finish his speech. I missed him thanking me and the rest of his supporters. It was too much to bear. His quitting meant the United States, a country I thought was spiraling out of control with the illegal wars in Iraq and Afghanistan, and the Bush administration's never-ending war on personal freedoms, was going to continue with its fascist march toward imperial injustice. It meant that George W. Bush would be reelected and the madness would only get worse.

The specter gnawed at me in a way I can't even begin to explain. If I could have, I would've grabbed the political establishment by the lapels and caved in its skull.

Political losses are bad enough when you're invested, but when you're a true believer? When that candidate marshals something in you that you once thought had been lost?

That's another matter altogether.

★   ★   ★

These Sanders supporters weren't typical Democrats.

Well, they were and they weren't.

Social media have branded them children in need of a timeout, and maybe that isn't far past the truth, but the majority were fringe-left activists who wanted to change the world. They were socialists. Anarchists. Members of movements like MoveOn and Democracy Spring and the like. They were the idealists of our culture who looked at the political circles you and I followed and felt disgusted by their shallowness and craven attitudes.

They were purists.

To them, there was right and then there was wrong.

Hillary Clinton, a career politician who had left decades worth of tracks, was to them most assuredly wrong. By their own accounts, she was just as bad as Donald Trump. That concept just caused some to roll their eyes, but consider this: To these people, there was business as usual and there was revolution. No in between.

Bernie Sanders was a once-in-a-generation figure whose genuine rebuking of standard politics was believable enough that he pulled into the Democratic Party—a party drifting toward the center, if not toward the right, for twenty years now ever, since Bill Clinton saw the writing on the wall and declared an end to the era of big government—a group of individuals who had all but given up on politics as a method of change.

For these people, the only option was to demolish the system and try again. So when they chanted "Burn it down! Burn it down!" they meant it. It wasn't a petulant tantrum. If given the matches, they would've burned the country to the ground like the flags they torched in the streets.

Bernie was their last chance. A politician who came so very close to the nomination and the levers of power that he gave them back something they didn't realize they'd lost or ever wanted in the first place: hope.

★   ★   ★

By Wednesday morning, the protestors seemed hungover. Lethargic, they lounged again in the park and listened to a speaker on the stage talking about GMOs and the need for organic food. There were signs everywhere, these less clever, more just a lashing-out against Clinton, including one that called her a "lying cunt" and another that said, rather simply, "FUCK YOU, HILLARY CLINTON, I HATE YOU."

Strung from the fences where they'd raged so hard and so long were their leftover trinkets. Bernie stickers stuck to the links. The DNC DO YOU HEAR THE PEOPLE SING? poster abandoned, I assume, when the owner went in search of more shade. Small pieces of cardboard left for future historians as explanation: DEM EXIT. On the streets were scrawlings that laid the blame at the feet of Hillary and the political establishment and promised days of rage and retribution.

THE SUMMER OF RAGE

RIP DNC

THIS WON'T END HERE

THE POLITICAL REVOLUTION IS OVER, REVOLT

THE PEOPLE ARE GOING TO RISE LIKE THE WATERS UPON
YOUR SHORE

That night, while President Obama called for unity and a higher cause, they'd have one last impotent outburst. In clashes with police, they'd break down the fences and attempt to swarm the area beyond, perhaps hoping to carry their burning flags to the convention center to start the fated fire they wanted so badly. They'd chant that democracy was dead and that the DNC had stolen their voice.

As they were being arrested, perhaps they'd wonder what it was they'd come for in the first place.

To maneuver their way into the seat of power?

To wrest control of the Democratic Party and the nomination from Hillary Clinton? A candidate whose platform was comparably liberal?

And how could they not look at Donald Trump and see him as an existential threat to all of their stated beliefs and principles?

CHAPTER 15
AGAINST ALL ENEMIES, FOREIGN AND DOMESTIC

THE TALK ALL MORNING HAD BEEN WHETHER DONALD TRUMP could get his shit together and stage something resembling an actual campaign for the presidency of the United States of America while rumors swirled that GOP officials were looking into any means necessary to steal the nomination. Other stories reported that top party officials and Trump confidants were planning an intervention of sorts.[75] Newt Gingrich, longtime Trump sycophant and certified space cadet, had even gone on the record saying Trump was rendering himself "unacceptable," a real treat coming from a man who had salted more earth than Sherman himself.[76]

No sooner had the pundits pondered and agreed that, yes, Trump would inevitably bring his campaign back to civilization, then Trump took a question on the morning of August 3 from a supporter in Daytona Beach and said that Hillary Clinton "should get an award" as "founder of ISIS."[77]

Later that day, pulling into a parking garage outside Jacksonville's Veterans Memorial Arena, part of me was prepared to find shortened lines and a conspicuous absence of Trump faithful. Hard times have a habit of making orphans in the political cycle, and these were much more than hard times. What Trump had stepped into in the last seventy-two hours was nothing short of an apocalyptic meltdown the likes of which hadn't been seen since the barbarians ransacked Rome.

It had seemed, finally, as if the fever might've broken.

But then, there they were. Dressed in their red, white, and blue. Their cheap-ass MAKE AMERICA GREAT AGAIN hats. Their HILLARY FOR

PRISON T-shirts, the first of which I saw in the stairwell down from the second floor of the garage as I followed a couple on the steps, the husband barely holding a smoking nub of a cigarette between his smudged fingers as he said, to no one in particular, "Trump's going to bring the jobs back. He's gonna do it."

"He does this all the time," his wife said, looking apologetic. "Ever since Donald came around it's all he talks about."

He wasn't alone. Outside the arena, the usual clumps of people fretted over terrorist attacks and what Hillary Clinton had said or hadn't said in the last news cycle, but, of course, the topic du jour was Khazir and Ghazala Khan, parents of slain war hero Capt. Humayun Khan, a Gold Star family that had had the nerve to speak out at the Democratic National Convention.

Riveting in their patriotism and grief, the Khans had kicked up quite a storm when Khazir pulled a pocket Constitution out of his suit coat and offered to let the Republican nominee read it should he need a lesson in American values. But the story would've undoubtedly died down had Trump not taken the bait and quickly lashed out against them. Chief among his concerns was Khazir's criticism that he had "sacrificed nothing and no one," a condemnation Trump denied on ABC News by claiming his businesses and "great structures" were proof of his sacrifice.[78] Further, Trump had insinuated that the Khans' faith had prevented Ghazala from addressing the convention.

"If you look at his wife, she was standing there," Trump said. "She had nothing to say. She probably, maybe she wasn't allowed to have anything to say."

When the full interview played on Sunday, July 31, the reaction was swift. Trump had attacked a Gold Star family. Traditional Republicans and segments of the Never Trump movement, a group of traditional Republicans who had impotently tried to keep Trump from the nomination, were quick to denounce him and express support for the Khans, a rebuke that led Trump to tweet, "I was viciously attacked by Mr. Khan at the Democratic Convention. Am I not allowed to respond? Hillary voted for the Iraq war, not me!"[79]

The crowd inside openly dismissed the Khans and their sacrifice, including a retired major I overheard tell a journalist, "They can say what they want, but what they did, going there and grandstanding like that?"

Many others were wondering whether the Khans were members of the Islamic Brotherhood, a rumor that'd gained traction on conspiracy websites and had been promoted by Roger Stone and Alex Jones.[80] Those who weren't convinced of their conspiring with jihadist organizations were certain of one thing: The story had been trumped up by the media to damage their candidate's momentum.

Before Trump had even arrived in Jacksonville, his opening speakers took turns decrying the media—a line that never failed to direct the ire of the crowd toward the press pit—and saying they would stop at nothing to derail Trump's winning the presidency. A man next to me wearing a chambray shirt pushed up his glasses, raised his TRUMP/PENCE 2016 sign, pointed at the journalists, and screamed, "You're disgusting!"

Later, after Gen. Michael Flynn tried to assuage worries—"You're hearing in the media today about some type of intervention that's going on in the Trump campaign . . . the intervention is the intervention by the American people against Washington, DC"—Trump took his turn and immediately criticized the press, drawing a massive round of applause from a primed crowd.

"By the way," he pivoted, "speaking of great people . . . speaking of our best people . . . we have, and I just visited with some incredible folks . . . I have no idea where they're sitting but I know they have a good location . . . some really amazing Gold Star families."

While the crowd cheered, he pointed them out, calling them "incredible" again, to which a man behind me yelled, "Not like the Khans!"

To further fluff and paint himself as the hero of veterans, Trump displayed a Purple Heart that'd been gifted him earlier in the week and then showed the crowd an envelope. "A gentleman handed me a check. I haven't even opened it yet. He said it's more money than we can afford but we want you to have it," he said before saying he wasn't going to tell how much it was and then peeking inside. "Wow," he said.

★   ★   ★

While Trump's feud with the Khans held the nation's attention, another story was brewing behind closed doors as the campaign, which Trump himself bragged that evening was more unified than ever, threatened to come apart at the seams. The rift had been there since the early days of the race and had only intensified as Trump began winning, a reality many of his acolytes had never even considered a possibility.

As the campaign shifted from insurgency to front-runner, and eventually turned its eye to the general election in the fall, several of his staffers had met this new reality with a growing sense of disbelief. Some had viewed Trump as the ultimate outsider, a chance to swing a sledgehammer at the system in order to dislodge the growing infection of corruption, while others saw it as getting in on the ground floor of a nascent media company many expected Trump to start following his defeat in the primaries. In essence, Trump's lack of communication, and his consistent vapidity on issues and direction, allowed his workers to imprint on his candidacy whatever higher value they aspired to.

But then he won.

Many of his staffers grew more and more despondent with each passing victory. They saw a window closing as the RNC and Trump feuded and then as Trump's rhetoric began to blacken with nationalistic and racist rhetoric. They couldn't remember anymore why they'd thrown in their hat in the first place and yet, here they were, along for the ride.

Trump's management style mirrored his corporate strategy of playing rivals against one another and watching them compete for his loyalty. Some days, offices had no idea who was calling the shots or who had garnered Trump's favor. The first public example of this came as Corey Lewandowski, Trump's first campaign manager, was pitted against Paul Manafort, a veteran politico who'd been hired to fend off a delegate coup at the Republican National Convention.

Lewandowski had long been considered a hard-ass, and this persona was only substantiated in separate incidents when he manhandled a reporter and a protestor at rallies. The anger that Trump prompted in his supporters was seen by some as an extension of Lewandowski, and as it boiled over many of the staffers watched with dread. They had planned to shake up the system, not to shake the country to its core. Over an eleven-day period back in March, the problem worsened as the seed of potential violence I'd witnessed came into full bloom. On March 8, Lewandowski grabbed *Breitbart* reporter Michelle Fields, prompting her to file a police report.[81] Three days later, in Chicago, a Trump rally was canceled as supporters and protestors raged against each other violently on live television.[82] In Phoenix, on March 19, Lewandowski grabbed a protestor by the collar.[83]

That month, Paul Manafort was brought aboard as it looked possible the RNC in Cleveland might be the first contested convention since 1976, when Manafort had served as a coordinator for President Gerald Ford.[84] As Lewandowski's tenure descended into chaos, Manafort managed to wrest control of the campaign's apparatus, leading to Lewandowski's ouster in June.[85] Staffers, however, had been uncertain who was pulling the levers well before Lewandowski's dismissal or Manafort's ascension.

Their confusion would only worsen as the race trucked on. Trump's own behavior was erratic and seemed at times uncontrollable. Day in and day out, he'd create a new controversy from thin air and then the entire team would be embroiled in cleaning up his mess. Manafort's inability to corral Trump was a giant problem all of its own, but even more troubling was the baggage he brought with him to the job.

One of the first moments that raised eyebrows occurred when the GOP met before the convention to outline the party's platform, a run-of-the-mill parliamentary maneuver that more or less sets the table for the candidate and party's agenda. A surprisingly contentious item was language that called on a Republican administration to provide "lethal defensive weapons" to assist Ukraine in ongoing conflicts with Russia.[86] First proposed by committee member Diana Denman, the language was promptly met by overwhelming resistance from Trump's campaign. When the dust settled, the platform only called for "appropriate assistance," a change that provided ample amounts of wiggle room and could be interpreted liberally. Manafort would later deny the campaign had insisted on the language despite contradictory accounts.

During the Democratic National Convention, Manafort's influence took an even darker turn. After WikiLeaks published its stolen DNC emails, members of the United States intelligence apparatus quickly suspected Russian involvement, a suspicion that dissatisfied members of the Trump campaign shared. Rumors circulated that Manafort had brokered a deal between Trump and the Russians, perhaps as far up as Vladimir Putin himself, whom Trump regularly heaped with praise, that would barter the election for Trump's assurance of cooperation.

Staff were obsessed with this rumor and promised enterprising reporters would be rewarded if only they dug deeper. Intrinsically, they mistrusted Manafort and his motives, and the more they stared into the growing story the more they saw evidence of a burgeoning conspiracy. The only thing they couldn't agree on was whether or not Trump had played an active role in that clandestine agreement. Some believed the businessman was a Machiavellian evil genius who played the fool in public while pulling strings behind the curtain. Others were convinced he was just easily controlled.

I wasn't sure what to believe. The Manafort angle certainly seemed to have legitimacy, especially in the wake of the DNC leak when Trump took to the podium and urged Russian hackers to find Hillary Clinton's missing emails.[87] On the surface, it seemed like a bizarre attempt to communicate with a foreign power, a move that bordered on treason, but others who maintained Trump's ignorance of the deal simply dismissed it as more of his inability to wrap his head around any given subject. A theory began to emerge that Trump had been targeted as a "useful idiot," a term that'd been popular during the Cold War to describe people who could be manipulated by Communist interests while remaining unaware of their handling.

Much like the rest of the 2016 election, the truth lay in the eye of the beholder. Trump's candidacy was so obtuse it had transformed into a Rorschach test of sorts in which anyone could see what they needed for their own narrative and there was more than enough circumstantial evidence to cast Trump as a Manchurian candidate happy to partner with a despot.

There was the financial support Franklin Foer of *Slate* uncovered in July that showed Trump had relied on Russian investors after American banks had been scared away by his multiple bankruptcies.[88]

There were his unending vocalizations of admiration for Putin, including stunning moments when he claimed the dictator had been a stronger leader than President Obama.[89]

There were his constant allusions to abandoning our NATO allies.[90]

There was his bizarre claim that Putin wouldn't "go into the Ukraine" despite the fact that Russia had seized the Crimean peninsula in 2014.[91]

There was Carter Page, a shadowy foreign adviser to Trump who was reported to have communicated directly with the Kremlin.[92]

There was Trump's daughter Ivanka vacationing in Croatia with Wendy Deng Murdoch, Putin's rumored girlfriend.[93]

There was a report that a server tied to Trump was communicating with a Russian bank.[94]

There was the continued Russian interference, whether it was the hacks, disinformation campaigns, fake news efforts, or an army of paid trolls.

And then there was the jaw-dropping discovery of a ledger in Ukraine that showed 12.7 million dollars of cash payments to Manafort that'd been paid by the party of President Viktor F. Yanukovych, a Russian loyalist Manafort had worked for as early as 2010.[95]

The ledger was what ultimately led to the resignation of Manafort on August 19 as the campaign was being swallowed by questions of international interference.[96] As he left, much of the suspicious activity and pro-Russian rhetoric disappeared with him, leaving staffers and critics to wonder whether Trump had decided to protect himself or if Manafort had been solely responsible for the questionable ties. If it was the former, that meant Trump was some kind of diabolical architect capable of manipulating geopolitical events to his nefarious ends.

If it was the latter, though, if he really was the useful idiot who could be swayed by a campaign manager into a dalliance with Russia, then what did that mean? Could the Republican nominee really be manipulated that easily? And, if so, what if another dangerous influence earned Trump's confidence?

★   ★   ★

In August 2016, outside the Veterans Memorial Arena, Trump supporters ran smack dab into a pen of protestors chanting "This ain't a Trump rally, it's a Klan rally!" Within minutes, tempers flared and supporters crowded the fence between the two parties, spitting on the protestors, threatening them, shoving their Trump signs in their faces, and yelling back, "All lives matter! All lives matter!"

Two separate fronts developed: one by the arena and the other across the street, where a small battalion of socialists with red flags readied themselves for the barrage. The overflow from the arena drove supporters straight into them, and it wasn't long until they moved from one scene to another, shouting and threatening to kick the protestors' asses.

On both fronts, Confederate flags with TRUMP 2016 lettering across the Stars and Bars appeared, and on both fronts the people displaying the flags shoved them in the protestors' faces and screamed threats and racist insults. Gone was any sense of civility or decorum.

One man holding the Confederate flag leveled a finger at a protestor being restrained: "You've been fucking brainwashed by the media."

Jacksonville police cleared out the scene the best they could, leaving stragglers from both camps to provoke each other in the streets and on the sidewalks. I walked behind a small group of Trump supporters, still wearing those hats, still wearing those shirts, and listened as they came across an African-American man standing on the street corner in a HILLARY FOR PRISON shirt with his arms folded. Just moments before, someone in the group had said, about the protestors, "They don't know how racist niggers are."

I waited to see how this interaction would play out. I was feeling sick, exhausted, relieved that police had broken up the scrum with the Confederate flags before real violence ensued.

"Finally," one of the men in the group said to the man on the corner, "a black guy with some sense."

In the parking lot, the stairwells were full.

Downstairs, as far as I could see, there were people wearing Trump shirts and chanting, "Trump! Trump! Trump!"

If it wasn't apparent already, the truth was setting in: The fever of the Republican Party wasn't about to break. There was no turning back.

CHAPTER 16
THE GREEN PARTY NATIONAL CONVENTION

THE STREETS RUNNING THROUGH THE UNIVERSITY OF HOUSTON'S campus were deader than the tumbleweed-ridden towns in a Clint Eastwood western where a gang of unsavory men has already gunned down all the locals. The August Texas sun beat the hell out of me as I strolled across the empty street and into the student center where the Green Party was birthing their own form of revolution to the delight of a few hundred supporters.

It was the first convention to grant me press credentials, so I'd come prepared in a navy-blue suit just a hair on the tight side after weeks spent eating fried food in every godforsaken bar from here to Cleveland and guzzling cheap beer to maintain a shred of sanity in the face of this insane election cycle. I huffed it up to the second floor and found the credentials area: a plastic foldout table helmed by a pair of white-haired women listening to Scott McLarty, the party's press secretary, marvel that things were miraculously going according to schedule: "We're the Greens!" he said, baffled. "How can we be on schedule?"

When asked, I told them I was there for *The New Republic*, and one of them fiddled with the list for a second, muttering, "Is this alphabetical?" before giving up and writing the publication on a scrap of paper. She handed me a pen. "You take care of the name."

The lanyard and "credential" looked like I was coming in for a kindergarten career day, which was made even more pathetic later when I heard the rumor spreading through press row that some asshole from *Breitbart* got thrown out of the convention for forging credentials, the equivalent of losing a game of Monopoly when opponents discover you're trying to pass off Post-It notes as fifties.

McLarty lead me inside to the three-fourths-full theater and a row of seats labeled MEDIA. Elijah Manley, a seventeen-year-old candidate for the Green Party's presidential nomination, was giving the best speech I'd ever heard given by a seventeen-year-old. He was firmly in Dr. Jill Stein's corner, lauding the nominee and physician as a candidate who would shake up the political status quo and lead the party into a new era. The crowd—predominantly white and granola-y, full of ponytails, bifocals, and scraggly beards, a gathering of people who'd probably hold up your local city council meetings every month over a recycling dispute—cheered and brandished their STEIN 2016 signs, some newly decorated with Sharpies: BERN THE GREEN.

In the wake of the Democratic National Convention the week before, with its contentious nomination of Hillary Clinton and the protests outside the Wells Fargo Center of the Bernie or Bust contingent, including members of the far left, anarchists, and career antagonists, the Greens had pushed their modest capital into the pot in a full-on effort to remake the party by poaching Sanders's revolutionary base, a gambit that didn't seem all that productive as they already owned the vote of the politically disaffected ultra-liberals, and any progress on their part would ultimately lead to a sequel of the 2000 election in which nominee Ralph Nader cost Al Gore the presidency and ensured the invasion of Iraq, a manmade disaster that had already cost more lives, money and influence, not to mention unrest, than it's even worth getting into.

But try telling them that.

They were all-in, even going so far as to invite WikiLeaks founder and alleged perpetrator of sexual assault Julian Assange to beam in like a supervillain addressing the United Nations with his demands. A giant screen loomed over the stage, and as the video flickered and Assange came into focus, his icy stare peered into the seats.

After an uncomfortably long effort to fix the audio—the problem solved after an audience member yelled out that the YouTube stream was fine, resulting in a bizarre and unsettling moment where Assange's answers ended in booming reverb: "Sanders . . . Sanders . . . Sanders . . ."—David Cobb, former Green presidential nominee, called Assange a "hero," a mantle the crowd conferred when they chanted, "WikiLeaks! WikiLeaks! WikiLeaks!"

Assange rambled about corporate political influence, an honest-to-god concern that he, in a way no one else, maybe in the world, could do, made so narcissistic and unpalatable that even someone who might agree—let's say, I don't know, me—had to grimace while fighting off an urge to go wash their hands until they were raw and bleeding.

"Google is like HIV," he said in the middle of a directionless rant that tied Clinton to the tech company and, by default, saddled her with responsibility for the coming singularity, wherein computers would gain sentience.

And that was his default analogy. Sexually transmitted diseases. After he described the choice between Clinton and Trump as "choosing between cholera and gonorrhea," my neighbor muttered to no one in particular, "Didn't that woman he raped say he gave her gonorrhea?"

The guy pulled out his phone, Googled.

"Huh," he said.

Less concerned were the party members calling out to the big face on the big screen.

"Where's the smoking gun?"

"Where's the big email?"

The "big email," as the audience member called it, was a piece of urban legend at that point in the campaign, a document members on the far right and far left were both waiting for in earnest: evidence that Hillary Clinton, as secretary of state, had either funded ISIS or had helped found it. All of the people I'd talked to at the Republican National Convention and now the Green Party Convention had believed in it despite no proof of its existence. Bizarrely enough, both the GOP and the Greens chanted "Lock her up!"

It was then, in that cramped theater, that I suddenly realized how little difference there was between the far far right and the far far left, particularly what lengths they would go to in order to gain power, the only real contrast being what they might do with that power should they ever attain it.

Assange signed off without answering whether he had the "big email" in his possession or not, and the Green Party faithful headed outside to grab a smoke or take a piss. I followed two of them around the corner, one in a burnt-orange Texas shirt and a cowboy hat. He was telling his buddy that back in the day it was "illegal to hang a Mexican and a black from the same tree," that back then they had "standards."

In the bathroom, I heard somebody say, "He sure as hell gave it to her."

"Hell yes," the guy at the urinal next to me agreed.

I noticed he was wearing a Bernie Sanders shirt with a BERNIE 2016 pin hanging from his lanyard. "You're a Bernie guy?" I asked.

"You bet," he said, ripping off some paper towel.

"And now you're with the Greens?"

He gave me a look like I'd misunderstood something. "Buddy, I've always been with the Greens."

★   ★   ★

It was only noon but I needed a drink so bad I couldn't take it anymore. When I got into the nearby bar I ripped off my tie, shed my suit jacket, and rolled up my sleeves. It was my intention, if I was going to sit in that auditorium another four hours, to get at least a good buzz going, if not a full-on drunk. Covering second-rate politics can do that to a man.

Two blocks from the student center was a campus bar completely empty except for me, a jukebox playing a string of alternative hits from the '90s, and a bartender who looked like she'd rather be anywhere else.

"Are you one of those people?" she asked in a tone indicating she was unsure what *those people* were all about. I assured her I wasn't, that I was just here to watch *those people*, and she nodded like that was the best answer. "They don't seem happy."

I was two beers in when the door opened and in walked one of *those people*. He had long, curly red hair and a beard that almost ran down to the neck of his Green Party shirt, and when he fell onto the stool down the bar from mine it was with a dissatisfied huff. He ordered a beer and sucked it down while playing on his phone.

After a trip to the bathroom, I came out and found his stool unoccupied.

"What happened to him?"

"Oh god," the bartender said, "that guy was a real fuckin' piece of work. He said he's over there at the conference or whatever that thing is, and he says everyone's lame as shit."

"He's not wrong."

"What crawled up their asses anyway?"

I did my best to explain the Green Party to this bartender and told her it was a group of the most liberal people you could ever imagine, a group so far left they'd actually more or less retreated from society at large and resided in a world where patting yourself on the back in the voting booth was more important than what actually happened in the country. That just that day they'd argued over the state of Texas's right to exist.

When I'm done she just stared at me. "Are you fucking kidding?"

I told her I was not.

"Do these people know about Donald Trump?"

★ ★ ★

After lunch, I settled back into the theater and felt the beer I'd just taken down in the past hour. I was fighting off the worst of all buzzes, the midday summer buzz, which is the kind of hell that befalls anybody who'd ever spent a day on the beach or woke up with little regard for the world. There was a hangover lurking in the back of my skull and my head was in no mood to put up with this Green Party shit.

"Howdy!"

I looked up from my shoes to find a guy dressed nearly identically to me. Middle-aged, he looked like he had some money in his wallet, which he sat on in the row of front of mine to shuffle his signs.

Eying the green ribbon that hung from my badge, he asked if I was from the press.

"Unfortunately."

"What do you think of this whole thing?"

I opened my mouth to answer but he cut me off.

"Me? I'm a Bernie guy. I felt the Bern. Ha. Ha. You know what I mean?"

I told him sure, and he started going on about how he was a fundraiser for the Democrats, how he'd been to every party in the city and had always given cash to the campaign. But not this time. Not after Sanders endorsed Clinton.

"Fuck," he said, "that's like Kirk Douglas in *Spartacus* endorsing the Roman Senate. I mean, really, that's like fucking Spartacus endorsing Caesar!"

He'd no sooner said that than another middle-aged guy, also with money, came walking in carrying a STEIN/BARAKA sign under his arm.

The guy I was talking to first pointed at him. "Here's another one!"

They went over some parties they'd seen each other at and how disappointed they were in Bernie. Earlier a speaker said that Sanders "sold out" his supporters and these two couldn't have agreed more.

"Tell your readers," the second guy said, "I'm tired of being held hostage. Maybe I can't change the course of an election, but I can vote my conscience."

The convention gaveled back into order a few seconds after I'd taken his note and the woman at the podium called for Alabama to come to the microphone and dispense their delegates, but before they did, presidential candidate Sedinam Curry, whose full name was Sedinam Kinamo Christin Moyowasifza-Curry, took the mic and yelled, "I have been discriminated against!"

Disarray in the crowd. Disarray at the podium.

"Tell me," she asked the delegates, "do you believe there are white supremacists in the Green Party?"

They answered back that they did believe there were white supremacists in the Green Party. Some of them raised their hands and wiggled their fingers, a sign of silent agreement. A woman not far from Curry banged a tambourine that quickly bored into the ailing parts of my skull.

Party officials scrambled to calm the situation, and Curry finally relented when she was told she'd have a hearing of her grievances later, but she didn't go away. Whenever a delegation read off votes for her, she yelled from her seat "Say my name!" and when they tried and failed she heckled them mercilessly.

Finally, after way, way, way too long, the exercise was over. Greens had championed all of their favorite causes, whether it was solar panels in Florida or fighting Texas's right to call itself a sovereign state, and now their leader, Dr. Jill Stein, strode out from the wings with Ajamu Baraka, her running mate, clasping her raised hand, and they walked straight across the stage and disappeared again.

There was more entertainment, including YahNe Ndgo, a Bernie or Buster who'd gotten a few shares on Facebook when she went on CNN to defend her stance. Ndgo took the microphone, stood at center stage, and delivered a disjointed speech in which she leveled the charge that

Sanders was a "sheepdog" who'd been charged with herding liberals back into the Democratic fold and then, the next minute, asked all the racists in the theater to stand up. Surprisingly, most of the delegates did just that.

"Those of you sitting," Ndgo said, "you've got some work to do."

Later, Dr. Cornel West took the stage. I'd seen him at every single convention that season, and all of his speeches remained the same. His delivery was all fire, though, and the crowd ate it up and lost their minds. The tambourine wouldn't stop banging and the hangover creeping over me was now banging in rhythm with it to the point where I thought I might actually go insane.

"Uh huh!" the girl next to me screamed with every one of Dr. West's applause lines. "Uh huh! That's right!"

I was keeping an eye on both of the exits, including the one closest to me, where a guy was hanging out wearing one of the most popular Bernie Sanders shirts, the one with just an outline of Sanders's glasses and unkempt hair. I'd lived through Cleveland with its nonstop onslaught of batshit-insane preppers and strong-jawed assholes, hundred-degree heat and riots in Philadelphia, and now, here I was, in an air-conditioned theater, struggling to overcome a fucking tambourine.

Miraculously, I made it to Dr. Stein. For those who have no idea who she is, you're not alone. After suffering staggering defeat after staggering defeat as a political candidate, including two runs at the governorship of Massachusetts, the first in 2002 garnering her 3 percent of the vote[97] and the last, in 2010, yielding just 1 percent, she ran for president as the Green Party nominee in 2012 and received 0.36 percent of the popular vote, charting above one point in only three states.[98]

But this one, Dr. Stein maintained, was the election where it all changed.

"You have completely changed the political dynamics going forward," she said in her acceptance speech. "It will never be the same and there will be no stopping you, there will be no stopping us . . . Voters are in revolt, are rejecting the Democratic and Republican candidates at record numbers . . . people are clamoring for more choices. We are that other choice."

In her address, she called Republicans the "Party of Hate" and Democrats the "Party of Deportation, Detention, and Midnight Raids," a portrait that left very little wiggle room for the socially conscientious voter to navigate. Like Dr. West, Ndgo, and Assange, Dr. Stein posited that this was an election where there was no difference between the party's candidates, that a vote for either Clinton or Trump was a vote for maintaining the status quo.

So, what if Dr. Stein could somehow manage to pull off the unthinkable and win the presidency? What would she do?

Hard to say as there was very little in the way of answers. After her speech was a press conference where the journalists in the crowd, for the most part, were Green-friendly blogs who lobbed softballs to Dr. Stein—one of the tougher ones being "What do you most look forward to in your CNN town-hall program?"

A few tough ones managed to get through as Eliot Nelson of *The Huffington Post* pressed Dr. Stein on WikiLeaks' association with Russia and concerns that Assange's organization interfered with the election. She waived him off, saying it was something state departments do to each other all the time. When Nelson tried to follow up, Baraka accused the media of hijacking the real story here: that Bernie Sanders was undermined by the DNC.

When the blogger next to me asked how a third-party president would get an agenda through a two-party Congress, Dr. Stein blinked before summarily dodging the question altogether.

And, all the while, the damnedest thing: The other bloggers, interspersed throughout the seats, their median age maybe twenty, were nodding along with her answers, smiling, literally offering Stein a thumbs-up and encouragement.

In the heat again, I was walking with Nelson and both of us were just stunned. It was a rinky-dink operation, for sure, but Nelson couldn't figure out why it wasn't more fun. "You'd think they'd have more of a sense of humor about themselves."

Still hearing that damn tambourine, I retreated back to the pub and reclaimed my seat at the bar, where the jukebox had transitioned from '90s alternative to '90s gangsta rap. "Nothin' but a G Thang" played as squares in Green Party T-shirts, their handmade lanyards still hanging from their necks, were slumping at the tables, at the bar, sipping their drinks and glancing at their phones, a striking contrast to the scenes in Cleveland and Philadelphia, where the Party of Hate and the Party of Deportation, Detention, and Midnight Raids were partying well into the morning, celebrating their halves of the world. There, bars and restaurants were stuffed with delegates, congressman, local party officials, and fame-clingers. The champagne popped in the wee hours and didn't run out until the next day's sun had breached the horizon.

This was a convention for losers, never-would-bes, a place to complain about issues beyond their control and go home feeling good about their political stance. But in one of the closest elections in the history of American politics, the few liberals the Green Party were able to siphon from the Democrats would certainly play a role in determining the outcome.

The bartender brought me another beer and leaned across the bar. "These fucking people," she said, eying the Green Partiers from corner to corner.

I raised my drink as if to toast. "These fucking people."

PART THREE

A NEW KIND OF RELIGION

CHAPTER 17
A VOICE FOR THE PEOPLE

THE FIRST THING I NOTICED WHEN I WALKED INTO THE CHARLOTTE Convention Center on August 19 were the teleprompters waiting on the stage where Donald Trump would emerge two hours later. Trump had never bothered with them in all of the events I'd been to. His remarks were rarely planned or contained anything nearing a logical order. His speeches had been rambling affairs that occasionally targeted his opponents, more or less stand-up routines serving as delivery systems to brag about his successes in the primaries and to prosecute those who had doubted him. In every instance, large swaths of the crowd that had come to chant along with his slogans and rage against the establishment had grown restless, dozens of them getting up and walking out in the middle of his rant as soon as they'd noticed others had had enough.

Something had changed, though.

When Trump took the stage, the first order of business was to address the recent flooding in Louisiana, the worst natural disaster in the United States since Hurricane Sandy in 2012, which had claimed thirteen lives and caused billions in damage. In the past, Trump would've preened and played with the crowd, but he was focused that night as he read the statement on one of his nearby screens.

"We are one nation," he began. "When one state hurts, we all hurt—and we must all work together to lift each other up. Working, building, restoring together.

"Our prayers are with the families who have lost loved ones, and we send them our deepest condolences. Though words cannot express the sadness one feels at times like this, I hope everyone in Louisiana knows that our country is praying for them and standing with them to help them in these difficult hours.

"We are one country, one people, and we will have together one great future."

I was astounded. Easily, it was the most presidential I'd ever heard Trump sound. As he delivered his remarks, I could, for the first time, imagine him standing behind a podium with the seal of the president of the United States, a far cry from the man who, the week before, had told a crowd not two hundred miles away in Wilmington, "If she [Hillary Clinton] gets to pick her judges, nothing you can do, folks. Although the Second Amendment people—maybe there is, I don't know."[99]

The remark had been just another gaffe in an overwhelming series of missteps that had plagued him. In his year of campaigning, he had now feuded with everyone from the pope to a Gold Star family while offending nearly every group outside of white males. The remark in Wilmington, which some worried might be a dog-whistle call for gun owners to assassinate his opponent, felt like the bridge too far that would finally, mercifully, put the nightmare that was Donald Trump out of commission.

Pivoting masterfully from the call for unity for Louisiana, he said, "Tonight, I'd like to talk about the new American future we are going to create together."

The transition was graceful, a piece of brilliant writing that felt so odd coming from Trump's mouth.

"On Monday, I laid out my plan to defeat radical Islamic terrorism. On Tuesday, in Wisconsin, I talked about how we are going to restore law and order to this country."

There was a cohesion to this speech, a logic that weaved all of the disparate elements of his campaign, the underlying xenophobia and the racism and the general ugliness, into a consumable, digestible appeal that relied on a portrait of America that many voters had sensed was true but hadn't yet been shown. It was the speech of a man running for the presidency rather than the directionless ramblings of a narcissist who found himself on a stage with a world's worth of eyes at his whim.

"The chaos and violence in our streets," he read from the teleprompter, "and the assaults on law enforcement, are an attack against all peaceful citizens. If I am elected president, this chaos and violence will end—and it will end very quickly.

"Every single citizen in our land has a right to live in safety. To be one united nation, we must protect all of our people. But we must also provide opportunities for all of our people."

The remark ended on a tailored applause line, the type speechwriters have relied on since there were speechwriters. The crowd applauded, and with that applause they were led into the next section of the speech and thus more receptive to the proceeding order of business.

"We cannot make America great again if we leave any community behind.

"Nearly four in ten African-American children are living in poverty. I will not rest until children of every color in this country are fully included in the American dream.

"Jobs, safety, opportunity. Fair and equal representation. This is what I promise to African Americans, Hispanic Americans, and all Americans.

"But to achieve this new American future, we must break from the failures of the past."

The night before, in Milwaukee's predominately white suburb of West Bend, Trump had given another prepared speech in much the same vein. That one, advertised widely as his appeal to African-American voters, had been another crafted narrative that had never delivered on an actual appeal. His remarks had nimbly tiptoed a thin line of racist rhetoric that seemed, at times, to hint that African Americans were either good citizens or criminals, a divide that could only be bettered if Trump were elected. The speech had little to nothing to offer black voters. It insinuated that the unrest and outrage following police killings had been a narrative spun by a media intent on enraging the population and inspiring riots in American cities.

Again, the speech in West Bend was never intended, as had been claimed, for African Americans. This was a new message for white voters who had wrung their hands at the thought of supporting Trump because of what it might mean about them. Traditional Republicans around the country had struggled with outwardly supporting their candidate lest they be considered a racist. But here, Trump was gifting them cover.

They weren't racist.

No, they were *concerned* about African Americans.

They wanted to help save them from themselves.

Standing in their way, however, were opponents who would do anything to undermine the necessary change. Hillary Clinton was the figurehead, but at her back was a machine much more sinister. Controlling her was an establishment, an unimaginably affluent conglomeration of international bankers and power brokers who saw Donald Trump as the greatest threat to their ongoing domination.

The speech in Charlotte entwined all of it into a simple narrative. Every crisp line litigated Clinton's perceived misdoings, her conflicts of interest, the supposed crimes that had Trump's followers calling for her execution. It built a formidable case and then, in the middle of that prosecution, Trump established himself as the alternative, a "champion of the people."

Their champion would right all the wrongs and put America back in good standing, but first, if he was to even get the chance, he'd have to overcome an adversary who'd been plaguing him even longer than "Crooked" Hillary Clinton.

"The establishment media doesn't cover what really matters in this country, or what's really going on in people's lives. They will take words of mine out of context and spend a week obsessing over every single syllable, and then pretend to discover some hidden meaning in what I said.

"Just imagine for a second if the media spent this energy holding the politicians accountable who got innocent Americans like Kate Steinle killed—she was gunned down by an illegal immigrant who had been deported five times.

"Just imagine if the media spent this much time investigating the poverty and joblessness in our inner cities.

"Just think about how much different things would be if the media in this country sent their cameras to our border, or to our closing factories, or to our failing schools. Or if the media focused on what dark secrets must be hidden in the 33,000 emails Hillary Clinton deleted.

"Instead, every story is told from the perspective of the insiders. It's the narrative of the people who rigged the system, never the voice of the people it's been rigged against.

"So many people suffering in silence. No cameras, no coverage, no outrage from a media class that seems to get outraged over just about everything else."

In the middle of his attack, a man near me turned to the press pit behind the railing and pointed an accusatory finger. "That's you!" he mouthed angrily. "That's you!"

Taking the cue, others came to the barrier and glared at the assembled reporters. Some snapped pictures of them with their phones, others scrawled notes before furiously stomping away.

"So again, it's not about me," Trump continued, turning the media's assault on his candidacy into an attack on his supporters. "It's never been about me. It's about all the people in this country who don't have a voice.

"I am running to be their voice. I am running to be the voice for every forgotten part of this country that has been waiting and hoping for a better future. I am glad that I make the powerful a little uncomfortable now and again—including some powerful people in my own party. Because it means I am fighting for real change.

"There's a reason the hedge-fund managers, the financial lobbyists, the Wall Street investors are throwing their money at Hillary Clinton. Because they know she will make sure the system stays rigged in their favor. It's the powerful protecting the powerful. The insiders fighting for the insiders.

"I am fighting for you."

Another applause line.

More applause.

★ ★ ★

In future examinations of Donald Trump's unexpected victory, there'll be plenty of arguments as to what exactly was the turning point. Many will focus on late-cycle revelations and Hillary Clinton's failures, but there is a case to be made that the presidency was won the morning of his speech in Charlotte when Trump accepted an embattled Paul Manafort's resignation and then handed the reins to the team of veteran pollster Kellyanne Conway and Steve Bannon, the then-little-known head of the alternative media company *Breitbart News*.

Conway was a tireless cable-television veteran who had an uncanny ability to stonewall hosts' lines of questioning until she found one she liked. She was reported to have had a calming effect on Trump and a much-needed influence that Manafort had never been capable of. In her, Trump found somebody who could manage him away from the day-to-day distractions long enough to get his campaign's messaging, which Conway helped sculpt, some sunlight between scandals.

The one who fashioned that message was Bannon, an unlikely pick for Trump's chief executive. Beginning with the speech in West Bend,

Bannon meticulously crafted long and powerful screeds against the establishment that took Trump's most unpalatable positions and softened them through a variety of advanced rhetorical tricks while effectively summarizing the message of the campaign and lionizing it as a growing movement. They were masterful pieces of speechmaking that appealed to voters who might otherwise eschew Trump and his bigotry while also flirting with members of the fringe right.

Bannon was no stranger to that juggling act. Since taking the helm of *Breitbart* after its founder Andrew Breitbart died unexpectedly in 2012, Bannon had succeeded in the task that had doomed the GOP: appealing to traditional Republican voters as well as the more radical members of its base, turning *Breitbart* into a platform for the alt-right, a group powered by a defining philosophy of misogyny and white supremacy.

During the course of the 2016 campaign, *Breitbart* established itself as one of the most powerful outlets for news. Whereas members of the site had fretted that Andrew Breitbart's untimely passing would lead to the venture's fall, under Bannon's tutelage the site took the right wing's media narrative a step further than traditional mainstays like Fox News had been willing to go. This daringness resulted in a boom that turned the site into the thirty-sixth-largest web designation in the United States, an achievement that netted it 300 million views in November 2016, in addition to its being declared by *NewsWhip* the owner of the country's number-one Facebook and Twitter political pages.[100, 101]

In many ways, *Breitbart* and Donald Trump enjoyed parallel ascents. Both had shunned traditional audiences and had instead focused on disaffected people who felt the forces of globalism and political correctness had led America astray. Both enjoyed the support of white supremacists while never officially accepting that support. Both had begun as fervent critics of the media but relied on that media to empower them, Trump having risen to prominence due to unprecedented coverage and *Breitbart* gaining traction via the embrace of traditional outlets.

And both benefited wildly from Fox News having opened its doors and given them substantial national platforms.

For Trump, it was the open invitation to come on FNC anytime to spout birther conspiracy theories, and with *Breitbart* it began in earnest in 2009 with Glenn Beck's all-out assault on the nonprofit ACORN, a community-organizing body that had been active for over forty years and had tenuous ties to President Obama. Andrew Breitbart had personally championed a set of undercover exposé films by "guerrilla journalists" James O'Keefe and Hannah Giles that purported to show members of the organization advising O'Keefe how to traffic underage prostitutes. ACORN and critics would argue the footage had been significantly doctored, but, regardless, the campaign resulted in ACORN shuttering its doors.

The ACORN fiasco, paired with Glenn Beck's success in costing Van Jones his job as special adviser to President Obama, was an undeniably important moment. With those tapes and the resulting controversy, conservatives now had proof of their suspicions that something was fundamentally wrong with Obama. The rumors regarding his birth and intentions had all been speculative, shots in the dark at casting the first black president as un-American, but O'Keefe's video provided the physical evidence that Americans who'd been predisposed to oppose Obama had been craving. The fire had been lit, and now Fox News needed more fuel to keep it going.

For those who weren't unlucky enough to pay attention to Glenn Beck back in those days, I can assure you his television program was dreadful. From 2009 to 2011, I watched every single episode, an exercise in self-harm that, although it prepared me to better understand what happened in the 2016 presidential election, undoubtedly inflicted severe psychological trauma. Every day, Beck would focus his program on some member of the Obama administration or some out-of-context remark the president had made and then draw a hazy line to the tenets of the Nazi Party. Later, Beck would embrace the caricature of a wild-eyed conspiracist and wheel out a chalkboard as a visual aid so he could juxtapose pictures of Obama with snapshots of stormtroopers on the march.

On *The Glenn Beck Program*, America mutated into an apocalyptic wasteland every single afternoon and viewers took heed. The rise of the Tea Party movement owes a great deal of its momentum to Beck and a motley crew of characters, many of them related either tangentially or directly to *Breitbart*. In 2011, Beck would leave Fox to form his own media company, but the damage was done. He'd injected an unstoppable virus into the body politic of the Republican Party.

While Fox News continued to offer a tamed-down version of Beck's apocalypse—the news channel has long relied on rhetorical devices to distance itself from more controversial topics, a strategy that led its hosts to sit and nod while Donald Trump wondered aloud if the sitting president was secretly a foreign-born Muslim—the viewers who had used Beck to assure themselves they didn't like Obama because of reasons other than race needed to find their fix elsewhere. In a way, Fox News became a starter course that whet their appetite, leaving upstart alternative media sources like *Breitbart* to sate their hunger.

Sometime after Beck left Fox, I started noticing more and more *Breitbart* articles popping up in my Facebook feed. The headlines would catch my eye, and I'd quickly scroll away from them. My relatives were almost unanimously conservative, and their insistence on believing Obama was the Antichrist or an Islamic Manchurian candidate was a tiring reality I'd tried and tried to forgive and ignore, but it was obvious the political climate was changing as the links kept coming and the narrative they told was unbelievably consistent with the horror story Glenn Beck had insisted on sowing.

An industry grew up around all of this fear, and my relatives bought in because they were inherently predisposed. Ever since I was a kid, my family had been telling paranoid stories of far-flung conspiracies, chief among them that a shadowy cabal had rigged the economic system and intentionally shortchanged my people, the working poor. They believed in smoke-filled rooms where the world's rich and powerful met to conspire against them. To defend themselves, they bought overwhelming arsenals of guns and maintained veritable armories in their houses and garages in preparation for a long-rumored invasion of the United States by the combined forces of the New World Order and the United Nations. They horded supplies and prepped for the fall of America, a dystopic horror companies advertising gas masks and rations and gold coins were too happy to use to peddle their wares.

Because of this irrational fear, many of my relatives and people like them were vulnerable to the manipulations of white supremacists. The election of Obama and the propagation of progressivism, including a vigorous fight for multiculturalism and equal rights, was seen as a scourge that threatened to undermine "traditional" American values. My family started talking about "political correctness," a term I'd only heard in my feminist-studies classes in college and occasionally on cable news. The phrase became something akin to a slur as my family hated anything that could fall under that umbrella, including social movements by African Americans, Muslims, and Hispanics. Racist memes originating from white-supremacy groups began appearing in conjunction with the articles on Facebook. My family was openly championing phrases like "white pride" and "European heritage."

Under Bannon's guidance, *Breitbart* turned into a one-stop destination for disgruntled people like my family. There, they were sold a reality that confirmed their darkest suspicions about how the world really worked while also receiving assurance that progressivism had been out to get them. When social-justice advocates demanded they "check their privilege," my dirt-poor, white family looked and saw no privilege to check. *Breitbart* and its growing stable of pseudo-academic alt-right voices assured them it was a political maneuver meant to further sell out the country.

It's unclear whether Bannon believed the narrative *Breitbart* built its platform on. There have been troubling reports of anti-Semitism and homophobia in the man's biography, not to mention allegations of spousal abuse.[102, 103] The one thing that is indisputable is that when he joined the Trump campaign that August, he affected immediate and long-lasting change as Trump was forever chained to teleprompters featuring Bannon's words and rarely went off-script, which was where most of his gaffes and controversies were born. And those words he read amounted to a new evolution for Trump as a candidate.

The fundamental elements of Trump's message—xenophobia and American-centric policies—were boiled down and concentrated into a doctrine, the "new American future" Trump referenced that night in Charlotte, that focused on key points of his message and strengthened it with a new populist tone of Bannon's creation. It was a message that had been tested on *Breitbart*, a message intended for people like my family, people who had been primed for fear by Glenn Beck in 2009, people who had grown up in households fearful of the New World Order and far-off machinations.

For the rest of the race, Bannon's story would be parroted by a tamer and more focused Trump. America had been sold out by an unbelievably affluent system of globalists and bankers more than happy to dismantle the once great nation in order to line their coffers. At times, it would sound like he was just seconds away from warning his supporters of the New World Order and the eventual occupying forces of the United Nations. President Obama had been an emissary of the coming destruction, but Hillary Clinton was the undoubted queen of the conspiracy, a threat so dire that her election would seal the fate of the nation.

Trump's embrace of Bannon's new vision delighted the fringe. Conspiracists embraced him as their liberator and supremacists were overjoyed that the white race had a new champion. Alex Jones turned his paranoid empire into a promotional tool dedicated to Trump's election, and when the votes were tallied, Richard Spencer, the man who had stood outside the Republican National Convention with a sign reading TALK TO A RACIST, an avowed white nationalist, waxed poetically: "When it happened, I thought I might have been dreaming."

"[Trump] is the first step," he told *The Dallas Morning News*, "the first stage toward identity politics for white people . . . That is something major. He's not your father's conservative. He's not in this to promote free markets or neoconservative foreign politics or to protect Israel, for that matter. He's in this to protect his people. He's in this to protect the historic American nation."[104]

★ ★ ★

After Trump said goodnight, supporters moved to the barricade and engaged with reporters. Some just stood there, glaring. In the crowd, the talk was how unfairly Trump had been treated. Somebody said the media was full of "perverts and retards," while a man in a TRUMP THAT BITCH T-shirt said, "All reporters need lobotomies." His friend suggested that President Trump might sign an executive order to that effect, but Mr. "Trump That Bitch" couldn't see that happening—a President Trump, that is. "You know there's no way they'll let him get in the White House," he said.

On the sidewalk outside, the familiar vendors were selling their offensive merchandise. People drifted toward the street to hail cabs or track down their Ubers. The conversation everywhere was about how corrupt the media was, how reporters were in league with Hillary Clinton and "them," a divisive pronoun I'd been hearing more and more, a designation for some shadowy group so threatened by Trump they'd take him down in the press or, if things got too dire, possibly have him killed.

There were pockets of people discussing taking up arms against the media and the government it served. There was somber reflection on the possibility of another Civil War.

Down a ways, in the shadow of the building, a pair of men were smoking cigarettes and shooting the bull. One wore a veteran's hat, the other a MAKE AMERICA GREAT AGAIN cap.

"It don't look good," the veteran said. "Biased media's gonna steal this thing."

"Yeah," his buddy said. "Reckon one of these days we'll have to take matters into our own hands."

CHAPTER 18
A TIGER BY ITS TAIL

HEADING INTO SEPTEMBER 26'S FIRST PRESIDENTIAL DEBATE, THE race somehow felt like a toss-up. Donald Trump had been effectively focused by his team of Kellyanne Conway and Steve Bannon, and a lack of new scandals or controversies meant the time was right for a surge and the inevitable comeback story the media world seemed destined to push. Meanwhile, Hillary Clinton had faltered after a headline-making swoon at the fifteenth anniversary of the 9/11 attacks in New York City.

The Sunday of September 11 had been a godsend for what had essentially amounted to a lull in a lull-less campaign. Trump had been behaving himself, or at least what passed for behaving himself, and the political world was bracing for the most eagerly anticipated debate of all time. While the grudge match loomed, the memorial was an opportunity to catch the most unlikely of pictures: Trump and Clinton standing just a few feet away from one another.

When that shot was broadcast, however, something didn't look right. Clinton seemed older and washed-out, pallid as the blouse under her navy pantsuit. It didn't take long for the internet to chime in. For weeks, the fringe right-wing media had been abuzz with rumors that something was medically wrong with the Democratic nominee. Alex Jones and his ilk examined footage like it was the Zapruder film and speculated that Clinton might have Parkinson's or that a concussion from a fall in 2012 had resulted in brain damage. Unbelievably, the conjecture infiltrated the mainstream as reputable publications covered the rumor, and soon even everyday conversations among liberals were punctuated by hushed gossip about what was *actually* wrong with

Clinton. In late August, Rudy Giuliani appeared on *Fox News Sunday* and told viewers to "go online and put down 'Hillary Clinton illness.' Take a look for yourself."[105] For days, the top searches all revolved around Clinton's imminent demise.

These swirling rumors, empowered both by the increasing influence of alternative media and the amplification of the mainstream, led to a damning decision by the Clinton campaign to obfuscate her diagnosis with pneumonia the Friday before the memorial. Strategists feared the illness would only reinforce the conspiracy theories, and so the campaign was mum.

That September morning was, by all accounts, muggy and uncomfortable, so it wasn't long before the pneumonia took its toll and the networks reported that Clinton had made an early exit. Speculation ran rampant before the campaign could release a statement that Clinton had become overheated and had gone to her daughter Chelsea's apartment to recuperate. In the time it took to right the record, the fringe's narrative was already spun: Clinton was on death's doorstep.

Furthering that dire rumor, the networks cut into their programming to air dramatic breaking-news segments with theatrical music and breathless speculation. Information was scarce, and so the viewer was left to fill in the blanks.

Was Clinton alive?

If she was unable to continue, would vice presidential nominee Tim Kaine take her place?

And then the video aired.

Somebody at the memorial had caught footage of a shaky Hillary Clinton being led into a security van by her detail. She looked out on her feet, as if she would've collapsed on the sidewalk had she not been carried.

While she recovered, the footage played incessantly on every channel. The conspiracy sites had already added commentary and folded it in with previous videos about her neurological debilitations, citing the incident as proof they'd been right all along. To combat this, Clinton strode out of Chelsea's apartment building later and waved to the crowd. A little girl in a flower-print dress made her way through the Secret Service and gave Clinton a hug before the nominee waved healthily on her way to the motorcade.

The photo op did little to quiet the noise. Now the conspiracists were combing over every nuance of the footage and claiming Clinton had been replaced by a body double, that she was either dying in the apartment or had already passed away.[106] Extensive exposés appeared on YouTube in which amateur sleuths compared the angle of Clinton and her supposed body double's nose and the curves of their bodies.

Almost immediately, the effects of the debacle affected the race's standing. Trump surged in the polls until most showed a dead heat. All of Clinton's post-convention bounce had been wiped away in virtually one afternoon. Now there was a renewed emphasis on the debates, one-on-one showdowns of historic proportions that would, it seemed more likely than ever, determine who would go on to be the forty-fifth president of the United States of America.

★ ★ ★

The scene in Hempstead, New York, home of Hofstra University, was a madhouse. Rubberneckers peppered the university's sidewalks, many of them holding inflammatory signs and chanting "Lock her up!" At the security checkpoint alone, I met no less than a dozen young men all convinced that Hillary Clinton had been replaced by a body double.

"Here's the question," one said: "Can that bitch impersonating her debate?"

I wanted to know more, but there was a confrontation at the nearby roadblock where an officer had denied entry to a couple wheeling a red wagon with a pile of fake feces and a TRUMP/PENCE 2016 yard sign.

"Lock her up!" one of the young men yelled and got a round of high-fives.

For a couple of blocks, I kept pace so I could eavesdrop. I heard them talking about a massive criminal empire that had manipulated the world's major economies and dictated wars designed to thin out populations. The story was something out of the fevered dreams of New World Order conspiracists and almost word for word what Alex Jones had said on a podcast I'd listened to on my flight from Savannah to JFK.

Closer to the event, it only got weirder. The assembled crowds represented every step on the political spectrum. There were anarchists decrying the entire system. Green Partiers clamoring for Jill Stein to be allowed into the debate hall. Trump supporters getting in the faces of Clinton supporters. Bernie or Busters chanting "Bernie beats Trump!" and calling for the Vermont senator to stage a last-second write-in campaign.

Searching for the shuttle that shepherded journalists inside the debate zone, I stopped a cop casing the closed-down street. He pointed me in the right direction and then grinned. "What do you think about all this?" he asked.

"This?" I said, nodding in the direction of the hall.

"No," he said. "That."

He'd hooked his thumb at the assembling crowd where somebody in a polar bear suit was taking pictures next to a man with a giant sign reading TRUMP VS TRAMP.

"It's something, huh?"

"You kiddin' me?" the cop said. "This ain't somethin'. It's the fuckin' apocalypse."

★ ★ ★

She destroyed him.

Unmistakably destroyed him.

With his tail tucked between his legs, a beaten Trump bucked tradition and joined his surrogates in the spin room. By most, it was seen as a concession, a sign that the Republican nominee knew full well he'd been bested. He was subdued and restrained, the pained look on his face telling the entire story. The post-debate polls concurred. A CNN/ORC poll scored it 62 to 27 in Clinton's favor, and the Democrats wasted no time celebrating their victory.[107]

By the next morning, Trump's faithful had already cooked up an explanation for their champion's poor showing. According to *The Baltimore Gazette,* Clinton's victory had only been made possible because she had been given the questions beforehand:

The first presidential debate was held and Hillary Clinton was proclaimed the winner by the media. Indeed Clinton was able to turn in a strong debate performance, but did she do so fairly? Multiple reports and leaked information from inside the Clinton camp claim that the Clinton campaign was given the entire set of debate questions an entire week before the actual debate.

Earlier last week an NBC intern was seen hand delivering a package to Clinton's campaign headquarters, according to multiple sources. The package was not given to secretarial staff, as would normally happen, but the intern was instead ushered into the personal office of Clinton campaign manager Robert Mook. Members of the Clinton press corps from several media organizations were in attendance at the time, and a reporter from Fox News recognized the intern, but said he was initially confused because the NBC intern was dressed like a Fed Ex employee.

The account is especially compelling because of the visual nature of the events unfolding, the attention to the subterfuge's details. Trump supporters could just imagine that NBC intern delivering that package.

Of course the media had seen it all happen and failed to report on it. The Fox News reporter was skeptical, but ultimately let it happen. Not to mention, there were sources *inside* the Clinton campaign. Certainly their consciences were getting the better of them after having realized they were serving the devil herself.

But the story was completely fabricated. Once upon a time, *The Baltimore Gazette* had been an actual paper, but it closed its doors in 1875. In the fast-paced world of the internet and social media, however, readers in search of favorable narratives are often in too much of a hurry to broadcast their chosen realities to notice where they're getting their information. *The Baltimore Gazette* sounded and looked like a newspaper. And, not to mention, there had been a previous story that interim DNC chair Donna Brazile, back when she was a pundit on CNN, had leaked a Democratic primary debate question to John Podesta, Hillary Clinton's campaign chairman.[108] That nugget of truth lent an air of authenticity to the NBC leak rumor, and soon it had been injected into the right-wing blogosphere.

Later, following the third and final debate, Trump himself would tweet, "Why didn't Hillary Clinton announce that she was inappropriately given the debate questions—she secretly used them! Crooked Hillary," a reference to the lie that would be retweeted and referenced over and over and would eventually be mentioned in mainstream publications who unwillingly gave cover to the growing untruths.[109]

Clinton, it seemed, couldn't win for losing.

☆ ★ ☆

On October 7, I was celebrating my birthday and waiting on Hurricane Matthew to strike my home in southeast Georgia. The storm had already raged through Haiti and the Bahamas, leaving a swath of destruction in its wake. In the morning, I was drinking my coffee and watching the National Weather Service's forecast update every hour, all the while keeping an eye on right-wing social media.

Matt Drudge, the provocateur behind the *Drudge Report*, a conservative aggregate site that rose to prominence and great influence after breaking the Monica Lewinsky scandal in 1998, had repeatedly tweeted doubts that Hurricane Matthew would amount to much, going so far as to insinuate that calls for caution and evacuation were attempts to further the left's climate-change agenda. Drudge needlessly endangered the lives of millions of people when he tweeted, "The deplorables are starting to wonder if govt has been lying to them about Hurricane Matthew intensity to make exaggerated point on climate."[110]

The fringe right took Drudge's bait and ran with it, filling their circles with criticisms of meteorological groups and the Federal Emergency Management Agency, claiming the hurricane was a fiction designed to further the fraud of climate change and enrich the government's coffers. Again, the fractured reality of Trump's America reared its head as people posted pictures of their unaffected backyards and calm patches of the ocean. While parts of the country hunkered down and prepared for the worst, others denied there was so much as a storm brewing.

After securing patio furniture and stocking up on supplies, I grabbed a beer out of the emergency cooler and watched the newest weather models. The storm was lumbering toward the Georgia coast and live cameras in Florida showed swelling waves and imperiled homes. For the duration of the day, I was glued to the coverage until, that afternoon, breaking news interrupted the forecast.

The Washington Post had obtained video from 2005 of Donald Trump aboard an *Access Hollywood* bus with host Billy Bush, the two of them engaging in explicit conversation about Trump's attempts to sleep with Bush's co-host Nancy O'Dell, a married woman. Trump had "moved on her like a bitch" before she got "big, phony tits." The bus had been transporting the pair to the set of the soap opera *Days of*

Our Lives, for which Trump was scheduled to film a cameo, and when Trump saw actress Arianne Zucker he was recorded saying, "I've got to use some Tic Tacs, just in case I start kissing her. You know, I'm automatically attracted to beautiful—I just start kissing them. It's like a magnet. Just kiss. I don't even wait. And when you're a star, they let you do it, you can do anything. Grab them by the pussy. You can do anything."[111]

It was nauseating, watching Trump exposed as the creep we all suspected him to be, but the added horror that he had more or less admitted to using his celebrity to sexually assault women was too much. Networks began openly speculating as to whether Trump would be forced off the ballot by Republicans, while experts asserted it was too late in the process to replace him. By the time Hurricane Matthew killed my power, it was more or less presumed we had finally come to the end of the Trump phenomenon.

Despite Matt Drudge's contentions, the storm was nightmarish. Throughout the night, strong winds pummeled my house, and against the dark sky the tall Georgia pines in my backyard swayed and threatened to snap. The gusts were so loud I could barely sleep for more than a few minutes at a time, and around 5 a.m. I found myself on my phone, perusing the fallout from the leaked tape. Already, clusters of Republicans had called on Trump to leave the race or had withdrawn their support. To staunch the bleeding, Trump had released a Facebook statement calling it a "decade old video" and saying his time running for office had "changed him," before labeling it a distraction and laying the blame on Hillary and Bill Clinton, who he claimed had actually hurt women.[112]

I clicked off the statement and put my phone away. Outside, the wind was still howling and the trees swayed threateningly in the distance, but it felt like something had fundamentally changed. For a year and a half, Trump had contorted the narrative and blamed everyone else, but surely this was the point where the lie broke down. It was, after all, the difference between claiming a deadly storm had been fabricated and then waking up the next morning to a disaster zone filled with downed limbs and lost lives.

Seeing was believing, and there was just no way even his most ardent supporters could deny reality when confronted with so much overwhelming evidence.

★ ★ ★

That Sunday, Trump held an impromptu press event ninety minutes before the second debate.[113] Flanked by four women who had all accused Bill Clinton of sexual impropriety, Trump used them to deflect questions about the tape and praised their bravery as Steve Bannon proudly watched from the corner.

Later, when the candidates were introduced, Hillary Clinton noticeably declined to shake Trump's hand.

The format of the second debate was a town hall where voters could address the candidates directly, and the first asked whether the nominees were setting an example for the country with their campaigns. When it was Trump's turn, he appeared subdued and even went so far as to agree with Clinton's answer that the race hadn't been much of an example. Then, co-moderator Anderson Cooper quickly brought up the *Access Hollywood* tape and asked Trump if he understood that he'd bragged about sexually assaulting women. Trump dismissed the recording as "locker room talk" and tried to shift the conversation toward his readiness to battle ISIS, but Cooper refused to let him escape so easily.

After Trump feebly attempted to pivot, Clinton was asked to respond and stated outright that Trump wasn't fit to be president. "I think it's clear to anyone who heard it," she said, "it represents exactly who he is." As she restated the broad set of evidence that Trump had disrespected women throughout his career, Trump fumed and waited his turn.

"If you look at Bill Clinton," he said, ". . . mine are words and his was action. His was what he's done to women. There's never been anybody in the history of politics in this nation that's been so abusive to women. So you can say any way you want to say it, but Bill Clinton was abusive to women."

To protect himself, Trump again dipped back into the deep and dark waters of conspiracy world, where audio of Hillary Clinton discussing a rape case she handled in 1975 had been circulated as proof of her monstrousness.[114] In that audio, Clinton was heard talking about the case and how her client, the accused rapist, had passed a polygraph despite his apparent guilt. Clinton had chuckled nervously while saying the case "destroyed her faith" in lie-detector tests, but the rumor had taken the exchange completely out of context.

Just as he had done all along, Trump had given his supporters something else to focus on instead of his critics. To push it further, he soon changed the subject to his favorite diversionary topic: Clinton's missing emails.

"But when you talk about apology," he said a few moments later, "I think the one that you should really be apologizing for, and the thing that you should be apologizing for, are the 33,000 emails that you deleted, and that you acid-washed, and then the two boxes of emails and other things last week that were taken from an office and are now missing. And I'll tell you what. I didn't think I'd say this, but I'm going to say it, and I hate to say it, but if I win, I am going to instruct my attorney general to get a special prosecutor to look into your situation, because there has never been so many lies, so much deception. There has never been anything like it, and we're going to have a special prosecutor."

Cornered and imperiled, Trump had done the unthinkable by threatening political retribution against his opponent. It was a threat without precedent in the history of American democracy, something more akin to the actions of a third-world strongman, but never the nominee of one of the two major American political parties.

The relentless needling over the audio unleashed something in Trump that would haunt the remainder of that debate and then the third and final contest. Throughout the town hall, he stood behind Clinton as she spoke, almost as if he were intending to physically intimidate her. Hardly a question passed when he didn't interrupt her or provide a running sarcastic commentary. Then, in the third debate, in a moment that would be played and replayed again ad nauseam, Trump interrupted Clinton and said, "Such a nasty woman."

In the aftermath, it was accepted that Clinton had wiped the floor with him and that the *Access Hollywood* video had opened a new lane upon which Clinton could coast to the presidency. After the contests, journalists and pundits alike were in agreement that the only question was by how wide a margin Clinton would beat Trump. After all, even the most ardent Trump voters would have to face the reality that their candidate was unfit for the office.

What wasn't discussed, however, was that Trump had effectively neutralized the sexual-assault charge by including Bill Clinton, a tactic that, while unfair, meant that Hillary would be dragged into the muck along with him. At the same time, important arguments, including Trump's wealth and successful avoidance of paying income taxes—a *New York Times* investigation had revealed his federal taxes in 1995 had declared a $916 million dollar loss,[115] meaning he was excused from paying taxes for up to eighteen years—as well as his questionable ties to Russia (Clinton, in her defense, had mentioned the link in the third debate by saying, "It's pretty clear you won't admit the Russians have engaged in cyber attacks against the United States of America, that you encouraged espionage against our people, that you are willing to spout the Putin line, sign up for his wish list, break up NATO, do whatever he wants to do, and that you continue to get help from him because he has a very clear favorite in this race") meant the vote in November would essentially come down to whether the public thought Trump's behavior was unacceptable or if they preferred Hillary Clinton, meaning they didn't care about the narrative of corruption that Trump and his supporters had weaved for months and months.

Even though the debates felt like a loss to everyone who watched them, and the consensus seemed that American politics had hit a new low, in the end it created a scenario wherein the public was able to head to the voting booths and make their choice depending on whether they felt Trump's behavior had crossed some ethical line. In all the hubbub, Hillary Clinton's legislative agenda, not to mention her readiness to assume the office, never factored into the decision.

CHAPTER 19
THE CULT OF THE MOVEMENT

ON OCTOBER 14, I WAS DRIVING TO CHARLOTTE, NORTH CAROLINA, for what I hoped would be a nearly empty Trump rally. In the days since the release of the *Access Hollywood* bombshell, matters had devolved as several women had stepped forward to accuse Donald Trump of inappropriately touching them in the exact manner he'd laid out for Billy Bush. It was bad enough to think a misogynistic braggart might be elected president, much less a sexual predator who'd been preying on women for decades. Even his most fervent supporters, I assumed, had to turn their backs on him at some point.

In a way, I'd always hoped Trump might suffer an attack of conscience after a long, hard look in the mirror and decide to save what little dignity he had left. With each successive controversy and every unwarranted and childish insult, I'd hoped the man's fever might break so he could finally recede from the public eye.

His first rally that day took place in Greensboro and quickly left no doubts that that wouldn't be the case. When addressing the accusations, particularly the claim leveled by Jessica Leeds that he'd fondled her in the first-class section of a 1980s flight to New York City, Trump not only denied the charges but attacked her looks: "Believe me, she would not be my first choice. That I can tell you."[116]

Similar was his denial of Natasha Stoynoff's claim that in 2005, while penning a story on Trump for *People* magazine, the mogul had shoved her into a wall and kissed her against her will. "Check out her Facebook page," he said, "you'll understand."

The crowd's response in Greensboro was to chant "We don't care!"

and laugh at Trump's belittling of women. In Charlotte, I found a
packed room itching to blame the victims and exonerate Trump. I
wasn't there a half hour before I heard a woman in a shirt reading
PROUD DEPLORABLE—a reaction to Hillary Clinton saying she could
put half of Trump's supporters in "a basket of deplorables"—say, "Let's
call them what they are. They're whores."

Generally, his supporters agreed. You couldn't walk a few feet
without overhearing someone referring to "these women" as "floozies"
and "opportunists," stories that Hillary Clinton herself had paid the
accusers to slander Trump.

The more extreme critics took it even further.

"Women say all the time they've been raped," said a man in a TRUMP/
PENCE shirt, whose friend had just seconds before ridiculously suggested
that maybe Fox News had put the victims up to it. "They lie all the time."

Men and women alike took turns attacking Trump's accusers, some
going so far as to concede that maybe Trump was guilty, including an
older woman shepherding her grandson, but whether he did it or not
didn't matter. "A man like Trump does that," she said, shaking her
head, "maybe take it as a compliment. Don't be so uptight for once."

Most were convinced the story had been created to derail Trump, and
many were visibly upset by the supposed smears, including a woman
who showed her group of friends her quaking hand as she said, "It
makes me shake to think they'd hurt a man like that."

Trump took the stage later surrounded by female supporters in pink
jackets that said WOMEN FOR TRUMP. Signs proclaiming the same
thing had been handed out to supporters as they entered the rally, and
now a sea of them buttressed the besieged nominee. "As you have seen,"
he told the crowd, "I am a victim of one of the great political smear
campaigns in the history of our country. They are coming after me to
try and destroy what is considered, by even them, the greatest movement in the history of the country. There's never been anything like it."

His supporters cheered wildly and chanted "Lock her up!" every time he mentioned an accuser and similarly called for the prosecution of every publication that had published their accounts. When Trump mentioned Stoynoff and *People* magazine, somebody yelled "Liar!" and received a round of applause from the section of the floor I was wading through.

As in previous rallies, there was an air of violence in the room. Many echoed the calls for Hillary Clinton to be executed for her treasonous actions while now including the accusers and members of the mainstream media who carried their false claims, all of them needing to be done away with for the good of the country. Later, as Trump assured the crowd he wouldn't assault a woman because "you would be very impressed, actually, with my life in so many regards, including *that* regard," and that the fabricated stories might be "the only way they're going to stop us," a protestor interrupted the speech. Most celebrated while he was led away, but a few broke off from the crowd to follow him as he was ejected, talking and joking loudly about wanting to drag him to death behind their trucks.

"So, folks," Trump returned to his speech, "here's the story: We are going to bring jobs back to North Carolina."

"Amen!" a woman near the back exclaimed and raised her hands in witness.

The gospel continued minutes later as Trump waxed nostalgically about his success in the Republican primaries, including his win in Indiana, which had been made possible, in part, by the endorsement of my childhood hero, basketball coach Bobby Knight. "It was like a miracle from God," Trump said, remembering how he'd come to find Knight's phone number. "Right? It was from God." Trump listened to the resulting ovation before pointing out a sign up front. "That says 'Jesus for Trump.' You're right."

★ ★ ★

It was in Sioux City, Iowa, nine days out from the caucuses, that Donald Trump delivered one of the most memorable lines of the 2016 presidential election: "They say I have the most loyal people. You ever see that? Where I could stand in the middle of Fifth Avenue and shoot somebody and wouldn't lose any voters. Okay? It's like, incredible."[117]

Certainly, Trump enjoyed the most loyal and enthused supporters of any candidate, even if that devotion effectively baffled experts. Many guessed it was because they were low-information voters, or people who made up their minds despite being acutely uninformed. Others pondered if his base was cemented by his popularity with the poorly educated, a group Trump himself had embraced when he said in February, "I love the poorly educated." And even more figured the real reason was forged in something deeper, particularly in the arenas of race and class.

There's truth in all of it, for sure. Even at the beginning of the campaign, it was easy to see that Trump's celebrity and personality attracted voters who would normally be uninterested in politics, and postelection autopsies seemed to prove a good number of voters were swayed by fake news stories that, one would think, a little critical thinking would've easily debunked. Entire books will be written about Trump's popularity with working-class whites, especially those who had grown disillusioned with a society in which they perceived globalism and multiculturalism as having essentially robbed them of their livelihoods and seat of power. But, at its heart, "the movement," as their leader began to refer to it, had less to do with any one characteristic and more with the sum of its parts and the narrative Trump used to bind it all together.

To fully grasp what happened in 2016, it's first necessary to glance back at the world-shaking upset pulled off in 2008 by a first-term senator from Illinois named Barack Obama. It's easy to forget now, after eight years of his administration, exactly how it felt to elect him, a transcendental figure who effortlessly blended a keen intellect and an undeniable charisma. In the wake of George W. Bush's tumultuous terms, Obama's promise of hope and change, both concepts that invited as much projection as Trump's call to make America great again, was like a long and heralded exhale. Liberals might pause at the notion, but it certainly felt at times like Obama might be something of a savior. Even Nobel Prize–winning economist Paul Krugman wrote in *The New York Times* in February 2008, "I'm not the first to point out that the Obama campaign seems dangerously close to becoming a cult of personality."[118]

Back then, this was a constant and favored criticism by members of the right-wing media. Oftentimes, Obama was ridiculed as a Christ-like fraud who promised to heal the world's ills and his supporters lambasted as sheep who basked in his glow. Hope and change, his favorite slogan, received its fair share of derision, as did his dramatic orations, from which his opponents cherry-picked the loftier pieces of rhetoric.

"I face this challenge with profound humility and knowledge of my own limitations," Senator Obama said in June 2008 after securing the Democratic nomination, "but I also face it with limitless faith in the capacity of the American people, because if we are willing to work for it, and fight for it, and believe in it, then I am absolutely certain that generations from now we will be able to look back and tell our children that this was the moment we began to provide care for the sick and good jobs for the jobless, this was the moment when the rise of the oceans began to slow and our planet began to heal."[119]

It was Obama's supposed mastery over the sea level that many fixated on and then mocked, including Rush Limbaugh, who still wielded considerable heft on the right. Limbaugh puzzled over his candidacy by saying, "It's not a political movement. It's a rock concert tour . . . it's a cult. It's a religious movement, whatever it is, it has gone beyond politics."[120]

Rush was both dead-on and misguided. What we had seen with Obama's victory was the evolution of politics in the modern age.

Candidate Obama recognized that speeches were better served by appealing to the individual's need to belong to a movement rather than how they communicated specific plans. Hope and change were vagaries that communed states of being, or, rather, how a citizen should view the world rather than whether they were for this tax or that stimulus plan.

"We all want to matter," Limbaugh continued. "We all want to have meaning in our lives. We all want to be relevant to something, and a lot of these people don't feel that about themselves . . . Obama gives them hope that he is going to make their life substantial and have meaning by virtue of his presence, his messianic—by virtue of his existence alone."

Certainly, Obama's strength as a campaigner was serving as a figurehead for a movement that reenergized a bloc of voters who had tired of George W. Bush's wars, social clashes, and wrecking of the economy. His name on the ballot represented a refutation of that era and the promise of new and better horizons.

More than anyone else in 2016, save for possibly Bernie Sanders, Donald Trump constructed his campaign as a cult of personality. Whereas Obama presented the American people hope for a fresh start, Trump appealed to voters who had lost their optimism and still remembered a time wherein the country had served their interests. Other candidates had gestured at that reality—it was, after all, a major component of modern conservatism—but only Trump was willing to give himself completely to the grotesque narrative. Obama had told his supporters they had staved off destruction from the rising waters, while Trump told them they were doomed to drown.

In politics, successful campaigns are usually cults of personality, but generally they only resemble those cults on the surface. The candidate at the center of the movement traditionally accepts the position as a means to gain momentum in the polls and marshal support, but once the campaign is won they shuck the mantle of messiah and settle into the role of executive. Trump was the exception to the rule, and because his machine more closely mirrored the structure of an actual cult, he found himself at the head of a dangerously devoted group of acolytes.

This devotion was born of Trump's propensity to unabashedly lie coupled with his willingness to vilify anyone who might stand in his way. As mentioned previously, John McCain and Mitt Romney had balked at enabling the more combustible elements of the party, but Trump had no qualms about presenting a horrendous picture of America in which certain destruction was inevitable unless he was given the levers of power. Along the way, he had said whatever was necessary to garner votes, and didn't hesitate if that meant denying that he'd said it at a later time, video evidence be damned. That contortion of the truth, however, never would have been possible had he not neutralized the press, the one entity that could have stopped him dead in his tracks if only it had done its job and discredited him before he could inoculate his followers.

Trump's masterstroke of the 2016 campaign was setting his sights on the media early in the race and planting the notion in his supporters' minds that any story that might depict him in a negative light was untrustworthy. By doing this, Trump cemented himself as the sole keeper of the truth, a position that gave him unlimited power to bestow veracity and legitimacy on whomever best served him at the moment. Later, when more and more stories focused on Trump's corruption and shady dealings, the wall around his supporters had already been sealed.

Within that confinement, Trump's movement became its own sub-culture, a group that banded together based on their shared interests and shared opposition to the world around them, but the wall had been under construction for years. Acting on marketing demographics, right-wing media and companies had created a standard existence that placed its inhabitants outside of popular culture. Conservatives had their own celebrities, their own movies, their own music, and their own reality that Fox News and talk radio fortified on a daily basis. They already shared a common existence when Donald Trump climbed the wall and spoke to them in a language they understood.

This loose conglomeration, despite assertions otherwise, included men and women from a variety of different social and economic backgrounds, and was something closer to a community when Trump acted upon their fears. This radicalization changed the makeup, though, and Trump and his movement effectively splintered off of the Republican Party in much the same manner cults often divorce from traditional faiths. When the split happened, the members of the movement found themselves isolated from their past contacts. On social media and in real life, they'd already cut off ties, or had their ties cut off, from anyone who might question their political stances or oppose their worldviews. Their options for escape were limited and their exposure to the outside world all but severed.

They only had each other and their dear leader.

As is often the case, the leader of a cult is eventually confronted with a multitude of sins that are the natural byproduct of a narcissistic personality capable of engineering a cult in the first place. Trump's near-constant stream of scandals—be they in his business dealings, his fascistic tendencies, his perceived reliance on Russian interference, his infinite supply of lies and exaggerations, or a flood of women claiming to have been assaulted by him—further insulated Trump's movement from the rest of the world. Again, cognitive dissonance is a hell of a motivating factor when processing information, and Trump voters were confronted, almost daily, with the choice between believing the media was corrupt and out to get him, which they had been told for a year and a half, or giving in and accepting the fact their candidate was the living embodiment of everything wrong with their country.

Assisting that decision was Trump's otherworldly ability to believe his own lies. For years, those around him had marveled at how easily Trump changed his mind to suit his situation, in the process apparently jettisoning his memory and understanding of past events in order to avoid any cognitive dissonance on his own part, a dizzying talent that, anyone who has ever dealt with a chronic liar can tell you, transforms life into a fuzzy and malleable reality. If Trump had ever stopped once to question his own string of untruths, if he had ever admitted on a single occasion that he had been wrong or caught in a lie, the entire illusion could've been interrupted. But Trump was shameless in his charade because he swallowed his own fabrications whole and then projected them back onto his flock, all of whom were more than ready to suspend their disbelief.

This cyclical relationship is terribly hard to break because either the incontrovertible reality of the godhead must be interrupted or the follower must decide to face their cognitive dissonance head on and choose to abandon their altered existence. In October of 2016, as more and more women came forward, including multiple Miss Universe contestants who claimed Trump had come backstage to see them as they dressed, a claim that Trump himself admitted to Howard Stern years ago by saying, "I'll go backstage and everyone's getting dressed . . . I'm allowed to go in because I'm owner of the pageant . . . I sort of get away with things like that," Trump's most fervent voters were forced to perform mental gymnastics, and ultimately betray their own morality, or else give up on the movement that had become synonymous with their identities.[121]

Unfortunately, the victims, and our country, never stood a chance

★ ★ ★

"These teleprompters haven't been working for the last twenty minutes," Trump said to a smattering of applause. "I actually like my speech better without teleprompters."

Leaving his podium, Trump moseyed over and playfully messed with one of the teleprompters, the screen falling off and landing on the stage. The crowd went wild.

"Get this thing out of here, will you? I like it much better without the teleprompters . . . I went through seventeen professional politicians, tough people, and I went without teleprompters, then all of a sudden they said, well now, you're running in the election, you need teleprompters."

Soon he turned his attention to the second screen and dismantled that one as well. Without Steve Bannon's words to read, Trump would settle back into one of his rambling standup acts that had been the norm at the beginning of his campaign. He riffed on his philosophy of when to stiff workers of their hard-earned wages and how the media was rigging the elections, all the while basking in the adulation of his followers. If he was a rock star, he'd be playing his greatest hits, coasting through another set in another one-stoplight town. He didn't seem like a politician fighting off a career-threatening scandal, and he didn't sound like a politician worried about hitting the right notes or weaving the right story.

Those screens had long since served their purpose, and he didn't need them anymore.

He had the people right where he wanted them.

CHAPTER 20
WE COME TO THE END

AROUND 5 P.M. ON ELECTION DAY, I WAS SITTING IN A TELEVISION studio on my university's campus and anxiously tapping my foot. I'd been asked to swing by and talk briefly about my experiences on the campaign trail, and I was feeling a bit antsy to get home to the fifteen-dollar bottle of La Marca prosecco I'd bought to toast Donald Trump's inevitable defeat.

As a disciple of the power of narrative, I felt extraordinarily confident about the election. When looking at the race, its characters, its twists and turns, it was quite obvious that Trump was not only the villain, but a once-in-a-lifetime scourge who would undoubtedly be summarily rebuked. Clinton's landslide victory would serve as future notice the United States of America was a country that didn't tolerate fascistic demagogues who spit in the face of democracy. No doubt we'd all look back on the debacle of 2016 and shake our heads in collective disbelief: Exactly how did *that* happen anyway?

The interview went fine. I sat down in a comfy chair and had a casual conversation with a colleague from the communications department about how I'd gone from hanging out in a small bar in Iowa to getting consistent threats from an army of alt-right trolls. I realized, while answering, that I was speaking like it'd happened sometime in the distant past. I guess I was looking forward to Trump being relegated to a sidebar in the history of the twenty-first century, an ugly anecdote I could use to warn my future grandchildren about the fragility of democracy, and a time when I could finally say goodbye to my days as a vocal and public opponent of Donald J. Trump.

I got home a little while later and settled down on the couch. Clicking on coverage, I unlaced my boots and slipped them off. Again, it felt like a turning of a page, the closing of a chapter of my life. All of the hard work, all of the analysis, all of the anxiety and the fear would be swept away in a matter of hours. Before midnight, if the projections held, that bottle of discount prosecco would be opened and we could all move on with our lives.

Early in the returns, everything seemed like it was going according to plan. My home state of Indiana was the first to go red, leaving me to wax nostalgic over Barack Obama's surprise win there in 2008. The map had changed that year, including the reliably conservative Hoosier State, which had been turned due in no small part to former DNC chairman Howard Dean's 50-State strategy, an initiative that directed the Democratic Party to begin investing money and resources into traditionally red states it had ceded for decades.

Electoral victory in the modern age has long been a game of vulnerabilities. Generally, Democrats enjoy a natural advantage due to their concentration in urban centers, while Republicans amass their votes in the South and the heartland. Going into November, it was understood that Hillary Clinton could count on at least 222 of the necessary 270 votes as her victory was assumed in seventeen states plus the District of Columbia. Trump's expected basement was 191 votes earned in twenty-three states. Only in the case of landslides, and many expected Clinton's victory to be just that, are these numbers really challenged, the most recent examples being Ronald Reagan's destruction of Jimmy Carter and Walter Mondale to the tune of 489 and 525, respectively; George H. W. Bush's drumming of Michael Dukakis in 1988; and Bill Clinton's pair of 370-plus victories in 1992 and 1996.[122]

The spotlight in 2016 was dominated by a key group of swing states, including Florida, Ohio, North Carolina, Pennsylvania, Iowa, New Hampshire, Colorado, Nevada, and a pair of surprise battlegrounds:

Georgia and Michigan. Conventional knowledge dictated that Trump had to virtually sweep the contests in order to win the presidency, the political equivalent of drawing an inside straight in a hand of poker. The more likely scenario, it seemed, was Clinton picking off the lion's share and sailing to a haul of well over 300 electoral votes.

Around 10:30 p.m. that prediction took a hit as Ohio and its eighteen electoral votes were called for Trump. Many had expected the Buckeye State to go red as Trump had led in most polls, but it was hard to deny that Ohio made Trump's inside straight more of a possibility. Not to mention that his vote totals were looking strong in Florida, Pennsylvania, and Georgia, and he held a slight advantage in North Carolina, the state some had said would ultimately determine the victor. There was still time, though, for all those Clinton votes to be counted.

In the next hour, Trump captured Florida and North Carolina. Both had been uphill battles for Clinton, but with Trump still winning in Michigan and Wisconsin, the scene turned dark. *FiveThirtyEight*, Nate Silver's data-projection site, had gone into the night giving Clinton a 71.4 percent chance to win the election.[123] *The New York Times*'s project "The Upshot" had given the former secretary of state an 85 percent chance.[124] By the time North Carolina was called, those numbers had swung dramatically.

Trump was now the favorite.

The mood on social media turned apocalyptic. Even the most hardened pundits were panicking. Dow Jones futures fell 750 points as Trump gained momentum.[125] Asian stocks faltered and the Mexican peso fell to a record low. Cable-network anchors appeared blindsided. Dumbfounded. On CNN and MSNBC, experts took to touchscreens to show where the votes in Michigan and Wisconsin were presumably coming from and doing the hard math of explaining how Clinton would more than likely make up the total, if not overtake her opponent.

Around one-thirty in the morning, Pennsylvania was called for

Trump. There'd been a lot of assurances that Clinton would ultimately carry the state, that suburban moms would make sure of it. The night before, Clinton had appeared with President Obama at a rally in Philadelphia, and the president's remarks had been an appeal for voters to make sure his eight years' worth of accomplishments wouldn't be swept away. With the Keystone State in Trump's column, a win in Michigan, Arizona, or Wisconsin would seal the election. He led in all three.

★ ★ ★

"There's just no way."

When I said that, I'd been sitting in a studio upstairs from where I would eventually give my election-night interview and guesting on a student-run radio show. I was busy explaining to one of the hosts that Trump stood literally no chance of winning the presidency. That, despite appearances, the campaign was a shoddily run operation that had neglected the most basic components of a winning effort.

"He has no ground game," I told him. "Offices in Ohio and Pennsylvania have been telling me they're not even able to get yard signs. He hasn't even bothered to try and win this thing."

The host I was lecturing had shown up a few minutes before we went on the air toting a sandwich from Subway and a bag of chips he'd wasted no time in destroying. He'd been wearing a white undershirt and a pair of basketball shorts he'd quickly wiped crumbs on when I offered to shake his hand. Between segments, he'd peppered me about why I thought Hillary Clinton should be trusted. By the last break, I'd gotten irritated.

"I'm sorry to piss on your parade," I snapped, "but it's not going to happen. Donald Trump will not be president."

Remembering that exchange is uncomfortable in retrospect. I can't believe I'd been so dismissive of that host. Late on election night, as it became increasingly obvious that Donald Trump would be president, I kept replaying the conversation while shaking my head. He'd been right and I'd been wrong. And not just wrong, but real, real wrong. I'd gone and done something that'd always pissed me off to no end. I'd crossed over into the media and started looking at politics as a game of chess instead of a process by which real people were affected in real and lasting ways.

Just that afternoon, before driving to campus, I'd been talking with a new friend of mine who travels in the usual political-media circles. He's well-connected, does talking-head appearances on the cable news shows, pens a column or two that characterizes trends in Washington's ecosystem. One by one, he'd taken me through the swing states and handicapped Trump's chances. He had no doubt Clinton would carry Florida, North Carolina, Pennsylvania, Iowa, and Nevada, and, after granting Ohio to Trump, he even predicted independent candidate Evan McMullin's interference in Utah would lead to a shocking victory there. He gave Clinton an easy 335 electoral votes and lamented that maybe he was being too conservative in his prediction.

Michigan and Wisconsin weren't even discussed.

I'd had many conversations like that one with other members of the media. There's a cloistered community once you reach a certain point of visibility, and everybody gets to know one another. There are inside jokes, rumors that never make it in print, a sort of high-school-clique mentality if high school were only full of nerdy writers wearing button-down shirts and slacks from Banana Republic. It was intoxicating to get a glimpse into that world, and when they told me, to a person, that election night would be over early, I believed them.

If only I'd kept my eyes open.

Trump had been surging in the days leading up to the election, and models showed Clinton needed a higher turnout than was predicted. When members of the media told me how they saw the night playing out, they kept referring to "Obama's coalition," the once-in-a-generation base that had been crafted by an otherworldly talented candidate. When they made their forecasts, it was with the assumption that the coalition would not only show up, but that Trump's offensive behavior would scare away groups I knew full and well it wouldn't.

The truth is that I had suffered from the same cognitive dissonance I'd spent so much of the cycle researching. While I was diagnosing Trump's supporters, I was forgetting to take a good, long, hard look in the mirror. I'd been in the room for several of his rallies and had witnessed firsthand the passion of his supporters, and yet, when Trump claimed he was building a movement, I stood in the middle of a fervent mass of people and rolled my eyes. When I opened this very book and read the chapters I'd written before the election, I saw it in my sentences. The narrative had been hiding in plain sight all along.

Everywhere I looked, I saw that the ground game and methods of traditional politics weren't going to matter this time. In Indiana and Georgia, I'd seen homemade Trump signs standing in the middle of fields. People wearing shirts they'd written pro-Trump slogans on using markers. It was scrawled into the dirt on the sides of eighteen-wheelers, scribbled on bathroom walls. The base-level support had never waivered because the true believers weren't going to desert Trump. He'd become so important to them, such a metaphor, that it truly had nothing to do with the man anymore. Trump was a symbol for them, a rallying point to communicate just how much they hated what America had become. It didn't matter how inept he was as a politician, how incompetent and clumsy his campaign. The people fueling his movement would push him over the line if they had to.

★ ★ ★

A little before three in the morning, Trump took the stage after the networks had announced Hillary Clinton had called to concede the election. "Sorry to keep you waiting," he told a jubilant crowd, "complicated business." Trump seemed as surprised as anyone. Sources inside the campaign told me later that virtually no one but the staff bordering on delusional expected the outcome. The Republican Party's models, as well as those belonging to the Trump campaign, were nearly certain he'd be defeated.[126]

Somberly, Trump was reading his plans for America off a teleprompter when somebody in the crowd yelled, "Hang Obama!"

I couldn't take it anymore. I put my head in my hands and listened to the newly minted president-elect prattle off platitudes and half-baked sentiments and didn't look up until the end was near.

"So, it's been what they call a historic event," he said, "but to be really historic we have to do a great job. I promise you that I will not let you down. We will do a great job. We will do a great job.

"I look very much forward to being your president. Hopefully at the end of two years or three years or four years or maybe even eight years, you will say so many of you worked so hard for us, but you will say that—you will say that that was something that you were really were proud to do.

". . . I can only say that while the campaign is over, our work on this movement is now really just beginning. We're going to get to work immediately for the American people. And were going to be doing a job that hopefully you will be so proud of your president."

When it was over, I turned the TV off and sat in the dark of my office. The anchors were so flabbergasted they hadn't been capable of any actual analysis. The joyous scenes inside Trump's victory party were too much to handle, especially in comparison to the heartbreaking scene at Clinton's headquarters, where supporters were openly weeping. I sat there in the dark and thought about all of the people who had harassed me and others in the press, the ones who had gone after Jewish writers and trafficked Nazi propaganda, the members of the alt-right and the KKK who were undoubtedly celebrating somewhere out there in the American night.

Eventually, I found my way into bed, but I didn't sleep. I lay there imagining it was some nightmare I could wake up from and tried to will myself to do just that. But there wasn't any waking up from it; the reality was that America had just elected Donald Trump, the walking, talking symbol of toxic masculinity, unrestrained greed, and cultural vapidity, president of the United States.

Groggy and downtrodden the next day, I skulked to my classes, each one populated with disheartened students who would weep spontaneously and without warning. An African-American student who had been deeply offended by Trump's so-called black outreach looked at me with red-rimmed eyes before losing control. Shoulders shaking, he fought through his sobs and said, "I feel like my country just told me they don't care about me."

A Hispanic student came to my office and slumped into the chair across from my desk. Crestfallen, she relayed the story of how her mother had called her the night before and worried over being deported until she'd gotten sick.

Since becoming a professor, I'd had to assume a mantle of authority. One of the things they teach you as you're trained to stand in front of a class is to project an air of confidence. Admitting ignorance is important, but too much can undermine a class altogether. Over the years, I'd grown into the role after having to pretend for semesters. I'd seen it all and heard it all, could field nearly every question a student could throw my way, but wasn't ready for the one thing every student wanted to know.

"What do we now?"

In the early afternoon, I was still shell-shocked, and in the hallways I kept meeting eyes with my colleagues, most of them similarly distressed and weary. We'd share a slight smile or a polite nod, but it was obvious everyone was just trying to make it through the day. The few conversations we shared were all stunted. No one had any answers. They couldn't believe they lived in a country capable of doing such a thing.

Later, as the last class let out and my students shuffled into the hall, a student passionate about social justice and civil liberties stayed behind and asked, tears in her eyes, the same question everyone had been asking.

"What do we do now?"

I answered without thinking. It was the one thing that'd been brewing in the back of my mind all day as the reality of the situation had set in. I realized it was the only acceptable answer. "We fight."

CHAPTER 21
ANATOMY OF A CAR CRASH

WHEN THE DUST SETTLED, THE POLITICAL WORLD WAS LEFT shaken and desperate for answers. In the era of hot takes and clickbait think pieces, there was no shortage of postmortems. The prevailing theory was that Trump had helmed a white, populist uprising that had been made possible by racist and economic resentment in an ever-diversifying country. Others pointed to missteps by the Clinton campaign. Some blamed the epidemic of fake news. What a majority of pundits missed, however, was that there didn't seem to be any single silver-bullet explanation as to what happened; rather, 2016 was a perfect storm, a potent mixture of the right people in the right place at the right time.

There is an argument to be made that a whole host of factors combined at exactly the ideal time in their development, including the usage and influence of the internet, the rise of social media as a tool for communication and understanding, and a noticeable shift in America's demographics and wealth, as well as the fruition of a decades' long indoctrination by the Republican Party. Any of these factors might have affected the election in a large and measurable way, but it was their synthesis that led to not only Donald Trump, but also the movement that carried him to the White House.

To begin, it must be acknowledged that Trump, while a largely ineffective campaigner, was incredibly adept at understanding how the country's media covered politics and how their viewers processed their information. A political rookie, but a veteran of cable news, Trump in the beginning campaigned as the candidate he would have wanted to watch on his television. For years, he had nursed what some of his staffers would later refer to as an addiction to cable news, and in the service of that dependence he had played armchair quarterback in the face of world events. The men and women on stage were boring to Trump, and their attempts to behave as statesmen left him cold. When it was his chance to take the stage, he bloviated and bragged, threatened and spoke off the cuff. He was, in essence, the pop and fizzle the cable networks needed to add to politics in the past to make them appointment viewing, but with Trump all they had to do was point a camera and hit record.

Those hours of featured speeches established Trump as a political force. Most imagined his stature would fade once he stood alongside his foes in the debates, but Trump's grasp of the media gave him a leg up against the competition. Beginning in the primaries, Trump showed an immense talent for collaring his rivals with devastating aliases— Jeb Bush as "low-energy" and Ted Cruz as "Lyin' Ted"—that fed into previously assumed weaknesses that could be pushed in the press and easily digested by the voting public, many of them simply reading the chyrons at the bottom of the networks' screens.

Obviously, this carried into the general election, as his most effective weapon against Hillary Clinton had been the ongoing corruption narrative, a story that cast the former secretary of state as the villainous mastermind behind every problem ailing the world. In past elections, there had been efforts to portray opponents as failed politicians pushing failed policies, and even smear campaigns intended to impugn character, but Trump's singular focus on Clinton's emails, not to mention his willingness to openly call her a criminal and threaten her with future prosecution, was certainly unique.

Trump's ruthless pursuit was aided by a media that had yet to adapt to the unique demands of covering a politician so unencumbered by integrity and so unabashedly shameless. Fact-checking every lie and fabrication proved impossible, and soon a whole host of untruths were going unchallenged. Then, as more Trump scandals materialized daily, the press, in the interest of fairness, juxtaposed the myriad Trump stories with the only thing they had on Clinton. This imbalance was further aided by Trump's continued war with the media, an assault that shockingly positively affected his coverage. It seems illogical, but it makes much more sense when compared to how a basketball coach's verbal tirade can lead to a makeup call a few seconds later. The referee, or in this case the media, is struck by an unconscious need to show the complainant and his/her fans that they aren't actually biased. Then the whistle blows.

Similarly, the networks failed in their charge to raise the level of discourse and instead focused on the stories that garnered them some of their highest ratings in their history. Statistics from the campaign's coverage are staggering. From the first of the year to October 21, the big-three nightly news programs combined aired only thirty-two minutes of policy coverage in comparison to a solid hundred minutes dedicated to stories about Clinton's emails.[127]

As previously discussed, Trump did his best to continue the controversy even after the FBI declined to prosecute in July, but that effort was largely to stanch the bleeding among his supporters. Had the issue been dropped then and there, swing voters might have considered the scandal put to rest. But then, on October 28, the director of the FBI again reared his head.

The now-infamous letter that Comey sent to Congress just eleven days out from the election will go down in history as one of the most stunning and infuriating October surprises. Addressed to committee members he'd testified in front of before, the letter was quickly leaked to the press by Representative Jason Chaffetz of Utah. It read as thus:[128]

Dear Messrs Chairmen:

In previous congressional testimony, I referred to the fact that the Federal Bureau of Investigation (FBI) had

*completed its investigation of former Secretary Clinton's
personal email server. Due to recent developments, I am
writing to supplement my previous testimony.*

*In connection with an unrelated case, the FBI has learned
of the existence of emails that appear to be pertinent to
the investigation. I am writing to inform you that the
investigative team briefed me on this yesterday, and I agreed
that the FBI should take appropriate investigative steps
designed to allow investigators to review these emails to
determine whether they contain classified information, as
well as to assess their important to our investigation.*

*Although the FBI cannot yet assess whether or not this
material may be significant, and I cannot predict how long
it will take us to complete this additional work, I believe it
is important to update your Committees about our efforts
in light of my previous testimony.*

*Sincerely yours,
James B. Comey
Director*

Immediately, the media latched on to the story and reported it with
eye-catching headlines like "James Comey, FBI Director, Reopens
Clinton Email Investigation," "FBI Director Says Investigation Into
Hillary Clinton Emails Back On," and "FBI Reopens Clinton Probe."
Quickly, those articles trended and were shared by millions of people
desperate to devour the latest campaign twist. The problem was that
the headlines were deceiving.

In truth, the FBI wasn't reopening the Clinton investigation. Seman-
tics here are important because a "reopening" meant the July announcement was suddenly null and void and there existed a real and legitimate

reason to reconsider the findings. Instead, the FBI's investigation into the alleged sexting of a fifteen-year-old by Anthony Weiner, the disgraced former representative and husband of Clinton's aide Huma Abedin, had revealed a new collection of documents only tangentially related to the Clinton matter, and when Comey sent his letter to Congress he had literally no reason to believe what the FBI would find in those documents would affect the Clinton probe. Comey was merely updating Congress about information that may or may not have been pertinent to the case.

The intelligence community has a long-standing tradition of not releasing findings so close to elections in order to avoid unnecessary influence, and the Department of Justice had warned Comey not to make public the development. The DOJ's concern was well founded as the letter, especially in how vaguely it had been written, was instantly turned into a powerful bludgeon against Clinton. That afternoon, in New Hampshire, an exuberant Trump told his crowd, "This is bigger than Watergate."[129] Surrogates took to the airwaves to spread the news that this time the FBI would get their woman.

One of them was Rudy Giuliani, who bragged openly about his close ties with the bureau and seemed to have insinuated that he'd been told beforehand about the development.[130] Later, he began alluding to divisions in the agency, saying, "There's a revolution going on inside the FBI, and it's now at a boiling point," an assertion that shed new light on a story Fox News ran on November 2 wherein an FBI leak from a New York field office characterized investigating Clinton's foundation as "high priority" while confirming there were tensions between its office, FBI headquarters, and the Justice Department.[131]

The same day Giuliani revealed the "revolution" inside the bureau, *The Guardian* reported "deep antipathy" toward Hillary Clinton within the FBI that had emerged in the wake of Comey's choosing not to pursue charges in July. One concerned agent was quoted as saying,

"The FBI is Trumpland" and that Clinton was "the antichrist personified to a large swath of FBI personnel."[132]

Two days before the election, Comey sent another letter, this one announcing the additional documents had been investigated in full and that nothing had been found.[133] The follow-up received only a fraction of the crazed attention the initial letter had earned. Even though the FBI had once more exonerated Hillary Clinton, the damage was done as the mere specter of another investigation, coupled with the media's continued obsession with covering the controversy, had unquestionably altered the trajectory of the race and led to toss-up voters finally swallowing the Crooked Hillary narrative Trump had been feeding them for months.

If it wasn't bad enough that the country's trusted institutions were falling down on their jobs of sorting the real from the fictitious, there was a developing industry that sought to further muddy the picture. This effort to distort the truth and inundate the internet with disinformation would eventually be labeled "fake news" and inflict untold damage. In the same vein as the *Baltimore Gazette* article that originated the rumor that Clinton had received questions in advance of the debate, websites camouflaged to appear like reputable sources had sprung up seemingly overnight to deliver deceptive revelations.

The spread of dishonest information has a multifaceted influence in that some accept it as fact because of their confirmation bias, or rather it confirms what it is they already believe, while for others it simply discredits all sources, meaning if a voter is inundated with questionable stories, they're more likely to just lose faith in all media.

For the former, fake news served as verification that the Crooked Hillary story line they had believed for years, and taken mostly on right-wing media and Trump's insinuations, had a basis in factual material. One of the most successful and widely shared fake news stories was "WikiLeaks CONFIRMS Hillary Clinton Sold Weapons to ISIS," published by *The Political Insider* on August 4.[134] The story instantly went viral despite it being patently false. The wording made it sound as if WikiLeaks had finally offered proof of Clinton having aided ISIS, a suspicion critics had been waiting on for months in the form of a leaked email. Instead, the story was built on an interview Julian Assange had given in which he intimated that to be the case.

Fake news ran the gamut from carefully worded mistruths to out and out lies, including one of the top shared stories in which it was claimed that Pope Francis had endorsed Donald Trump. Their content didn't matter though—Craig Silverman of *Buzzfeed* discovered that over the course of the campaign, fake news had outperformed actual stories on Facebook, the top method by which voters now received their information.[135] From February to November, Silverman found that the twenty best-performing fake-news pieces "generated more engagement than the top stories from major news outlets such as the *New York Times*, *Washington Post*, *Huffington Post*, NBC News." Fake news stories were interacted with 8.7 million times, more than 1.3 million times more than traditional and trusted outlets. Of the top performing fake news links, all were meant to either assist Donald Trump or discredit Hillary Clinton.

This success could be attributed solely to confirmation bias, but something larger and more disturbing was at play. Facebook's vaunted algorithms made the epidemic of fake news a possibility, particularly when considering its filters were designed to give users what they wanted. The confluence of confirmation bias and the filter meant the ideological bubble that had always been present was amplified to a staggering degree, and, to make matters worse, much like how the media had been abused into false equivalencies, Facebook had been exposed in May of 2016 of having intentionally stifled conservative trends on the platform, leading to an overcorrection in its algorithm that meant the social-media platform was now ripe to serve as an incubator for right-wing news, real or imagined.[136]

This conducive environment meant literally anyone with an internet connection and enough free time could affect the presidential election in ways before unheard of. Groups of Macedonian teenagers played on the fervency of Trump's supporters and penned fake news designed to elicit reaction and earn money.[137] Others followed suit and used social-media traffic to charge exorbitant prices to advertisers who only cared about views. Marco Chacon, a fake-news writer, wrote in *The Daily Beast* that he'd been "aghast" as he watched his completely fabricated stories gain traction in the mainstream press.[138] These fake-news writers had manipulated readers for a whole host of reasons, be they malicious or mischievous, but that vulnerability opened the door for more malevolent actors to influence America's democratic process.

In the end, there's no telling how many people were convinced to vote for Donald Trump because of fake news, just as it's unknown how many people read the headlines and finally gave up on a political process they'd already lost faith in. Some went ahead and sided with Trump as a metaphorical middle finger, while some turned to third parties. Undoubtedly, a large number of them decided to stay home as voter turnout for the 2016 election hit a twenty-year low.[139]

It's easy to look at the race and conclude the electorate had been primed for Trump's victory. The GOP had inundated the American public with a duplicitous vision of the country that readied them to believe that Hillary Clinton was the mastermind behind a globalist criminal syndicate and Trump, with the help of the nascent online world and an overmatched media, successfully used that vision to position himself as the champion of a group of people who had long been in search of one. But it would be disingenuous not to lay at least a portion of fault at the doorstep of the losing campaign.

First and foremost, Hillary Clinton was a problematic candidate in this particular election. Her position as a veteran lawmaker pinned her down as establishment in a change election, and while her choice to keep a private server for her emails did not rise to the level of criminality that Trump claimed and the media pondered over, the resulting explanation, or rather a lack of one, lent to the perception. For months, Clinton attempted to dodge questions relating to the investigation and, no doubt owing to her training as a lawyer, her answers felt pedantic.

More troubling, however, was Clinton's ties to her husband's NAFTA agreement, a trade deal that plagued her chances in Michigan, Wisconsin, and Pennsylvania, three states that would go on to cost her the election. Before she ever won the nomination, workers in the Midwest were predisposed not to support her, and making her the face of the decline of manufacturing was child's play, but Clinton didn't do herself any favors in those states either. The campaign, citing polls showing a healthy lead, advocated for "mandate building," meaning Clinton's resources and time were spent more on nontraditionally Democratic states like Arizona and Georgia, as well as focused on congressional races that could give their candidate a working majority in Washington. As far as spending, the campaign allocated to Michigan and Wisconsin only 3 percent as much as was designated for Florida, Ohio, and North Carolina, all of them losing efforts.[140]

In the aftermath of the loss, more light was shed on just what happened in terms of ground-game politics. The Clinton campaign trusted its models that showed her as a favorite in Michigan and Wisconsin and wrote them off as potential swing states. In Michigan, the Service Employees International Union begged to go to work, but the campaign wanted it to serve as a decoy in Iowa to distract Trump's operation in the Hawkeye State. Local operatives were stunned by the lack of attention and focus they received, and, in many cases, they failed to marshal the voter turnout that would have made the difference.

The predominant narrative that Trump had raised a movement of disaffected whites in the Midwest seemed to fit with the failures in these states, but the numbers show a more complicated story. In a postelection piece for *Slate*, Konstantin Kilibarda and Daria Roithmayr examined the statistics and found that, while GOP gains in the Rust Belt were modest, Democratic losses were substantial.[141] Whereas Trump gained a little over half a million white, working-class votes, the Democrats lost well over one million.

There's no doubt the Democrats had squandered their position as the "Party of the Working Man," as my grandma had put it, well before the 2016 election. Reacting to the GOP's pandering to "Real America," or the subculture of rural whites blaming urban elites and minorities for economic difficulties, the Democrats had actively ceded that territory for years. In the past, economic populism had been one of the main party planks, but in 2016 there was nary a word from the top of the ticket.

Instead, there was a concentrated effort to wage war on Donald Trump's temperament. Nearly every single advertisement focused on the offensive things he'd say or his explosive temper. In one particularly haunting commercial called "Role Models," the children of America were shown watching the Republican nominee cursing, calling Mexicans rapists, referring to Megyn Kelly's menstrual cycle, and mocking a disabled reporter.[142]

The ad was pitch-perfect and evocative. It flawlessly communicated the danger of a Trump presidency and the consequences for an entire generation if we chose to normalize his ugliness. For Democrats and progressives alike, it was a summation of exactly why they so ardently opposed Trump. Members of polite society recognized his behavior as disqualifying and the necessity of handing such a monster a resounding defeat.

Unfortunately, working-class people, people like my family, are no strangers to offensive language and behavior. Political correctness has no place in a lot of working-class homes. These are factory people. People who curse. People who say misogynistic and homophobic things. To tell them that someone who uses brusque language or utters shameful things is thus unworthy is to tell them, in essence, that *they* are unworthy, that their children are unworthy. To win the vote of Midwestern poor whites by citing language is only possible if you can convince mothers and wives that their sons and husbands are as much of a lost cause as Donald Trump.

Oftentimes, it's not a pleasant reality. If the rest of America could gaze inside working-class homes and hear the things that are said at the dinner table, they'd be shocked. Truthfully, the conversations are often several degrees worse than those things Trump was being lambasted for. Racial slurs are common. So is misogyny. Homophobia, in many cases, is a given. When working-class men talk about politics, more often than not they talk about it ignorantly in the same way Trump does. Comparing someone who wants to "bomb the shit out of ISIS" to someone who thinks the Middle East should be utterly wiped out isn't a winning strategy. Neither was relying on working-class women in the Midwest who have, night after night and day after day, heard much worse.

In the months leading up to the election and afterward, I received the most blowback from people when I argued this case. Should Clinton have pointed out the vulgarity and backward nature of Trump's campaign? Shouldn't we expect more out of working-class whites? And these people who behave like Trump, who see nothing wrong with him, do we really want their votes anyway?

Yes, yes, and yes.

The unfortunate political truth is that, in this election at least, it was integral for Clinton to capture more of the working-class vote in order to win the Electoral College. And it's next to impossible to undo generations' worth of behavior in one cycle, meaning it was unrealistic to expect rural working-class whites to suddenly realize their behaviors were unacceptable because of a political candidate, especially one who more or less absolved them of those behaviors. Perhaps they suspected that about themselves and Trump, but the lecturing tone of the campaign actually harmed the possibility, especially in a polarized country where right and left identities are so stringently defined.

Trump's ugliness, and the problems in rural America he came to represent, needed to be addressed and changed, but Clinton would have had a much easier time doing so as a president with the bully pulpit at her disposal. That wouldn't happen, however, because the campaign missed a glowing opportunity to find common ground.

Following conversations with members of the Clinton team, and after reviewing campaign documents leaked by WikiLeaks, a cohesive picture emerged of just what had gone wrong. According to what was supposed to have been the Democratic opposition file on Trump, the main talking points against him meant to outline that Trump lacked principles, had run a divisive campaign, was, despite appearances, a failed businessman, advocated irresponsible policies, and was racist, xenophobic, and terribly sexist.[143] These were all valid reasons why Donald Trump didn't deserve to win the presidency, but none of them meant much to the working poor.

I've now heard that several members of the campaign had advocated for more outreach, but were wholly rebuked. Unfavorable numbers showed that Trump had suffered because of his behavior, and so time and resources were going to be focused on hammering away at those facets. The problem with that strategy was that Trump's numbers remained incredibly consistent throughout the race. Considering he'd opened his campaign with an explicitly racist and belligerent speech, there wasn't much further he could fall.

What the Clinton campaign failed to realize was that Trump's own narrative provided the antidote to his candidacy. His base consisted primarily of working people who saw him as an advocate, but that could've easily been counteracted. Instead of framing Trump as a failed businessman with multiple bankruptcies, the Democrats should've portrayed him as a gaudy billionaire who had been born into his money. The story of how his father, Fred Trump, had not only given Donald his start, but had actually bailed him out, should've been a centerpiece of the attack. Not to mention that Trump's prominence in the American consciousness was built on his character on the television show *The Apprentice*, a character whose most famous catchphrase was "You're fired."

Essentially, in criticizing his behavior and language, the Democrats were giving cover for the "blue-collar billionaire" persona the Trump campaign had created. He was rude and crass and spoke his mind, all of these being things his supporters cited outside his rallies as being draws. Because he was boorish and tactless, they saw him as one of their own. Clinton played directly into that characterization by tossing Trump's supporters into the same basket of deplorables right along with him.

There was still a place, obviously, for censure of Trump's indecency. His rampant sexism and racism have no place in the twenty-first century, and the attacks played well for the modern Democratic base. Other than those still faithful to the Bernie or Bust movement, progressives were suitably motivated to work against Trump, but the working class was never given a reason. In 2012, Mitt Romney had been effectively depicted as a wealthy businessman whose time at Bain Capital made him the heartless CEO who bought your factory and sold its parts before laying you off. Everything was there for Trump to be seen as the rich fat cat who refused to pay taxes before shipping your factory to Mexico and then partying on his yacht while your family starved.

That attack isn't the easiest one, for sure; however, in this case it would have worked had the Clinton campaign tried a two-pronged approach for the base and the working poor. In urban centers, Democrats could have run their condemnations, and in the Rust Belt all it would have taken was footage of Trump from *Lifestyles of the Rich and Famous* and his garish, gold-laden home set to quotes of him bragging about his wealth and stiffing workers.

In essence, the Clinton campaign assumed the American electorate would be capable of seeing the danger of Trump as president and do the right thing. What it didn't recognize was that identity politics extended far beyond the confines of race and gender. Trump ultimately succeeded because he was able to present himself as a member of Real America, an alternate country created from whole cloth by the right-wing media. Because of Trump's addiction to cable news, primarily Fox, the originator of the myth, he was uniquely fluent in its language and customs.

Though it won't be written into history books, 2016 was an inimitable opportunity for the spell of that myth to be broken. Though critics will harshly criticize the working poor as "uneducated" and "ignorant," there is at least one thing they are exceptionally talented at: detecting bullshit when a rich person is trying to manipulate them. Trump's entire "blue-collar billionaire" persona was fragile and could have been effectively dismantled had the Democrats even tried. Working-class people are suspicious of outsiders, especially wealthy ones, but the moment they saw urban elites criticizing Trump for his political incorrectness, he was welcomed with open arms.

Clinton's strategy drove them further into Trump's camp, and, with the aid of Steve Bannon's populist rhetoric, he positioned himself as the voice of the common man. He was lying and, I suspect, deep down in their guts, his supporters knew as much. If only they'd been given half a reason, the portion of Trump's working-class base that gave him the presidency would've evaporated and all the lies, exaggerations, internet manipulations, and cognitive dissonance in the world wouldn't have saved his candidacy.

CHAPTER 22
WAITING FOR THE END OF THE WORLD

ON JANUARY 6, 2017, BEFORE A JOINT SESSION OF CONGRESS, the final electoral votes for the 2016 election were counted. The final tally: Donald Trump, 304. Hillary Clinton, 227.[144] During the Electoral College's meeting on December 19, a pair of faithless electors had abandoned Trump, but, much to the chagrin of the Democratic faithful, five had forsaken Hillary Clinton. Voters who'd gotten their hopes up that an electoral uprising would deny Trump the Oval Office were summarily disappointed. In Congress, there were last-second challenges by a few Democrats, but the protest was ended by Vice President Joe Biden, who said, most fittingly, "It is over."

The numbers coming out of the election suggest a perplexing divide within the country. Though Clinton lost in the Electoral College, she bested Trump by nearly 3 million in the popular vote.[145] Undoubtedly, Trump had not earned a mandate that would bestow upon him a wide berth and an unassailable bully pulpit, a fact that obviously irked the newly minted president-elect. Trump repeatedly tweeted that he could've won the popular vote if the contest would have depended on it, and then, in one of his more inexplicable and irresponsible moments, fired off on November 27 that he "won the popular vote if you deduct the millions of people who voted illegally."[146]

Unprecedented as always, in his eagerness to explain away his popular shortcoming, Trump had actually called into question the legitimacy of the election he'd just triumphed in.

Of course, Trump's obsession with rehashing his electoral battles, both in the general and the primaries, was perhaps the least concerning of the developments following his victory. In the seventy-three days between his upset and his inauguration, Trump would plunge the country into an unrelenting anxiety attack where Americans were forced to sit in fretful contemplation as to what hell they'd just unleashed on the world.

Perhaps the first sign that business was anything but usual was the spate of hate crimes that erupted in the wake of Election Day. The Southern Poverty Law Center reported that in the ten days following November 8 there were 867 hate crimes reported in the United States.[147] Of these, 202 occurred the day after, and over a quarter of them took place in public settings. The list of offenses is depressingly varied and spans all genders, sexual orientations, races, and ages. Children were called racial slurs and threatened with deportation. Families had racist and threatening notes slipped under their doors. Women in hijabs reported being attacked. Minorities suffered threats and egregious disrespect. Across the country, swastikas and demeaning graffiti like BLACK LIVES DON'T MATTER AND NEITHER DOES YOUR VOTE appeared on walls, along with the word TRUMP that carried with it an obvious connotation.

Most disturbingly, the hate filtered into our schools. In a survey conducted by the SPLC, school employees reported the election's troubling tone afflicted children, with 80 percent of those surveyed observing "heightened anxiety" in their students, 40 percent hearing derogatory language, and 2,500 explicitly describing "specific incidents of bigotry and harassment."[148] CNN documented two such incidents, including one in Kansas when students chanted "Trump won, you're going back to Mexico," and at a high school in Tennessee where a pair of white students blocked a black student from entering a door and chanted, "Trump, Trump."[149]

Bigotry and ugliness had been granted a foothold in the culture at large, and suddenly white nationalists like Richard Spencer weren't on the outside looking in anymore. Spencer's think tank, the National

Policy Institute, would host its annual conference in Washington, DC, on November 19 and make headlines around the world. After referring to the media as *"Lügenpresse,"* a term resurrected from the Third Reich meaning "the lying press," Spencer punctuated his white-centric remarks by shouting, "Hail Trump! Hail our people! Hail our victory!"[150] Many in attendance took his cue, rose from their seats, and proceeded to shower their leader with the same Nazi salutes I'd seen members of the crowd give Trump outside the Republican National Convention.

Milo Yiannopoulos, the speaker at the event where I'd previously had my brief run-in with Spencer, would similarly benefit from Trump's victory. It was announced in December, just days after he'd insulted a transgender student during a speech at the University of Wisconsin, Milwaukee, that Yiannopoulos had been given a book advance of a quarter of a million dollars by Threshold Editions, an imprint of publishing giant Simon & Schuster.[151] The deal was met with nearly universal scorn, but Yiannopoulos, in his usual flamboyant style, told *The Hollywood Reporter,* "I met with top execs at Simon & Schuster earlier in the year and spent half an hour trying to shock them with lewd jokes and outrageous opinions. I thought they were going to have me escorted from the building—but instead they offered me a wheelbarrow full of money."[152] Later, Yiannopoulos's book deal would be terminated after comments were discovered in which the provocateur seemingly advocated pedophilia, but it set an obvious precedent for controversial right-wingers getting rewarded for their offensive views.

It seemed the alt-right and fringe news had become big business. After all, even though he had lost the popular vote, Donald Trump had convinced 63 million people to pull the lever attached to his name. That meant nearly 20 percent of the country's population had been able to look past his innumerable scandals or else had sequestered themselves by relying on biased outlets that would never challenge their worldviews.

One such consumer of fake and alternative news was twenty-eight-year-old Edgar Welch, a North Carolina man who carried an AR-15 semiautomatic rifle into Washington, DC's popular Comet Ping Pong restaurant and proceeded to fire off three rounds.[153] In an interview with *The New York Times* after his arrest, Welch told the paper he just "wanted to do some good" and "had went about it the wrong way."[154]

The "good" Welch had wanted to perform was to interrupt a child sex-slave ring that was purported to have been housed inside the pizza restaurant, a child sex-slave ring websites had claimed involved Democratic nominee Hillary Clinton.

The conspiracy theory that led Welch to carry his semiautomatic into a restaurant had become known as "Pizzagate," and it had its roots in a tweet authored by a white supremacist in late October.[155] *Buzzfeed* followed the rumor's development after that posting and found that Clinton had been tied to an underage prostitution ring as it circulated around fringe-right websites, including Alex Jones's *Infowars*.[156] Over time, the gossip gained traction and heft via numerous fake-news outlets, and then Clinton's campaign manager John Podesta's leaked emails were used to "decipher" a code that, in some way, ensnarled the Comet Ping Pong restaurant into the burgeoning untruth.

Pizzagate was just another cog in the relentless operation to smear Hillary Clinton's name, but the damage done extended well beyond the election. Though Welch's rifle hadn't been aimed at any of the customers, it's still worth considering what would've happened if it had been. Welch wasn't alone either, as many consumers of fake news flooded the restaurant with threats and harassment, and, even in the wake of his arrest, rumors persisted that he'd only been an actor and the incident staged to discredit alternative media.

Just like that, another man with a gun had disrupted American life and put lives in danger, and just like that, the lessons needing to be learned were swept away. Welch was a potential Dylann Roof in the making, as is the next unstable man who believes the lies a little too much.

It goes on and on and on.

. In a better world, we would've addressed this problem decades ago, but it seems we are doomed to repeat this awful cycle. Perhaps we could've built on President Obama's legacy and began to tackle it in the coming years, but instead we are now face-to-face with the once inconceivable task of enduring a Donald Trump presidency.

$$\star \quad \bigstar \quad \star$$

Nine days after the election, Vice President–elect Mike Pence attended a Friday-night performance of the wildly popular Broadway musical *Hamilton*, and, following the final number and curtain calls, the cast thanked the audience and addressed Pence, saying they hoped they'd inspired and reminded him the new administration would represent all Americans.[157] On Saturday, Donald Trump responded by harshly criticizing the musical and claiming his running mate had been "harassed."[158] Ironically, the candidate who had won largely due to his continued disparagement of political correctness and his followers' disdain for "snowflake" liberal culture insisted the theater must "always be a safe and special place."[159]

By Saturday afternoon, Trump was feuding with the cast of the most critically acclaimed and beloved musical in the United States of America. In that moment, it felt like Trump's ever-growing list of rivals and disputes was turning into a game of ad libs. There was no telling who would earn the president-elect's ire or what minute indignity would set him off.

Throughout the campaign, Trump had used the 140-word tweet, his favored means of communication, to spread his point of view. Much like streaming services had found a way around distributors, Trump's harnessing of the tweet to bypass traditional media channels and have his message amplified by supporters and opponents alike had given him an edge in defining not just who he was as a candidate, but how the world appeared to his base. This change was as groundbreaking as the emergence of television in the debates between Kennedy and Nixon and President Obama's harnessing of the organizing and fund-raising powers of the internet. With the press of a button, Trump could answer any question, address any controversy, and disseminate talking points to his waiting followers.

In the time between his election and swearing-in, Trump would repeatedly focus the power of his social-media pulpit on private citizens, companies, and sovereign nations, and with the immediacy of tweeting—as well as its inherent lack of context, not to mention Trump's penchant for jumping before looking—the first Twitter president could instantly destabilize the world and create dangerous situations out of thin air.

In December, after a union boss in Indiana criticized Trump's characterization of a deal with Carrier, an air-conditioning manufacturer that was given a sweetheart deal to maintain some jobs in the Hoosier State while moving a majority to Mexico, Trump called him out by name, saying, "Chuck Jones, who is president of United Steelworkers 1999, has done a terrible job representing workers. No wonder companies flee the country!"[160] Almost immediately, Jones began receiving threatening phone calls and an intense amount of harassment.[161]

Much like his ability to upend a person's life at a moment's notice, Trump also discovered he was able to manipulate the stock market with only a few seconds of typing. Four days after siccing his followers on Chuck Jones, Trump tweeted his displeasure with arms manufacturer Lockheed Martin by saying, "The F-35 program and cost is out of control. Billions of dollars can and will be saved on military (and other) purchases after January 20th."[162] Lockheed's shares dropped by 2 percent following the tweet, forcing Marilyn Hewson, the company's CEO, and Dennis Muilenburg, CEO of Boeing, another company Trump had publicly chided (this time in regards to the cost of a new Air Force One), to meet privately with the president-elect and attempt to earn his favor.[163] Later, Trump would again use his Twitter to attack the company, this time pitting Lockheed and Boeing against one another and effectively lowering both their stock prices once more.

This method of manipulation hasn't gone unnoticed in the corporate world. Already an app has been created that alerts stockholders when a company they own shares of has been mentioned by the president, while tech companies on the West Coast have hired people specifically to track Trump's tweets in the morning.[164, 165] With his election, there's a developing sense that not only does Trump not believe in free-market principles, but that he's increasingly interested in putting his thumb on the scales.

This certainly seemed to be the case on the world stage as Trump used his platform to upend relations and, in the case of China, put other superpowers on notice. As soon as he was elected, he began taking congratulatory calls from other world leaders, a customary tradition, only these calls were being taken without the appropriate vetting and on unsecured lines.[166]

This chaos led to a bizarre conversation with Pakistan's prime minister, Nawaz Sharif, in which Trump promised, "I am ready and willing to play any role you want me to play to address and find solutions to the outstanding problems," a sentiment that, while benign at first glance, angered our allies in India as "outstanding problems" could easily be interpreted to mean the two countries' ongoing hostility over the territory of Kashmir, a conflict that has seen the rivals at the brink of nuclear war.[167]

It's unclear whether Trump understood the consequences of what he had said, much as it still remains uncertain whether he was aware on December 2 that, by taking the phone call of Taiwanese President Tsai Ing-wen, he not only broke thirty-seven years of American foreign policy but put our relationship with the Chinese at risk.[168] China has long been touchy about Taiwan and considers it a breakaway province, meaning it opposes any and all references to its independence or sovereignty. Because of this, the United States had not publicly communicated with Taiwan for nearly forty years before Trump took the call, an action that led China to lodge a formal complaint.[169]

In true Trump fashion, the president-elect took to Twitter again and escalated tensions with the rival superpower. On December 5, in back-to-back missives, Trump sniped at the country, "Did China ask us if it was OK to devalue their currency (making it hard for our companies to compete), heavily tax our products going into [sic] their country (the U.S. doesn't tax them) or to build a massive military complex in the middle of the South China Sea? I don't think so!"[170]

Repeatedly, in his tweets and public statements, Trump criticized the Chinese at length and signaled that relations with the country might dramatically change under his administration. Later, he insinuated that the United States might produce more nuclear weapons and declared, "Let it be an arms race," a frightening proposition that signaled his willingness to let relations with China, and any other rival, worsen to the point of war.[171] In January, China would see Trump's threats and respond with its own in the form of a warning printed in a state-run newspaper that advised the United States to "prepare for a military clash."[172]

Every single day, there were new things to fear from a Trump presidency, so much so that concerned Americans began wondering if the man who'd just been elected was unhinged. The schizophrenia that'd characterized the Trump campaign had evolved into everyday existence in America. The most frightening part of the confusion, however, was the uncertainty as to whether it was the result of a man trying franticly to adapt to a job beyond his capabilities, or a well-designed plan coming into fruition.

★   ★   ★

As soon as the results were final, the transition from campaign to administration began in earnest. Trump's team announced its choices to fill offices so quickly, and the Republican majority in Congress so expedited its approval hearings, that the Office of Government Ethics accused those responsible of rushing in order to undercut the vetting process.[173] There appeared to be reason to circumvent the procedures as Trump continued to surround himself with highly questionable people.

To begin, he chose for his chief strategist Steve Bannon, the man who had concentrated the central message of the campaign and effectively gave the presidency to Trump. For his work, Bannon received the new president's ear, a frightening prospect as the former editor of *Breitbart* had shown a penchant for running alarming stories and had effectively chained Trump to the white-nationalist scourge of the alt-right. Perhaps even more disquieting, as displayed in David Farenthold and Frances Stead Seller's illuminating *Washington Post* examination, was Bannon's ability to not only frame Trump's message, but to lead him into questionable theoretical territory.[174] After reviewing Trump's appearances on Bannon's former radio show *Breitbart News Daily*, Farenthold and Sellers found that Bannon, by using a mixture of flattery and semantic tricks, was able to goad Trump into more palatable positions. That manipulation went further, however, in December 2015, when Bannon essentially talked the candidate into questioning NATO's support of Turkey, an ally since 1951.

To the dismay of Bannon's opponents, the adviser position didn't need the approval of the Senate. Trump's cabinet picks were another story, and with each announcement concerned observers were only given more and more reason to worry. Throughout the campaign, Trump had repeatedly voiced the slogan "Drain the Swamp," a nod to Washington, DC's origins and its transformation into a city of greed and self-preservation. His nominations not only contradicted that notion, but seemed to imply he was interested in deepening the bog while tearing down any impediments.

Another position needing no confirmation, that of national security adviser, was given to the deranged Gen. Michael Flynn, a onetime potential vice presidential candidate who trafficked in conspiracy theories on social media. Flynn, by all accounts an unpleasant colleague, lasted all of twenty-four days before his lying about conversations with Russian ambassador Sergey Kislyak prior to Trump taking office came to light and cost him the job. Later, investigative journalists would find that Flynn, while working as a surrogate for Trump's campaign, was actually being paid by Turkey and served as a foreign agent.[175]

For a cabinet, Donald Trump assembled a motley crew of billionaires and millionaires, a team worth in excess of thirteen billion dollars.[176] This included secretary of commerce nominee Wilbur Ross, a player in the subprime mortgage crisis, and secretary of the Treasury nominee Steve Mnuchin, a former partner at Goldman Sachs, a pair that signaled Trump's criticism of Wall Street during the campaign amounted to little more than rhetoric.[177] His other nominees were notable because, upon first glance, their politics and worldview put them in direct opposition to the departments they'd been nominated to helm.

Retired neurosurgeon Ben Carson, a long-standing critic of social safety nets, was nominated to head the Department of Housing and Urban Development.[178]

Another primary foe, former governor of Texas Rick Perry, was Trump's pick to lead the Department of Energy, a surprising choice as Perry had famously forgotten its existence during a debate in 2011 while expressing a desire to eliminate the department.[179]

Oklahoma Attorney General Scott Pruitt was tapped to lead the Environmental Protection Agency, an interesting choice considering his continued skepticism of climate-change science and past lawsuits against the agency.[180]

Andrew Puzder, CEO of Hardee's/Carl's Jr., was chosen to be secretary of labor—though he would later withdraw his nomination after accusations of spousal abuse—despite his longtime opposition to minimum wage and paid leave while openly advocating for increased automation.[181]

For secretary of education there was Betsy DeVos, a fierce promoter of privatized schools and a wealthy lobbyist who raised ungodly amounts of money for Trump. Her post would put her in charge of America's public education despite her record of effectively destroying Michigan's educational system.[182]

Jeff Sessions, one of the first Republicans to back Trump's bid for the presidency, was selected for attorney general, a post responsible for ensuring the rights of Americans, even though his questionable history on civil rights caused him to be denied a federal judgeship in 1986 when racist allegations came to light.[183] Later, after appearing to lie about his own interactions with the Russian ambassador while under oath, Sessions, under siege from calls for his resignation, would recuse himself from any future investigations into the Trump campaign's dealings with Russia.[184]

Each one, on the surface, seemed like a bizarre pick, but a pattern soon emerged and it became obvious that Trump and his team had one domestic goal: dismantling decades' worth of progress. In essence, every worldview and priority that had run in opposition to the interests of the American people had bought a seat at the table. The foxes were given free rein in the henhouse.

Meanwhile, on the foreign-policy end of things, a sinister plan years in the making was just coming to light.

⋆   ★   ⋆

Secretary of state nominee Rex Tillerson's hearing before a Senate committee began the morning of Wednesday, January 11, and did not go as smoothly as the former CEO of Exxon/Mobil might have hoped. Particularly probing in his questioning was Senator Marco Rubio, who pressed Tillerson to admit that Russian President Vladimir Putin was a war criminal.[185]

"I would not use that term," Tillerson responded.

By the day's end, Rubio wouldn't say whether he'd vote for Tillerson's confirmation, a blow to the oil executive's chances that had been exacerbated by his continued tap-dancing around the issue of Russia, a country he'd enjoyed such close relations with he'd been awarded in 2013 with the Order of Friendship that recognized "special merits in strengthening friendship, peace, cooperation, and mutual understanding between peoples."[186]

While Tillerson was answering for his ties to Russia, Donald Trump was wrestling with his own. In New York City on January 11, the president-elect held his first news conference in six months, and before he ever took a question his press secretary, Sean Spicer, lambasted *Buzzfeed* and CNN for a pair of reports alleging there'd been uncovered proof that Russia had compromising material on Trump[187] and that intelligence officials had briefed both President Obama and Trump on the matter.[188]

During the course of the contentious press conference, Trump would deny the *Buzzfeed* story outright—calling the news organization "a failing pile of garbage"—and refer to CNN as "fake news," but would fail to respond to a question as to whether or not his campaign had been in contact with emissaries from the Russian government.

That non-answer seemed to fall in line with a *Washington Post* report after the election in which Russian Deputy Foreign Minister

Sergei Ryabkov confirmed that elements of the government had been in touch with members of the Trump campaign. It was another chapter in a bizarre story that refused to go away and only seemed to grow in intrigue and import by the day.

Public rumblings that Russia had deliberately interfered in the 2016 election went as far back as the July hacks of the Democratic National Committee, and it was in those days that I was first alerted to the rumors by people inside and outside the Trump campaign. For the most part, it was background chatter that would be immediately dismissed whenever voiced in public, the originators of the theory called paranoid and partisan, but in early 2017 a cadre of intelligence agencies compiled a report for President Obama that ascertained that not only had Russia willingly influenced the election, but that Putin himself had ordered the operation in order to assist Trump's candidacy.[189]

This process included multiple fronts, including the leaking of hacked documents, continued probing of our electoral infrastructure, the spreading of misinformation and fake news, and armies of paid Russian trolls who flooded news feeds, comments sections, and harassed liberals and journalists alike, all in an effort to undercut Democratic nominee Hillary Clinton and promote Donald Trump. The agencies, including the FBI, the CIA, and the NSA, were in agreement that such an operation had originated from the highest levels of Russian government and had been underway for years.

The report was a bombshell and thrust the United States into unheralded waters. President Obama expelled thirty-five Russian diplomats as uncertainty swirled as to whether we'd simply been victims of manipulation by a foreign power or if the president-elect himself had been privy to the exercise.[190] Opponents and critics called for the election results to be overturned. Civil-rights legend Representative John Lewis cited the Russian interference when saying, "I don't see Trump as a legitimate president."[191]

True to form, Trump did little to answer his critics other than insulting them. He openly questioned the intelligence communities who compiled the report and praised Putin for his response to Obama's sanctions, calling him "very smart!"[192] To kick off the Martin Luther King Day weekend, he insulted Lewis, who'd marched at King's side, by saying he was "all talk" and should focus on "the burning and crime infested inner-cities."[193]

The only times he directly responded to the Russian threat he'd argue it would be an improvement if the two countries worked together, that it'd be beneficial if the murderous dictator liked him. In an interview with *The Guardian*, he again derided NATO as being "obsolete" and floated the possibility he might arrange to drop sanctions against Russia.[194]

In *The Times* of London, he offered, "we should be ready to trust Putin."[195]

As always, Trump's base took its cues from its dear leader. In a shocking poll conducted by *The Economist* and YouGov, 35 percent of Trump voters reported having a favorable opinion of Vladimir Putin in contrast to 8 percent of people who voted for Hillary Clinton.[196] Among Republicans, Putin's standing had skyrocketed from a net negative of 66 percent to a net negative of 10 percent, a full fifty-four points higher than President Obama's Republican net negative of 64 percent.

In the end, whatever its motivation was, Russian's interference was successful. It discredited Hillary Clinton, a longtime adversary, and tipped the scales in favor of its preferred candidate. Whether Donald Trump liked it or not, Russia had accomplished the improbable in influencing the free elections of the United States of America, and because of Trump's continued insistence on praising Vladimir Putin, and championing policy and worldviews in line with Russian interest, the American people were quickly shifting into a mind-set favorable of Russia.

Trump's most outspoken critics alleged that it was part of a plan the president-elect played an integral role in carrying out. They pointed to Paul Manafort, his adviser's ties to Moscow, his continued backing and flirtation with Putin, the continual criticisms of the systems and apparatuses that were designed to keep Russia in check. They said Trump is nothing but a compromised puppet, a marionette dancing on Putin's string who will open his mouth only for the dictator's voice to emerge.

But, as is the case with so many facets of Donald Trump's world, the truth seems unknowable. Is he a mastermind or the face of a more sinister thing? Is he a chronic liar who so believes his own untruths that they're not actually lies, or is he the most talented embodiment of misinformation, a force of chaos that keeps his opponents chasing after his motivation, the world has ever seen?

Every time we think we have an answer, the question seems to change.

Is Donald Trump a Russian agent tasked with dismantling America, or is he the unwitting beneficiary who's been outsmarted and outmaneuvered the entire way?

And which of those possibilities is better?

In the weeks leading up to Donald Trump's swearing in as the forty-fifth president of the United States of America, the world watched with bated breath, all the while realizing, with grim certainty, that none of the answers were worth a damn.

EPILOGUE: We the People

THE TV IN THE CORNER OF SAVANNAH'S AMTRAK STATION WAS tuned to CNN when I walked through the doors. Across the bottom of the screen a breaking-news chyron reported that Treasury secretary nominee Steve Mnuchin had failed to disclose $100 million dollars in assets. Seated under the television, oblivious to the report, was a middle-aged couple in matching MAKE AMERICA GREAT AGAIN hats, on the wife's lapel a red-white-and-blue brooch, on the husband's a button with Donald Trump giving a thumbs-up over the words THE 45TH PRESIDENT OF THE UNITED STATES OF AMERICA.

Not having the strength to navigate the dissonance between the news and the supporters, I found a seat on the opposite side of the station and popped in my ear buds. I'd been listening to Arkady Ostrovsky's *The Invention of Russia*, a narrative of how his country had devolved from Mikhail Gorbachev's *glasnost* into Vladimir Putin's despotic reign, a transformation that saw television and nostalgia for a Soviet past play an integral role. Ostrovsky was talking at length about how Putin's power depended on Russian citizens succumbing to the temptation of tuning out politics and allowing government to go unchecked, when a man talking on his cellphone fell into a chair a few feet away and said, in a beleaguered voice, "I'm exhausted."

Always fascinated by the assumed privacy of cellphone users and their resulting honesty, I paused the book and listened as he talked to some nameless, faceless person about how Trump's victory had resulted in days that dragged on and felt like months.

"I never understood people saying dog years. 'Dogs live the same years as us,' I thought. But now I get it. Every year's gonna be like seven."

When the Silver Meteor to Washington, DC, boarded a little before 8 p.m., I stashed my bag and made a beeline for the café car, where I found a Mennonite family stuffed into the booths picking at pretzels and sandwiches. When I asked the attendant for a couple of Miller Lites, he shrugged.

"We've got Bud Light."

Forking over eleven dollars for two cans of beer I didn't want anyway, I returned to my seat to try and settle in. My plan for covering the inauguration was brutal and meant I'd be on the train until 8 a.m. the next morning and then back on another for Georgia at 7:30 that evening. I'd have to try and catch some sleep somewhere along the way, a problem as there is absolutely no proven method for getting comfortable on a train. As soon as your eyes close and you relax, the car shifts and the brakes squeal, and you're left wondering if derailment is only a curve away.

I was on the second Bud Light when the car door slid open and a man wandered in wearing a HILLARY FOR PRISON shirt. Behind him was a friend who, I'd find out later after he'd removed his coat, had on a shirt with a picture of an idyllic-looking little girl with a dialogue bubble reading SOMEDAY A WOMAN WILL BE PRESIDENT and then, on the back, in bold letters, NOT THIS TIME, BITCH. I'd find them later in the dining car with two other men, one in a Confederate flag cowboy hat and the other wearing a homemade BUILD THAT WALL shirt and sipping a Corona.

Eleven dollars later, I had more beer to try and nurse myself to sleep. I needed it for therapeutic purposes, though, as I'd just read a report in *The New York Times* that law-enforcement and intelligence agencies were investigating intercepted messages to determine if Paul Manafort and other members of the Trump campaign had been in contact with Russia.[197] It was another in a long line of rumors and innuendo I'd heard on the campaign trail that'd sounded too salacious to be true before finding their way into the headlines. I was reading and rereading the article as the Trump supporters talked about how relieved they were to have a president they could believe in again.

After a fitful night, I got out in DC to find Union Station filled to the brim. There were Trump supporters and there were people wearing I'M WITH HER shirts, others with the trademark pink hats that would come to signify the giant Women's March the next day. In nearly every corner of the station, people were arguing. In a bagel shop, a group of young men in UFC shirts and Trump scarves needled a woman with a #NOT-MYPRESIDENT sign as she bought coffee. By the gates, senior citizens with VETERANS FOR TRUMP buttons saluted as a man in a sports coat belted out "The Star-Spangled Banner" in an operatic voice so impressive it raised goose bumps on my arms. Nearby, an African-American woman in a Washington Redskins hat flipped them off, yelling, "That's not *my* flag! That's a racist flag!"

A few steps outside, another protest brewed as the first rays of morning began to play on the Capitol's dome in the background. These were college-aged students, some hoisting signs calling Trump a fascist and others with portraits of Vladimir Putin and Trump engaged in a sensual kiss. They chanted, "Down with Trump! Down with Trump! Down with Trump!" as supporters nearby sipped their coffees and laughed.

"Get a job!" one yelled.

"You should've gotten off your ass in November!" his buddy contributed.

All around Washington, the streets were cut off for security. Chain-link fences corralled pedestrians while buses and military vehicles blocked intersections. A man in a red hat shouted to a group of National Guardsmen keeping watch, "Are you here to stop Obama's coup?"

After passing a crowd of protestors, including a street preacher who accused everyone through his bullhorn of "worshipping at the altar of the gods of entertainment," the conversation in security lines mostly centered on how relieved everyone was to be through with President Obama, some of them joking they were only a few weeks from trying to assassinate him themselves. One man with his family shook his head as a slight drizzle fell and wondered aloud, "You don't think he's going to repeal the Second Amendment before Trump swears in, do ya?"

Inside the perimeter was another demonstration, this one concentrating on the media's culpability for gifting Trump a platform and billions worth of free advertising. A man at the microphone declared, "This is on CBS! This is on CNN! This is on everyone who thought a reality-TV star running for president would mean good ratings!" Ten feet away, a man in a BIKERS FOR TRUMP vest, a wife and children in tow, taunted, "Got to make sure I don't drop my wallet so a bunch of faggots don't bump up on me."

The closer I walked to the Capitol, the worse they got. Trump supporters were talking openly about "the gays," "faggots," "niggers," and "bitches." When a protestor would walk by with a sign criticizing Trump, supporters rained down insults, calling them "queers" or asking if their "libtard feelings" were hurt.

Just as the rain began in earnest, I found a spot by a building on the corner with a decent sightline of the Capitol. Attendance was sparse—a minor controversy would emerge the day after when Trump, true to form, claimed his crowds had been record-breaking while the photos told another story—but those who had made the trip were in the mood to celebrate. To my left was a young couple in MAKE AMERICA GREAT AGAIN sweatshirts and to my right a pair of men wearing a hot item I'd seen all over the Republican National Convention that featured Trump driving a motorcycle with Clinton being thrown from the back, his shirt reading IF YOU CAN READ THIS THE BITCH FELL OFF. One lit a cigar with a lighter he'd snuck through security and the other, after noticing two men walking by while holding hands, yelled, "This isn't your country anymore!"

Not far away, at the barricade, a guy wearing the MAGA hat cat-called a female police officer: "Hey, sexy! Hey, sexy, over here!"

When she ignored him, the cigar smoker joined in, "What? You too good to give us a smile? Come on, sweetheart." A few minutes later, as a group of high-school students on a field trip walked by, he focused on an underage girl. "I don't care if she's fifteen," he said with a chuckle, "she's got the twins out."

All around us, people were loudly calling Obama every derisive name and slur imaginable. "Ape." "Monkey." "Nigger." "Darky." Some joked he'd probably head back to Kenya now that he didn't have to pretend to be an American anymore. Another yelled, "Thank Allah Obama's gone!" Leaning on the barricade and pantomiming like he was staring through a scope at the inaugural platform, a man joked as to whether he could've gotten the outgoing president in his cross hairs if only he'd brought his hunting rifle.

When the ceremony began, I got out my phone and listened to the livestream as the supporters around me continued to raise their arms in triumph and celebrate with clumsy high-fives. There was a broadcast delay, so often someone would be speaking in my ear as cheers rang out from the crowd by the Capitol. Most of those around me weren't paying much attention to the proceedings, and were instead laughing, some continuing to tell protestors as they passed that they'd lost their country. Trump was still taking the oath of office on my screen when the celebratory cannons went off and a man yelled, "What happened? Did they shoot Obama?" Others cheered. Some chanted, "Lock her up! Lock her up! Lock her up!"

For Trump's inaugural address, I left the side of the building and waded into a cluster of young white men by the barricades closest to the Capitol. I'd been watching them harassing protestors the last few hours and wanted to hear their reactions. Instead of listening to their renowned leader's speech, a nightmare of paranoia and nihilism that described a dying country and coined the signature phrase "American carnage," they were busy celebrating and talking to the press, one of them pointing to an iPad playing the address and saying, "Government belongs to motherfuckers who pay taxes again," and when a journalist had the temerity to mention Trump had dodged paying taxes himself, the man twisted his face in disgust. "What kind of fake fuckin' news is that?"

As his friends loped their arms around each other's shoulders and cheered, the man spread his own arms out wide, leaned back, and accepted the rain as if it were deliverance.

"I just got so many rights back!" he shouted, the words sounding like so many hallelujahs.

✫ ★ ✫

For lunch and a beer, I stopped at a hole-in-the-wall where, inside, a bar full of young liberals sipped craft IPAs and stouts as they watched footage of the ceremony and talked shit about the table of Trump supporters a few feet away. The contrast was remarkable. The liberals were in either tailored suits or the trademark clothes of the urban hipster, an appropriation of the rural working class they were making fun of. The Trump supporters all wore matching hats, almost like they were on a family vacation to Disneyland, the dad wearing a shirt with a bald eagle clutching the American flag, his wife in a seasonally inappropriate sundress. While she continued to rub her mittened hands together and tried to warm up, her children, dressed in their Sunday best, picked unhappily at their faux-haute salads.

My beer was nine dollars and the food north of twenty, but I didn't have time to enjoy either. I was just about to dig in when the men at the bar next to me, amateur comedians who'd been competing over who did the best Trump impression, said in unison, "Holy shit."

The TV over the bar that'd been airing an inaugural lunch was now broadcasting protestors smashing windows in a Starbucks and a Bank of America.

As I listened to the liberals praise them and the conservatives condemn, I reached for my wallet. "Where is that?"

"Looks like K Street," a bartender answered.

I laid forty dollars on the bar next to my untouched food and half-drunk craft brew and sprinted out the door and in the direction of K Street, a few protestors and journalists hoofing it alongside me. We dodged traffic, tiptoed across congested intersections, and knew we were in the right place when we came to broken glass strewn across the sidewalk like sleet. A block away, police had quarantined the protest into three separate actions, the people pressing against them at each point.

At one, there weren't many people, but this is where members of the alt-right, most in suits, some of them wearing Pepe the Frog pins, all of them grinning ear-to-ear, engaged and argued philosophies. The separate groups raged against one another, the protestors calling them fascists and the alt-right men grinning and insulting them. One told a young woman criticizing Betsy DeVos's nomination for secretary of education that she might be "more eloquent" and "more successful" if she'd gone to a private school instead of "a pathetic state university."

With each insult, the protestors would back away and regroup, almost like they were ready to swarm into their antagonists and overwhelm them. In the background, police stood in militaristic armor, riot shields and weapons at the ready. A few inched toward them, appealed to their consciences, asked if they really believed in the system they were protecting.

Breaking the tension, a young woman called, "Over here!"

I turned and saw over two dozen people dressed in black, masks and bandanas obscuring their faces, swarm through an alleyway. I gave chase and followed a block over, where a larger demonstration was developing in Franklin Square. In the street, people were lined up against the police, some in gas masks, others holding signs with Donald Trump's face transposed onto the body of a pig. On the sidewalks, protestors and journalists were congregating around cars with smashed windows, the journalists going so far as to climb on them to get their best angle, including a stretch limousine filled with shattered glass, broken champagne glasses and bottles. On the side, somebody had spray-painted in gold WE THE PEOPLE.

"Who does that?" somebody asked me, and I was about to answer that I didn't know when a man in a green parka climbed atop an SUV and began jumping and stomping on the windshield. He cracked it with his first blow, but it refused to shatter. Over and over he stomped before he climbed to the roof and dropped an elbow. Still, the window held. He tried again. A crowd member snatched a windshield wiper from the vehicle and began stabbing at the glass. The man in the parka joined in and soon the window relented.

In the street, somebody had started a fire in an overturned trashcan. It wasn't large, by any means, but then protestors began throwing the telltale red MAKE AMERICA GREAT AGAIN hats on the blaze and it grew in size. Protestors were climbing on top of the bus stops and in the neighboring trees to get a better look.

A man emerged from the crowd carrying a tire he'd stolen off a nearby vehicle. "This belongs to a Trump voter!" he said and tossed it on the pyre.

Choking black smoke began filling the air as the tire burned. I moved to get out of its path and into the park, and while I was maneuvering somebody must've thrown the tire into the stretch limo because soon the car ignited and bright flames curled out of the windows.

I watched them for a second, transfixed by the glow, unable to make my legs work, when somebody screamed that the car was going to explode.

Dozens of people stampeded away from the burning car and through the park. Women carrying children stumbled as they escaped.

Protestors cheered as they sprinted. We made it to the back of the park and watched the smoke leak into the sky, obscuring, for a second, the police helicopter circling the protest. Something popped, maybe a tire, maybe a device belonging to the police, and then the smoke changed colors from black to white. Police had managed to extinguish the fire and now protestors stepped out of the park and back into the street.

Inside the park was a stage with a banner of Trump having sex with a bomb. It had been set up for a protest concert and whoever had been helming the speaker system put on Black Sabbath's "War Pigs" and cranked the volume. Heavy metal roared through the park as protestors clashed with police, and when I stepped onto the street a flash-bang concussive grenade exploded thirty feet away and momentarily blinded me. Out of instinct alone, I stumbled back into the park and recovered. As I did, I was hit by two separate and distinctive smells: pot smoke and tear gas.

In the distance, some protestors were gathered by the stage smoking joints. Others were down on their knees coughing and gagging. I saw a woman on the ground vomiting, a friend pressing a wet handkerchief over her eyes. All around us, people were in the trees, some of them videotaping the police, others chanting "Hey hey, ho ho, Donald Trump has got to go!"

When I left the riot, there were still people suffering from the gas, some bleeding from having fallen during the stampedes, others regrouping and planning further actions, further protests. With watering eyes, I escaped Franklin Square and slipped through a line of bystanders watching the chaos and clutching their chests or else pressing their hands over their mouths in disbelief. Three blocks down, well-coiffed, wealthy-looking men in tuxes were escorting women in elaborate gowns to inaugural balls. Surrounding them, more police made sure protestors didn't ruin their evenings.

"Hope you have a good time at your fucking Nazi dance!" one called to a couple dressed to the nines who chose not to respond and instead checked their appearances in a nearby window.

At the train station, I took a moment to catch my breath. My clothes reeked of fire and teargas. Nothing had changed from that morning. People were still milling about, still clashing in the walkways, still relitigating the election. A man in a LOVE TRUMPS HATE button pointed at another man carrying a TRUMP 45 tote and told him he was what was wrong with the country. A few gates away the people chanted.

Trump.

Trump.

Trump.

The name like the drumbeat of war.

On TV, scenes from the riot played out. More footage of men breaking windows. Police cutting off streets, tackling people and carrying them away. I watched and let my mind drift back to 2015, to the June night I'd spent on a bed in a cheap hotel room in Illinois, the television broadcasting glimpses from a world that was just beginning to come apart at the seams. Next door, the men I'd just drank with in the parking lot had been fighting, slamming one another into walls, and, with the click of a button, I could exchange one reality for another.

On this channel, the country was in flames.

On this channel, there was still time.

It occurred to me then—there was no changing channels anymore. The show that had been airing, the alternate reality that had been subscribed to, digested, regurgitated, and monetized, had seeped into everyday life. The election that was supposed to have stemmed the tide and settled all matters had only worsened the divisions and muddied the waters.

I realized, with frightening clarity, the people had become the monsters they'd feared, and the battle, it seemed, was only beginning.

ACKNOWLEDGMENTS

THIS BOOK WOULD NOT HAVE BEEN POSSIBLE IF IT WASN'T FOR THE support of a whole host of people, all of whom I owe an incredible debt, including Stacie McDaniel, my agent Christopher Rhodes, Dan Smetanka of Counterpoint Press, Dan Cafaro, Patti McKee and Jon McKee, Bernie Hoseman, Josh Sanburn, Clayton Haldeman, Ryan Kearney of the *New Republic*, Clay Risen of *The New York Times*, Dr. Dan Bauer and the Department of Writing and Linguistics at Georgia Southern University, Dr. Curtis Ricker, Benjamin Drevlow, Christina Olson, Dr. Lisa Costello, Dr. Michael Pemberton, Dr. JoAnna Schreiber, Dr. Melissa Carrion, Dr. Laura Agnich, Dr. Bryan Miller, Dr. Dustin Anderson, Dr. Richard Flynn, Dr. Patrick Novotny, Amanda Miska, Amanda Malone, Christopher Wolford, Jarrett Haley, Kaj Tanaka, Bronwen Dickey, Michael Meyerhofer, Alysha Hoffa, Andy Berger, Chris Smith, W. T. Pfefferle, Robert James Russell, Aubrie Cox, Jim Warner, Matt Bell, Eric Shonkwiler, Tasha Coryell, Cliff Schecter, Nick Hauselman, Chauncey DeVega, Don Armell, Chrissy Tiegen and John Legend, Jon Cryer, Rhea Butcher, my inspiring students who were so patient and so understanding, and every single person who took a moment to drop a note of encouragement and fortified my belief that, while these are dark and trying days, the possibility remains to better the world one word at a time.

Portions of this manuscript have previously appeared in the Atticus Review, Lit Hub, *and the* New Republic.

NOTES

1. www.msnbc.com/rachel-maddow-show/jeb-bush-doesnt-know-charleston -shooters-motive.
2. www.cnn.com/2015/06/20/politics/hillary-clinton-race-guns.
3. www.usatoday.com/story/news/nation/2015/06/20/mitt-romney-remove -confederate-flag-south-carolina-statehouse-capitol-grounds/29031185.
4. www.slate.com/articles/news_and_politics/chatterbox/2002/12/the_ legend_of_stroms_remorse.html.
5. gawker.com/here-is-what-appears-to-be-dylann-roofs-racist-mani- fest-1712767241.
6. fox59.com/2015/06/19/dylann-roof-says-he-almost-backed-out-because- everyone-at-church-was-so-nice.
7. www.dailykos.com/story/2015/6/18/1394261/-Fox-News-Charleston- shooting-is-an-attack-on-faith-not-race-calls-for-pastors-to-arm-them- selves.
8. www.splcenter.org/fighting-hate/extremist-files/group/council-conserva- tive-citizens.
9. www.washingtonpost.com/news/post-nation/wp/2016/12/07/as-dylann- roof-trial-begins-prosecutor-describes-each-victims-life-and-how-they- died/?utm_term=.af84d8b5ce41.
10. www.nbcnews.com/politics/2016-election/hes-not-war-hero-donald- trump-mocks-john-mccains-service-n394391.
11. abcnews.go.com/Politics/john-mccain-pow/story?id=32574863.
12. www.washingtonpost.com/politics/poll-trump-surges-to-big-lead-in-gop- presidential-race/2015/07/20/efd2e0d0-2ef8-11e5-8f36-18d1d501920d_ story.html?utm_term=.abed0979c278.
13. www.youtube.com/watch?v=DfWH2s9rc30.
14. www.realclearpolitics.com/epolls/2016/president/us/2016_republican_ presidential_nomination-3823.html?utm_source=hootsuite.
15. www.insidepolitics.org/ps111/candidateads.html.

16. www.youtube.com/watch?v=PmwhdDv8VrM.

17. www.thenation.com/article/exclusive-lee-atwaters-infamous-1981-interview-southern-strategy.

18. articles.latimes.com/1987-04-25/entertainment/ca-959_1_broadcasters.

19. web.archive.org/web/20050429070116/http://www.opinionjournal.com/columnists/dhenninger/?id=110006626.

20. www.nytimes.com/1994/12/12/us/republicans-get-a-pep-talk-from-rush-limbaugh.html.

21. www.washingtonpost.com/news/post-politics/wp/2015/07/19/bernie-sanders-draws-his-biggest-crowd-yet-in-arizona-of-all-places/?utm_term=.fed13b6803bf.

22. www.king5.com/news/politics/bernie-sanders-to-draw-thousands-at-safeco-field/102422243.

23. www.latimes.com/nation/la-na-sanders-california-20150811-story.html.

24. www.cbsnews.com/news/bernie-sanders-draws-28000-in-portland-rally.

25. electoralmap.net/PastElections/past_elections.php?year=1972.

26. www.journalism.org/2016/05/26/news-use-across-social-media-platforms-2016.

27. bigstory.ap.org/article/8ffa5f79fe8848f9bd9150fa9ec863a4/divided-america-constructing-our-own-intellectual-ghettos.

28. www.ncbi.nlm.nih.gov/pmc/articles/PMC4797953.

29. www.bostonglobe.com/news/politics/2015/11/05/bernie-sanders-draws-differences-with-hillary-clinton-oil-pipeline-and-trade/Lr5NoMApOsAtrMc4aR0ShI/story.html.

30. politicalticker.blogs.cnn.com/2008/02/25/clinton-gets-sarcastic-mocks-obama.

31. www.realclearpolitics.com/epolls/2016/president/mi/michigan_democratic_presidential_primary-5224.html.

32. www.upi.com/Top_News/US/2016/05/17/DNC-chair-Wasserman-Schultz-slams-Bernie-Sanders-after-violence-at-Las-Vegas-convention/9671463526538.

33. www.theatlantic.com/politics/archive/2015/10/here-comes-the-berniebro-bernie-sanders/411070/?utm_source=SFFB.

34. www.washingtonpost.com/news/monkey-cage/wp/2016/02/24/

these-6-charts-show-how-much-sexism-hillary-clinton-faces-on-twitter/?utm_term=.aea3e9a15bb6.

35. www.ibtimes.com/bernie-bros-obama-boys-echoes-2008-medias-clinton-sanders-pundit-clash-2300707.

36. bigstory.ap.org/article/4c9c850385c84b12ad5b85fda49743f9/after-weekend-wins-clinton-cusp-democratic-nomination.

37. www.cnn.com/2015/07/10/politics/nikki-haley-confederate-flag-removal.

38. www.winthrop.edu/news-events/article.aspx?id=42042.

39. thinkprogress.org/south-carolina-trump-supporters-say-theyll-never-forgive-nikki-haley-for-removing-confederate-flag-8a6cd2c0a83e#.398my-8a6l.

40. www.publicpolicypolling.com/main/2016/02/trump-clinton-still-have-big-sc-leads.html.

41. www.nytimes.com/interactive/2016/us/elections/primary-calendar-and-results.html.

42. www.scientificamerican.com/article/calling-truce-political-wars.

43. www.scientificamerican.com/article/organization-and-political-leanings/.

44. www.fbi.gov/news/pressrel/press-releases/statement-by-fbi-director-james-b-comey-on-the-investigation-of-secretary-hillary-clinton2019s-use-of-a-personal-e-mail-system.

45. www.nytimes.com/2016/07/04/us/politics/hillary-clinton-president.html.

46. datascience.columbia.edu/new-study-highlights-power-crowd-transmit-news-twitter.

47. adage.com/article/media/cnn-charging-40-times-usual-price-commercials-republican-debate/300185/.

48. www.marketwatch.com/story/trump-has-gotten-nearly-3-billion-in-free-advertising-2016-05-06.

49. www.washingtonpost.com/blogs/erik-wemple/wp/2016/12/07/study-clinton-trump-coverage-was-a-feast-of-false-equivalency/?utm_term=.87bafbb8c898.

50. fortune.com/2016/09/12/trump-foundation-bondi-florida-ag.

51. www.nbcnews.com/news/us-news/25-million-settlement-reached-trump-university-lawsuit-n686026.

52. bigstory.ap.org/article/67444ec825f3460ba4aadefc0d29d22f/trump-university-model-sell-hard-demand-see-warrant.

53. www.newsweek.com/2016/11/11/donald-trump-companies-destroyed-emails-documents-515120.html.

54. www.wctv.tv/content/news/Authorities-investigating-crime-scene-at-Valdosta-apartment-complex-386009191.html.

55. www.huffingtonpost.com/entry/new-york-post-dallas_us_577fae7fe4b01edea78d7313.

56. www.thewrap.com/drudge-report-conservatives-republicans-gop-black-lives-kill-dallas-police-shooting-racism-headline-backlash.

57. www.infowars.com/will-blm-dallas-massacre-start-race-war.

58. bigstory.ap.org/article/c894476bcbcf4d98b68ae98b27e0a0ff/authorities-highway-gunman-motivated-police-shootings.

59. ktla.com/2016/07/08/officer-shot-near-st-louis-suspect-in-custody.

60. www.atlantamagazine.com/news-culture-articles/what-really-happened-to-the-man-found-hanging-in-piedmont-park.

61. abcnews.go.com/US/dallas-shooting-suspect-wanted-kill-white-people-white/story?id=40431306.

62. www.nydailynews.com/news/national/dallas-shooter-micah-johnson-military-exercises-backyard-article-1.2705573.

63. www.cbsnews.com/news/baton-rouge-police-shooting-suspects-information.

64. www.cnn.com/2016/07/17/politics/cleveland-police-baton-rouge-security-open-carry.

65. www.washingtonpost.com/news/the-fix/wp/2016/07/18/rep-steve-king-wonders-what-sub-groups-besides-whites-made-contributions-to-civilization/?utm_term=.0276a5387c83.

66. www.buzzfeed.com/charliewarzel/twitter-just-permanently-suspended-conservative-writer-milo?utm_term=.moO9YjPeo#.cnlymJjoG.

67. www.businessinsider.com/mike-pences-most-controversial-stances-on-gay-rights-abortion-and-smoking-2016-11.

68. www.nytimes.com/2016/07/20/magazine/how-donald-trump-picked-his-running-mate.html.

69. www.nytimes.com/2016/07/21/us/politics/donald-trump-issues.html.

70. www.independent.co.uk/news/uk/home-news/jo-cox-murder-trial-tommy-mair-britain-first-thomas-mp-killer-court-latest-a7416021.html.

71. www.nytimes.com/2016/07/23/us/politics/dnc-emails-sanders-clinton.html.

72. theintercept.com/2016/07/22/new-leak-top-dnc-official-wanted-to-use-bernie-sanderss-religious-beliefs-against-him.

73. www.thegatewaypundit.com/2016/07/flashback-video-wasserman-schultz-says-conspiracy-theory-say-dnc-wanted-hillary.

74. www.politico.com/story/2016/07/sanders-wasserman-schultz-should-resign-now-after-leaks-226083.

75. www.nbcnews.com/politics/2016-election/trump-allies-plot-candidate-intervention-after-disastrous-48-hours-n622216.

76. www.cbsnews.com/news/gingrich-trump-is-making-himself-unacceptable-next-to-hillary-clinton.

77. www.usnews.com/news/politics/articles/2016-08-03/the-latest-trump-claims-unity-in-his-campaign.

78. abcnews.go.com/Politics/donald-trump-father-fallen-soldier-ive-made-lot/story?id=41015051.

79. twitter.com/realdonaldtrump/status/759743648573435905?lang=en.

80. thehill.com/blogs/blog-briefing-room/news/289976-roger-stone-suggesting-khizr-khan-part-of-muslim-brotherhood.

81. www.politico.com/blogs/on-media/2016/03/trump-campaign-manager-breitbart-reporter-220472.

82. www.usatoday.com/story/news/politics/elections/2016/2016/03/11/trump-rally-canceled-due-to-security-concerns-protesters/81671860.

83. thehill.com/blogs/ballot-box/273674-trump-aide-lewandowski-grabs-protesters-collar-at-rally.

84. www.nytimes.com/politics/first-draft/2016/03/28/donald-trump-hires-paul-manafort-to-lead-delegate-effort.

85. www.foxnews.com/politics/2016/06/20/trump-splits-with-campaign-manager-lewandowski.html.

86. www.npr.org/2016/08/06/488876597/how-the-trump-campaign-weakened-the-republican-platform-on-aid-to-ukraine.

87. www.politico.com/story/2016/07/trump-putin-no-relationship-226282.

88. www.slate.com/articles/news_and_politics/cover_story/2016/07/vladimir_putin_has_a_plan_for_destroying_the_west_and_it_looks_a_lot_like.html.
89. www.motherjones.com/politics/2016/10/trump-putin-timeline.
90. www.theatlantic.com/news/archive/2016/07/trump-nato/492341.
91. www.cnn.com/2016/07/31/politics/donald-trump-russia-ukraine-crimea-putin/index.html.
92. www.yahoo.com/news/u-s-intel-officials-probe-ties-between-trump-adviser-and-kremlin-175046002.html?soc_src=mail&soc_trk=ma.
93. thehill.com/blogs/in-the-know/in-the-know/291465-ivanka-trump-vacationing-with-putins-rumored-girlfriend.
94. www.slate.com/articles/news_and_politics/cover_story/2016/10/was_a_server_registered_to_the_trump_organization_communicating_with_russia.html.
95. www.nytimes.com/2016/08/15/us/politics/paul-manafort-ukraine-donald-trump.html?mtrref=undefined.
96. www.politico.com/story/2016/08/paul-manafort-resigns-from-trump-campaign-227197.
97. www.cnn.com/ELECTION/2002/pages/governor.
98. www.fec.gov/pubrec/fe2012/federalelections2012.pdf.
99. www.nytimes.com/2016/08/10/us/politics/donald-trump-hillary-clinton.html.
100. www.breitbart.com/big-journalism/2016/11/19/breitbart-news-hits-300-million-pageviews-45-million-uniques-last-31-days.
101. www.newswhip.com/2016/06/biggest-politics-publishers-social/?utm_source=NewsWhip+Newsletter+-+news+media+%26+publishers&utm_campaign=1ad6c7b4ac-NewsWhip_Note_June_17_20166_17_2016&utm_medium=email&utm_term=0_268c0aa396-1ad6c7b4ac-199129445#SCgBTBrvGYxqDLCp.97.
102. nymag.com/daily/intelligencer/2016/11/yes-steve-bannon-asked-why-a-school-had-many-hanukkah-books.html.
103. www.politico.com/story/2016/08/steve-bannon-domestic-violence-case-police-report-227432.
104. www.dallasnews.com/news/politics/2016/11/16/

trumps-rise-first-stage-white-nationalist-movement-says-alt-right-leader-dallas.

105. www.nbcnews.com/politics/2016-election/giuliani-fuels-clinton-health-rumors-again-again-n635841.

106. www.usatoday.com/story/news/nation-now/2016/09/13/internet-thinks-hillary-clinton-has-body-double/90297312/.

107 www.cnn.com/2016/09/27/politics/hillary-clinton-donald-trump-debate-poll.

108. www.bloomberg.com/politics/articles/2016-10-31/dnc-s-brazile-said-to-have-leaked-debate-question-to-clinton.

109. twitter.com/realdonaldtrump/status/789117930801926148?lang=en.

110. www.npr.org/2016/10/07/496996886/matt-drudge-suggests-government-may-be-lying-about-hurricane-matthew.

111. www.washingtonpost.com/politics/trump-recorded-having-extremely-lewd-conversation-about-women-in-2005/2016/10/07/3b9ce776-8cb4-11e6-bf8a-3d26847eeed4_story.html?utm_term=.f4639fc70630.

112. www.cnn.com/2016/10/07/politics/donald-trump-women-vulgar.

113. www.foxnews.com/politics/2016/10/09/trump-holds-press-conference-with-women-whove-accused-bill-clinton-sex-assault-rape.html.

114. www.politico.com/blogs/2016-presidential-debate-fact-check/2016/10/trump-is-wrong-hillary-clinton-did-not-laugh-about-the-rape-of-a-12-year-old-229455.

115. www.nytimes.com/2016/10/02/us/politics/donald-trump-taxes.html.

116. www.washingtonpost.com/news/post-politics/wp/2016/10/14/trump-mocks-sexual-assault-accuser-she-would-not-be-my-first-choice/?utm_term=.e8ceed338a41.

117. www.cnn.com/2016/01/23/politics/donald-trump-shoot-somebody-support.

118. www.nytimes.com/2008/02/11/opinion/11krugman.html?_r=0.

119. www.nytimes.com/2008/06/03/us/politics/03text-obama.html.

120. www.rushlimbaugh.com/daily/2008/02/20/the_cult_of_barack_obama2.

121. www.cnn.com/2016/10/08/politics/trump-on-howard-stern.

122. www.270towin.com/historical-presidential-elections.

123. projects.fivethirtyeight.com/2016-election-forecast.

124. www.nytimes.com/interactive/2016/upshot/presidential-polls-forecast.html.

125. www.marketwatch.com/story/dow-futures-plunge-450-points-on-election-turmoil-2016-11-08.

126. www.politico.com/story/2016/11/rnc-model-showed-trump-losing-231074.

127. mediamatters.org/blog/2016/11/02/how-media-s-email-obsession-obliterated-clinton-policy-coverage/214242.

128. www.washingtonpost.com/apps/g/page/politics/oct-28-fbi-letter-to-congressional-leaders-on-clinton-email-investigation/2113.

129. www.politico.com/story/2016/10/fbi-clinton-new-probe-trump-hails-230460.

130. www.thedailybeast.com/articles/2016/11/03/meet-donald-trump-s-top-fbi-fanboy.html?via=desktop&source=twitter.

131. http://www.foxnews.com/politics/2016/11/02/fbis-clinton-foundation-investigation-now-very-high-priority-sources-say.html.

132. https://www.theguardian.com/us-news/2016/nov/03/fbi-leaks-hillary-clinton-james-comey-donald-trump.

133. http://www.independent.co.uk/news/world/americas/us-elections/fbi-director-issues-new-letter-saying-it-has-not-changed-conclusion-on-hillary-clinton-since-a7401561.html.

134. www.thepoliticalinsider.com/wikileaks-confirms-hillary-sold-weapons-isis-drops-another-bombshell-breaking-news.

135. www.buzzfeed.com/craigsilverman/can-facebook-trending-fight-off-fake-news?utm_term=.mkZ5LxkoZ#.khwqe3n4B.

136. gizmodo.com/former-facebook-workers-we-routinely-suppressed-conser-1775461006.

137. www.nbcnews.com/news/world/fake-news-how-partying-macedonian-teen-earns-thousands-publishing-lies-n692451.

138. www.thedailybeast.com/articles/2016/11/21/i-ve-been-making-viral-fake-news-for-the-last-six-months-it-s-way-too-easy-to-dupe-the-right-on-the-internet.html.

139. www.cnn.com/2016/11/11/politics/popular-vote-turnout-2016/.

140. www.politico.com/story/2016/12/michigan-hillary-clinton-trump-232547.

141. www.slate.com/articles/news_and_politics/politics/2016/12/the_myth_ of_the_rust_belt_revolt.html.

142. www.youtube.com/watch?v=mrX3Ql31URA.

143. gawker.com/this-looks-like-the-dncs-hacked-trump-oppo-file-1782040426.

144. www.washingtonpost.com/news/powerpost/wp/2017/01/06/trump-victory-becomes-official-as-congress-tallies-electoral-college/?utm_ term=.08488d5a57f8.

145. www.cnn.com/election/results.

146. www.bostonglobe.com/news/politics/2016/11/27/donald-trump-says-without-illegal-votes-won-popular-vote-too/B6KClZcV7x2whk4Jjn6aZP /story.html.

147. www.splcenter.org/20161129/ten-days-after-harassment-and-intimidation-aftermath-election.

148. www.splcenter.org/20161128/trump-effect-impact-2016-presidential-election-our-nations-schools.

149. www.cnn.com/2016/11/29/health/school-survey-post-election-negative-incidents.

150. www.theatlantic.com/politics/archive/2016/11/richard-spencer-speech-npi/508379.

151. nymag.com/thecut/2016/12/milo-yiannopoulos-usd250k-simon-and-schuster-book-deal.html.

152. www.hollywoodreporter.com/news/milo-yiannopoulos-strikes-250k-book-deal-959745.

153. www.courier-tribune.com/news/20161206/religious-zeal-drives-nc-man-in-8216pizzagate8217.

154. www.nytimes.com/2016/12/07/us/edgar-welch-comet-pizza-fake-news .html.

155. www.buzzfeed.com/craigsilverman/fever-swamp-election?utm_term= .aqlV2WXPn#.ohea5wrkD.

156. www.infowars.com/pizzagate-is-global.

157. www.nytimes.com/2016/11/19/us/mike-pence-hamilton.html.

158. twitter.com/realDonaldTrump/status/799972624713420804?ref_src= twsrc%5Etfw.

159. twitter.com/realDonaldTrump/status/799974635274194947?ref_src=
twsrc%5Etfw.

160. twitter.com/realDonaldTrump/status/806660011904614408?ref_src=
twsrc%5Etfw.

161. www.washingtonpost.com/news/wonk/wp/2016/12/07/donald-trump-
retaliated-against-a-union-leader-on-twitter-then-his-phone-started-to-
ring/?utm_term=.4f71d8b7d587.

162. twitter.com/realDonaldTrump/status/808301935728230404?ref_src=
twsrc%5Etfw.

163. www.cnbc.com/2017/01/11/lockheed-martin-shares-fall-after-trump-
targets-f-35-programs-cost-again-during-press-conference.html.

164. www.latimes.com/business/technology/la-fi-tn-trump-trigger-finance-
20170109-story.html.

165. us11.campaign-archive2.com/?u=47c9040f6ff957a59bd88396e&id=
ac7d0f9073.

166. www.salon.com/2016/11/17/australias-prime-minister-could-only-reach-
donald-trump-by-getting-his-unsecured-cell-phone-number-from-a-golf-
ing-buddy.

167. www.independent.co.uk/news/people/donald-trump-pakinstan-prime-
minister-nawaz-sharif-india-anger-a7452571.html.

168. www.nytimes.com/2016/12/02/us/politics/trump-speaks-with-taiwans-
leader-a-possible-affront-to-china.html.

169. www.cnn.com/2016/12/02/politics/donald-trump-taiwan.

170. www.bbc.com/news/world-asia-china-38167022.

171. www.politico.com/story/2016/12/trump-nuclear-arms-race-russia-
232944.

172. www.independent.co.uk/news/world/asia/rex-tillerson-south-china-sea-
state-media-prepare-military-clash-donald-trump-global-times-a7525061
.html.

173. thehill.com/homenews/senate/313175-ethics-office-accuses-gop-of-
rushing-trump-cabinet-confirmations.

174. www.washingtonpost.com/politics/how-bannon-flattered-and-coaxed-
trump-on-policies-key-to-the-alt-right/2016/11/15/53c66362-ab69-11e6-
a31b-4b6397e625d0_story.html?utm_term=.6e480ab9502f.

175. www.nytimes.com/2017/03/10/us/politics/michael-flynn-turkey.html.

176. www.bostonglobe.com/metro/2016/12/20/trump-cabinet-picks-far-are-worth-combined/XvAJmHCgkHhO3lSxgIKvRM/story.html.

177. www.forbes.com/sites/chasewithorn/2016/12/22/heres-how-much-trumps-cabinet-is-really-worth/#229afb236f02.

178. www.washingtonpost.com/national/hud-job-to-pit-carson-ideology-against-long-standing-housing-policy/2016/12/05/6e7e8d76-bb25-11e6-94ac-3d324840106c_story.html?utm_term=.63f7bbbd2502.

179. time.com/4598910/rick-perry-department-energy-oops-gaffe.

180. www.usatoday.com/story/news/politics/elections/2016/2016/12/07/donald-trump-scott-pruitt-environmental-protection-agency/95104512.

181. www.nytimes.com/2016/12/08/us/politics/andrew-puzder-labor-secretary-trump.html.

182. www.washingtonpost.com/news/answer-sheet/wp/2016/12/08/a-sobering-look-at-what-betsy-devos-did-to-education-in-michigan-and-what-she-might-do-as-secretary-of-education/?utm_term=.14b7f1423d03.

183. www.rollingstone.com/politics/features/why-lawyers-are-freaking-out-about-jeff-sessions-as-ag-w460272.

184. www.nytimes.com/2017/03/02/us/politics/jeff-sessions-russia-trump-investigation-democrats.html.

185. www.nytimes.com/2017/01/11/us/rex-tillerson-confirmation-hearings.html.

186. money.cnn.com/2016/12/11/investing/rex-tillerson-exxon-russia-putin.

187. www.buzzfeed.com/kenbensinger/these-reports-allege-trump-has-deep-ties-to-russia?utm_term=.ylJkoMXwJ#.gf24AW1Rq.

188. www.cnn.com/2017/01/10/politics/donald-trump-intelligence-report-russia.

189. www.nytimes.com/2017/01/06/us/politics/russia-hack-report.html.

190. www.theguardian.com/us-news/2016/dec/29/barack-obama-sanctions-russia-election-hack.

191. www.nbcnews.com/politics/politics-news/john-lewis-captures-spotlight-after-calling-trump-illegitimate-n707146.

192. www.washingtonpost.com/news/powerpost/wp/2016/12/30/trump-praises-putins-response-to-sanctions-calls-russian-leader-very-smart/?utm_term=.a25a7a898893.

193. www.nytimes.com/2017/01/15/us/politics/trumps-race-john-lewis.html.

194. www.theguardian.com/us-news/2017/jan/15/trumps-first-uk-post-election-interview-brexit-a-great-thing.

195. www.thetimes.co.uk/article/donald-trump-interview-brexit-uk-trade-deal-theresa-may-phthbjsmw.

196. today.yougov.com/news/2016/12/14/americans-and-trump-part-ways-over-russia.

197. www.nytimes.com/2017/01/19/us/politics/trump-russia-associates-investigation.html?smid=tw-bna.

ABOUT THE AUTHOR

JARED YATES SEXTON's political writing has appeared in *The New York Times*, the *New Republic*, *Salon*, and elsewhere. He is the author of three collections of fiction and a crime novel. Currently he serves as an associate professor of creative writing at Georgia Southern University. You can follow him at @JYSexton.